Fly to

JAMAICA

Via **PAA**...

for the grandest vacation of your lifetime!

One of the most beautiful spots in the Caribbean, this mountainous isle, with its world-famous beaches and magnificent scenery, combines the leisurely atmosphere of a British colony with a wealth of native color.

Just to mention a few favorite vacation pastimes: you can swim, fish, shop for devalued pound bargains, dance to Calypso music, float down the scenic Rio Grande on a raft, or enjoy Jamaica's lovely sights.

See your travel agent or PAA ticket office NOW for reservations to Jamaica.

GROWING WITH JAMAICA!

Ever since Pan American started serving Jamaica, 20 years ago, the island and the Airline have progressed together.

As Jamaica's tourism, industry, and agriculture have flourished -- so have PAA's routes and fine service . . . linking Jamaica with the entire world.

T.M. REG. PAA, INC.

ME-516

PAN AMERICAN
WORLD AIRWAYS

PASSENGERS • MAIL • CLIPPER* CARGO

iii

All the year round . . .

. . . this glorious beach resort on the beautiful blue Caribbean is fanned the year round by soft day and night breezes. The long stretch of reef-protected white sand is as lovely as any in the West Indies.

SILVER SANDS BEACH CLUB is unique in the Caribbean. Comfortable furnished bungalows provide first rate secluded accommodation. First-class meals are served in the dining-room. There is bar and lounge accommodation for sociable hours, and your own private quarters when you prefer privacy and seclusion.

Rates are inclusive. Special attractive rates for Summer, for long stays, and for family parties.

SILVER SANDS BEACH CLUB
Near DUNCANS . JAMAICA

PLEASURE ISLAND

BOOKS BY ESTHER CHAPMAN

PLEASURE ISLAND

The Book of Jamaica

edited by

ESTHER CHAPMAN

assisted by

MARJORIE THWAITES

★

Historical Section by H. P. JACOBS, B. A.

Bibliographical & Geographical Section by MARY M. CARLEY, B. Sc. (Econ.)

Drawings by RHODA JACKSON

The illustration on page eleven by ANGUS GRANT

★

44 EAST STREET, KINGSTON, JAMAICA, B.W.I.

To
Mrs MAY BELLE EWEN
affectionately called
'MA EWEN'
by thousands of visitors to Jamaica
this book is dedicated in appreciation
of her services to the
TOURIST INDUSTRY

Printed for The Arawak Press (West Indian Publishing Co. Ltd.)
by Robert MacLehose and Company Limited
at The University Press, Glasgow, Scotland

CONTENTS

ILLUSTRATIONS

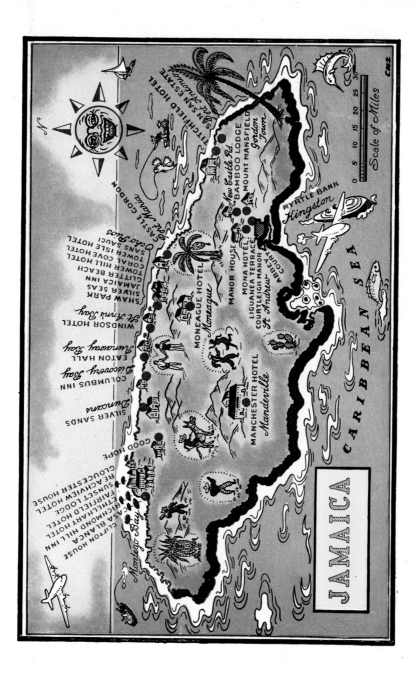

Gloucester House, Montego Bay

Several years ago, GLOUCESTER HOUSE was built upon modern luxury lines as a small, quiet, comfortable hotel opposite the Doctor's Cave beach (to which it has its own private entrance) and adjacent to the fashionable centres, but away from the hurly-burly. It speedily gained a reputation for excellent food, perfect service and absolute comfort.

The hotel has now been greatly enlarged, and brought in every respect to the ultimate standards expected in the world's leading resorts by travellers of experience, judgment and taste.

A new luxury hotel with an established reputation

Every possible aid to comfort has been incorporated in the design, and the visitor is offered hotel service, including a first-rate cuisine and wine cellar, in keeping with the highest conception of hotel management. Proximity to the pleasures of this famed resort is maintained, with peaceful and restful nights assured.

THE BEACH

YACHTING IN THE BAY

HORSE RACING — MONTEGO BAY

TENNIS — THE COUNTRY CLUB

ONE OF MANY DELIGHTFUL RIVER SPOTS

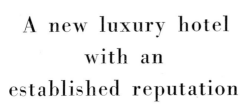

One of the lovely beaches at

SAN SAN ESTATE

near

PORT ANTONIO

Exquisite view from each site

Driving road, main water and power

to every lot

FOREWORD

PLEASURE ISLAND! Truly a happy title for a publication depicting the most lovely Tropic Isle in the world.

In its pages the Editor has described and pictured some of Jamaica's four thousand square miles of exquisite and ever changing scene. The tropical landscape, the stately mountains and rolling hills, the rivers and streams, the plains and palm strewn beaches and coves—that is *Jamaica*.

To catch the Ah's and the Oh's of the visitor travelling through this piece of God's creation, and in descriptive form pass them on to the armchair occupant, is a formidable task, but not beyond the ability of the Editor of *Pleasure Island*.

Jamaica was created for the very purpose of becoming a Pleasure Island—in reality it is all that. The vacationist or holiday-maker will find the natural charm of creation unspoiled despite Western man's occupation for the past four and a half centuries since its discovery by Christopher Columbus.

The addition of man-made amenities in the form of both luxury and modest hotels, with their appendages of recreation and entertainment, has provided that other ingredient. Mixed together by competent cooks and sprinkled with the proverbial hospitality of its people, it is today a real Pleasure Island for the visitor.

If *Pleasure Island* can capture the imagination of its armchair readers to the point of 'packing their bags' and coming to enjoy a holiday in the place they have read about, then this new publication will prove a worthy and outstanding addition to Jamaica's tourist literature and the Editor will deserve much credit.

F. H. ROBERTSON
Tourist Trade Commissioner
Jamaica, B.W.I.

Welcome to Jamaica!

Off Tower Isle

Look Magazine

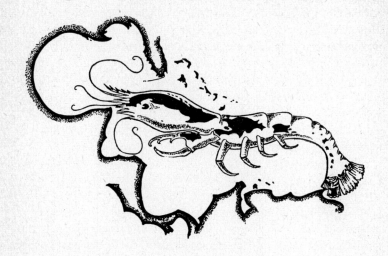

Jamaica: A General Picture

THE WEST INDIES

If you look at a map of the West Indies, you will see that it lies like a great prawn in the bowl of the Gulf of Mexico. The head is Cuba, the body stretches in a great arc through Haiti and the Dominican Republic (which together form the Island of Hispaniola) to Puerto Rico, and so by way of the long tail to the Leeward and Windward Islands down to Trinidad. Jamaica is a claw. It is situated southward of Santiago on the eastern end of the great island of Cuba and, across another expanse of sea, its easterly end at Morant Point looks toward the western end of the big Haitian Peninsula, at the eastern end of which is Port-au-Prince.

The life of this group of Caribbean islands, and of the mainland colonies that help to compose it, is diverse and fascinating. It varies from country to country, with the differences of racial origin, and form of government, and social conventions that distinguish one portion from another.

On the island of Hispaniola, Haiti, dominated by the French influence and using the French language, has preserved its status as a (so-called) Black Republic for more than a century, almost without interruption. The Dominican Republic, on its part of the same island, has a mulatto population under the rule of the Dictator Trujillo. Across a narrow arm of sea, Puerto Rico, a colony of the United States, has a people predominantly light in hue, and is now experimenting with a native-born Governor. Cuba, the largest of the islands, is dominated by Spanish influence; it has produced a lively and cosmopolitan capital in Havana, the Paris of the West Indies.

Throughout the group, national affiliations and economic associations vary, the treatment of the colour problem differs, there are great variations in the industrial and agricultural life, in the political outlook, in the scenery. Only climate and geographical location (though the distances are considerable) are similar; and even so, the climate varies, for some countries are mountainous, some are flat.

OUTLINE OF JAMAICA

But of the entire area, the most fascinating is the British Colony of Jamaica. It is perhaps not the most beautiful, though it has greater variety of beauty than any other. The grandeur of Hispaniola, the wild loveliness of Dominica, the charm of Grenada . . . you will hear them all extolled, but none offers the contrasts and the variety of choice. The political situation is more engrossing, however aggravating may be the immediate effects on a country in violent flux. The life is more vital. The earth burgeons with richness, though tropical agriculture is neither so easy nor so profitable as the novice imagines.

But just as this rich prolific life of the soil is not always blessed with rewards, so the proliferating life of the people does not always carry immediate blessings. The colour problem, though still having its thorny edges, has been solved in essence; and while the professors in the universities are analysing statistics and solemnly pointing morals, Jamaica is successfully working out one of the most interesting social experiments of modern times. Politically, the country is progressing, the gait rather that of a kangaroo, which proceeds in a series of great jumps, ignoring the ground over which it leaps, and sometimes coming down heavily upon the earth. Nevertheless, its progress is onward, as the figures prove.

Industrially, vast improvement has been made in recent years. As a tourist resort, the island is gradually coming into its own. It has more to offer than most other places on the earth, including a surface apparently unruffled by such troubles as the menace of war or the threat of the atom bomb. It is a small island, and its people are insular . . . of course they are. But they have the advantage of easy air communication, a close relationship with two great continental centres, Europe and North America, and a lively curiosity, allied with a great ambition, which keeps their insularity from becoming too narrow or confined. They certainly have more breadth and cosmopolitanism of outlook than is evinced by those who live in land-locked places remote from a sea-board; and this applies to all classes of the people, for the peasant who stares out from his hut at the passing visitor may have a son who, having passed through great English universities, is a doctor or a dentist or a lawyer or a Government official. A people freed from slavery only in the course of the last century or so has reached with a long arm for all the privileges of democratic civilisation; and has secured most of them without great effort of its own.

THE ECONOMY

This is not to say that the country is prosperous and successful. The island as a whole is a poor one, for as new inventions, new enterprises, industrial developments, improved methods come to it, its population increases at a rate alarmingly high in proportion to the world's figures. There is great poverty, and there is much unemployment. Nevertheless, these troubles do not press so hardly as they do in countries which have to endure the hardships of cold.

There is no weather problem in Jamaica; and, although the people sometimes have to endure the consequences of an up-heaval of Nature, a storm or occasionally even a hurricane, and their suffering may be intense at such times, the recovery of the fertile earth is so rapid that the effects are not protracted.

It was once possible to say that Jamaica was prosperous be-cause she had a large and satisfied peasant population . . . a strong and stable class of small landed proprietors who, despite their faults of improvidence and of unscientific husbandry, were the salt of the country. This peasantry was helped and supported by the existence of a class of large landed proprietors. They too had their faults, the chief of which were the neglect of estates under absentee ownership and insufficient regard for the rights and privileges of the labourers. But they gave stability to the island's agricultural economy; and they also provided employ-ment, for it was the habit of the peasant owner to work two or three days a week for wages (real money as distinct from the life-supporting product of his own fields), while devoting the rest of the week to his own cultivation.

From this fact, a legend of laziness grew. It is quite true that the habit of physical industry is not so deeply ingrained in manual workers in tropical countries as it may be elsewhere; but it is wrong to attribute to idleness the fact that workers preferred to work only three or four days for their bosses. They worked at least as hard for themselves on their own plots.

If this custom could have continued, perhaps none of the in-dustrial troubles would ever have come about, perhaps the seething political cauldron would never have boiled over. It used to be possible to say, as I have said, that the salvation of Jamaica lay in the fact that everybody had a grandmother. By this I meant that remote in a country parish was the little family estate.

When the servant girl in Kingston had a baby, it could be sent to Grandmother in the country, and Matilda could go on with her job.

When James lost his employment, he could go home to

COCONUTS LOVE THE SEA!

Long Bay
Portland

F. J. Vaculik

The Cove

Tourist Board

Grandmother for a time, and at least would find shelter and food.

But with the dwindling of the available land, due to wasteful farming methods and to subdivision into ever-smaller units after the death of the owner, and the ever-mounting increase in the population figures, the Grandmother has become less and less dependable as a refuge in time of trouble. The people stream into the towns, particularly into Kingston, creating problems of unemployment, hooliganism and crime, and forming a new social pattern by which the population is at the mercy of discordant and disruptive elements.

SYSTEM OF GOVERNMENT

Jamaica has 'inherited' many of her privileges by right of her affiliation to the British Commonwealth; and some of these benefits of progress she has assumed without ever having had the necessity to work for them. This has created some of her immediate troubles, particularly her political and industrial problems. It is customary in Jamaica to blame the Colonial System for the fact that today the island is over-populated and under-employed. Perhaps it is not fashionable to say it quite as baldly as that, for very few people—here as elsewhere—will face the fundamental facts. But the fact is that, under the Colonial System, Jamaica has enjoyed a quite remarkable and steady forward progression, in every department of life. Politically, the advance (apart from an occasional set-back) has been steady, and has taken the island (some people think prematurely) right to the edge of self-government.

In 1944, with no pressure from the population, but as the result of forward-thinking colonial officials, the Colony was given an advanced Constitution under universal suffrage. There has been a continuing desire to develop the abilities of the island's own people to the maximum of their capacity, and educational facilities are the first step on a journey which may lead to some of the highest positions available.

Jamaicans have often distinguished themselves, inside and

outside their own country, in sport, in politics, in business, in administration, occasionally in art.

There is absolutely no colour distinction except in the narrowest social sense. The position of Governor is filled by a Colonial Office career man, and as a rule, the highest governmental appointments are made from England. But this is a matter of Colonial Office technique, for some of the highest positions in the administrative service—either in their own or in other colonies—are filled by West Indians, many of them with coloured blood. There *is* distinction, there *is* a certain social discrimination, but it is becoming less and less, as far as the island's own internal life is concerned; and what there is, is due to the imperfection of the individual in his attitude to Society, rather than to any discriminatory rules or practices in the life of the community.

INDUSTRIAL RELATIONS

One of the respects in which the country has 'inherited' reforms without having to work for them is in the matter of industrial relationships. Trade union practices have been introduced quite painlessly . . . as far as the unions are concerned! The country, however, suffers from haste and the lack of organisation. The workers of Jamaica have suddenly found themselves with the facilities and the machinery without much understanding or appreciation of the values involved. Unhappily, this places them at the mercy of unscrupulous leaders; and, in addition, there has arisen a conflict of political interests which are struggling for control of the unions as a step toward political control of the country. The visitor to Jamaica will hear much of the so-called injustice of the employing classes; but he may turn a doubting ear, for most employers in the island welcome the advent of trade unionism . . . if only the unions would play fair and would obey the rules. Unfortunately, they sometimes do not, and the restlessness of the industrial scene is the result of too many privileges imperfectly understood and too rapidly gained, and the exploitation of the workers by some of their own leaders. This is not an altogether surprising manifestation in a young and developing community, the members of which were for many years under a serious disadvantage because of colour prejudice and discrimination.

THE POLITICAL SITUATION

A bitter struggle is being waged between a moderate but politically immature group and a left-wing Socialist faction. A description of the political machinery will be found in the Appendix, but this sketch would not do justice to the scene if it failed to take note of the conflicting personalities of the two cousins, William Alexander Bustamante and Norman Washington Manley, who for several years have fought a passionate battle for political domination.

The situation is a peculiar one.

Bustamante seems set for the villain of the piece, for he is a flamboyant character with a high flavour of egotism to his remarkable and outstanding personality. But he came up the hard and riotous way, and first entered the public life of the island as a labour agitator who was scarcely the darling of the employing class. Nevertheless, he has conquered Jamaica by force of character, and has developed into a personality still often unpredictable but in many ways admirable. With the entire working class behind him, he swept into political power in 1944, at the first elections under universal suffrage, and as head of the elected portion of government (with the courtesy title of Prime Minister) he has wielded his very considerable power with great deftness, shrewdness and tact.

Although his political group is called the Jamaica Labour Party, and his adherents are mostly of the working classes, he is opposed to Socialism, and believes in the encouragement of private enterprise, properly controlled and regulated. To many of us, this seems an admirable doctrine, especially for a country on the edge of its development and without any large immediate resources of its own; and, despite his occasional unique personal aberrations, Bustamante has emerged as a stabilising force in the affairs of the country, and is backed by most responsible sections of the population against the extremists on the other side.

But at the election at the end of 1949, a change had manifested itself. Kingston changed its allegiance, and went almost solidly over to the Socialist group. Bustamante and his Party were returned by a very much smaller majority than in 1944, and, although they are still solidly in power, the situation causes anxiety to those who are afraid that a change might mean a change to irresponsibility.

Just as Bustamante might have been considered the villain of the piece so might his first cousin Manley have been expected to appear as its hero. Of much darker complexion than his cousin, he is a man of superior education. An athlete who was by way of being a bit of a hero to his Jamaican schoolfellows, he was awarded a Rhodes Scholarship and proceeded to Oxford University, whence he applied for a commission in the British Army at the outbreak of the 1914-18 war. This was refused, presumably on the ground of his colour, and this is said to have had an embittering effect on his life, and by virtue of it perhaps upon the life of Jamaica. However, he has had a successful career as a skilful barrister, a King's Counsel, and a man who is still honoured and respected for his personal qualities.

His political ideas, however, are anathema to the majority of his fellow-countrymen . . . as has been proved at the polls up to the present. In the 1944 election he was defeated; in 1949, he was successful in gaining a seat in the House of Representatives. Some people think he is at the extreme left wing of his Socialist party; some think that he acts as a moderating influence. Certain it is that as time goes on his political group (the People's National Party) tends to be more and more dominated by its trade union elements, under the leadership of men less popular in the public regard than Manley himself.

The cousins are not a pair, they are a trio; for first cousin to both of them is Edna Manley, wife of Norman, and a sculptor of distinction. She shares her husband's political views, and is a worker and agitator for the Socialist cause.

BENEATH THE SURFACE

In the succeeding pages of this book, the reader will be told something of the story of Jamaica, a romantic island in the earliest-known portion of the New World, the hunting ground of the warriors of the past, the scene of adventures in which the Caribbean and the Spanish Main were overrun by figures from the history books. Swashbuckling figures people its pages, dressed in the picturesque costumes of another day, their deeds hallowed or at least condoned by time and the glamour of the past. But to me the true romance of the Caribbean lies in the story being enacted today under our eyes, the story of men and women of different habits, different backgrounds, and different races learning to live together under the smiling sun.

The sun shines three hundred and sixty-five days every year in Jamaica. There is no record of towns, hotels or communities presenting forfeits to visitors on the exceptional days of rain; for the sunshine is part of the accepted life, so commonplace that it is not worth remarking. Sometimes, of course, the rains come, and sometimes the waters race down the gullies and even through the streets. But this aberration is soon over, and the skies smile again.

The skies smile upon one of the most beautiful places on the earth's surface, with every variety of scenery and all (pleasant) varieties of climate. Of these things, also, the reader will be told in detail in subsequent pages. I have tried in this book to present a comprehensive picture of the Jamaica of yesterday and the Jamaica of today. Within so limited a space, it cannot be detailed and complete; but it is a portrait, or at least a sketch, of a very lovely portion of the earth's surface, which is also a very fascinating spot.

Many visitors come to this lovely island, and skim the cream from its beauty, its climate, and its life. They enjoy the scenery, they bask in the sunshine, they swim in the caressing waters. They stay in the luxury hotels, and they tip the civil and efficient servants. But they will gain a more personal satisfaction from their visit if they will peep a little beneath the surface, at the rich, pulsating life beneath. All is not well, all is not happy, all is not perfection; for these are human beings essaying the task of living, and the failures are many.

But, though these faults and these failures are seen so clearly in a small country, where details are magnified as under a microscope, they are not more numerous nor more heinous than those of human creatures in other communities. The faults are the defects of people who have developed over-quickly in an insular environment; and they are being corrected by the natural process of evolution and by the contacts with a broader world made possible by modern travel facilities. To this end, the change that has come about in recent years is to be welcomed. Every winter through the past, and all the year now that the tourist season is expanding, visitors have come and will come to enjoy the charms and beauties of the island. More and more its peace and serenity are sought by those who want to build or

buy a winter home and by those who, tired of the stringencies and austerities of northern lands, have chosen Jamaica as a permanent abiding place. As these tendencies spread, the life of the country will be modified, and the process of assimilation between races and peoples will be hastened.

The visitor who is bored or offended by differences in manners and modes will not appreciate this exciting country, this microcosm of scenic beauties and social experiments. But the man who is keenly interested in life and its manifestations, who is enthralled by the spectacle of human beings working out their salvation in a new manner and in a different type of environment, will be fascinated by the varied and vital life of the island of Jamaica; just as he will be enraptured by its loveliness.

ESTHER   CHAPMAN

CHAPTER ONE

The History of Jamaica

The first inhabitants of Jamaica may possibly have been the primitive cave-dwellers known in Cuba as Ciboney. But from about A.D. 1000 the island was occupied by Arawak or Taino Indians related in language and stock to those mainly found by the Spaniards in the Greater Antilles and the Bahamas.

The Arawaks burnt patches of bush, grew crops, and burnt more bush when the soil was exhausted. The chief crop was cassava: corn, sweet potatoes, tobacco, and cotton may also have been grown. The Arawaks were skilled fishermen and had large dug-out canoes. They shot or snared the Indian coney, various birds, and the iguana.

Tainan culture was still in the Stone Age. Crude hand-shaped fire-baked pottery was made, probably also wicker-work, and apparently cotton cloth. Weapons included bows and clubs, probably spears and knives.

The Arawaks were unwarlike, and in Jamaica their physique was poor. Little is known of their social, political, and religious organisation, except the fact that they had chiefs, or *caciques*.

DISCOVERY AND CONQUEST

Jamaica may be the *Babeque* reached by Martin Pinzon in 1492. Columbus, on his second voyage, landed on May 1, 1494, at St. Ann's Bay, which he called Santa Gloria. Conquest and settlement were delayed for several years. Columbus was marooned at Santa Gloria for over a year (1503-4) on his third voyage. The Crown granted the island to Ojeda and Nicuesa, who may have settled it, but Diego Colon, son of the discoverer, on becoming Viceroy, sent as Governor Juan de Esquivel, who founded the first capital (Seville) on a hill above St. Ann's Bay.

The Crown sent out a new Governor, Garay, who cowed the

Arawaks into Christianity, and reduced them to peonage, in which condition they rapidly died out, probably from European diseases. After their extinction (about 1540) some Indians were apparently imported.

JAMAICA UNDER THE SPANIARDS

The capital was moved to the unhealthy coastal plain, and fortified. It retained its name of Seville, but in 1534, the Spaniards moved to the south, where they built the Villa de la Vega (or Santiago de la Vega), now Spanish Town, which with one short interval remained the capital for nearly two and a half centuries. Some sugar mills existed, but cassava remained the chief crop, and labour shortage reduced most of the country to a pastoral stage, with Indian peons as ranch hands at small wages. The chief exports were hides, pimento and cassava. A few Negro slaves were imported.

As a source of food, arms, horses and soldiers, Jamaica played a part in the conquest of Cuba and much of the mainland. Afterward its importance waned. As the property of the family of Columbus (Dukes of Veragua and Marquises of Jamaica), the island suffered from dual control and was both neglected and badly governed.

About 1550, French, Dutch, English, Italians and Portuguese began to poach in Jamaica, trading or plundering. Sir Anthony Shirley seized Spanish Town in 1597; Christopher Newport attacked it in 1603, but was bravely repulsed; Jackson took it in 1643. A dozen turbulent years followed Jackson's departure, until on May 10 (O.S.), 1655, the armament of Penn and Venables, sent by Cromwell to attack San Domingo and repulsed there, arrived in Kingston Harbour and forced Governor Ramirez to capitulate.

II

ENGLISH CONQUEST AND SETTLEMENT (1655-1664)

When the heads of the Spanish community realised that the English meant to establish a colony, and that their expulsion

F. J. Vaculik

Fort Charles, Port Royal

J. Dougall

The Old Fort

was part of the design, they organised resistance and maintained a five years' war. The command eventually devolved on Don Christoval de Ysasi Arnaldo, member of an old settler family, who made use of Negro hunters in an active guerrilla warfare. The English were pressed hard in spite of their greatly superior numbers: and in October, 1655, the King of Spain made Ysasi Governor and seriously planned the recovery of the island.

The defeat of two Spanish expeditionary forces at Las Chorreras (1657) and Rio Nuevo (1658) and the defection of some Negro hunters (1660) destroyed the hopes of Ysasi, who abandoned the island in May of 1660.

With the end of the war, civil government was established, at first with an elected council, and later (1664) with an elected House of Assembly and a nominated Council—the Governor possessing the executive power, while the legislative initiative and the right to vote taxes rested with the Assembly. This type of Government lasted for 200 years (to 1866).

The island was now gradually divided into parishes, each of which sent two or three representatives to the Assembly and had its Vestry to look after roads, poor relief, police, and other local Government functions. In each parish or group of parishes, there was a *Custos rotulorum*, appointed by the Governor to head the magistracy and the Vestry. Freeholders were the only voters.

III

RISE OF THE 'PLANTOCRACY' (1664-1728)

Although Negro slaves were introduced by the English as early as 1656, it was intended to make Jamaica a white colony with many small proprietors and a white labour force of indentured servants (criminals and political offenders sentenced to transportation). But the whole purpose of the colony was deflected by the exploits of the buccaneers.

Though Spain ceded the island in 1670, it remained a base for operations against the Spanish Empire, by the buccaneers— French and English adventurers—the greatest of whom was Henry Morgan, who became a knight and Lieutenant-Governor of Jamaica. Port Royal, the chief buccaneering base, became a large and important town.

The hectic life of the buccaneering period brought wealth to the merchants and great planters, but ruin to the small proprietors. White bondsmen, who were badly treated, deserted to the buccaneers, and while the large proprietors could replace them by Negro slaves, the small landowner could not do so. Jamaica began to be a land of large estates and Negro slaves.

A terrible earthquake destroyed Port Royal in 1692, and though the town was rebuilt, it was replaced as the chief trading town by Kingston, which arose after the earthquake on the other side of the lagoon.

THE FRENCH ATTACK

The closing of Jamaica to the buccaneers threw those adventurers into the arms of France, which created a colony similar to Jamaica in what is now the Republic of Haiti. Ducasse, the French counterpart of Morgan, delivered a serious attack on Jamaica in 1694, plundering many plantations on the south coast, and carrying off hundreds of slaves. Landing at Carlisle Bay, the French fought a three days' battle with the colonists, but withdrew after suffering heavy losses. This was the last battle between Europeans on Jamaican soil.

THE GOVERNING CLASS

A body of island-born proprietors had now arisen with great power and wealth—what is generally known as 'the plantocracy'. Unlike the plantocracy in other slave colonies (except Virginia), the Jamaican governing class was closely related to the English governing class in outlook and habits. It shot its coverts in swamps and woodlands, loved races, fine equipages, balls and receptions, practised a lavish hospitality, monopolised the magistracy, sent its sons to English public schools and universities, furnished officers for the Imperial army and navy, dominated the militia, took a prominent part in local government, provided most of the members of the Council and many Assemblymen, intervened in the elections with money and influence: a member of it would occasionally be Acting Governor.

For nearly 150 years, this class dominated Jamaica. It was white and Anglican. The Test Act excluded Jews from office, and the electoral law excluded Roman Catholics and dissenters. The whites excluded from the franchise (1721), and from every public post (1712), all Negroes, and all coloured people except those born of octoroons and whites. Yet the governing class did not regard itself as English; and it is mentioned that 'they will not allow themselves to be called Englishmen'. They even attempted to exclude Englishmen from office.

The 'Creole interest' was in fact perpetually at odds with one or more of the other 'interests'—with His Majesty's Government or its local representative the Governor, with the slaves, with the merchants, and eventually with the dissenters and the free people of colour.

CONSTITUTIONAL COMPROMISE

In 1728, the 'Creole interest' wrung from the British Government the confirmation of the laws on which the independence of the Assembly rested (such as the Militia Act and the law regulating the composition of the Assembly), and also admission of the right of Jamaica to the benefit of certain English statutes. (The design to make the Habeas Corpus Act part of Jamaica's legal system was defeated but the Writ of Habeas Corpus subsequently crept into use.) In return, a 'perpetual revenue' of £8,000 was voted for certain expenses of the central government. All other charges would have to be met by votes of the Assembly, the financial power of which was thus a barrier to encroachments on the liberties of the governing class, and attacks on its interests by any Governor.

IV
JAMAICA UNDER THE PLANTERS (1728-1808)

The domination of the planters continued almost unbroken until the abolition of the slave trade stopped the forcible immigration of Africans into the country and so gave the slave population a new unity.

Institute of Jamaica

The Parish Church (from a lithograph by J. B. Kidd, *c.* 1835)

Institute of Jamaica

A view of King Street (from a lithograph by Benoist after Duperly, *c.* 1845)

DIFFERENT CLASSES OF SLAVES

The mass of unorganised and unrooted plantation workers, speaking no common language and with no common rallying point, was singularly helpless. In view of their numbers, they could be taught English only by putting them for a time to live with earlier immigrants. Thus the Creole or native-born slaves, who talked a relatively intelligible patois, were sharply differentiated from the Africans. In addition, a subordinate field staff of 'head Negroes', called *drivers* or *bosuns*, was created, and must have been chosen, as a rule, from the more heavy-handed and intelligent of the Creole slaves.

A quite separate class consisted of servants, who might be either Creole or African, though Creoles were better. Nurses, housemaids, butlers, cooks, valets, ladies' maids, coachmen, and grooms had a comparatively easy time, and dreaded above all punishments to be relegated to field labour. They were essentially a 'faithful' class unless abominably treated: and nurses in particular were known to betray conspiracies against the whites.

The isolated 'Great House', with broad acres, a mill, and the 'Negro houses', was a distinct economic unit needing experienced sugar boilers and certain craftsmen—coopers, joiners, carpenters, and masons. These in the early days were all white. Slave 'tradesmen', however, began to appear and formed another distinct group.

In the towns, there were many domestic slaves and 'tradesmen'. In addition, there were the slaves who provided the labour for heavy work on wharves and in warehouses, and a certain number of boatmen and even sailors.

THE FIRST COROMANTEE AND MAROON WARS

The settlers were involved in a series of Negro wars, first with the Varmahalys (Spanish Negroes), then with their own Coromantee (Gold Coast) slaves. Amalgamation of these produced a people called Maroons whose chief bases were in the wild central plateau—the country of the Varmahalys—and the Blue Mountains where they had a stronghold called Nanny Town.

After many reverses, Government troops stormed Nanny Town in 1734, and Cudjoe, one of the Blue Mountain chiefs, broke away to the plateau and joined the Maroons there. He was hard-pressed, however, and in 1739 was meditating suicide, when he was unexpectedly offered peace, freedom, and land, in return for the services of the Maroons as a rural police to bring in runaway slaves. Cudjoe accepted, and settled at Trelawny Town (the present Barracks in St. James). Quaco, chief of the Maroons left in the Blue Mountains, took similar terms and settled ultimately at Moore Town.

By this stroke of policy, the Government armed the Maroons, who knew the wild uninhabited areas, against all new runaways, who could not know the ground. In future no rebellion could be maintained in the mountain fastnesses. (*See also Chapter Two*.)

CONTRABAND AND WAR PROFITS

Spanish America was virtually closed to British trade; but Kingston built up a flourishing contraband trade, with 'Jamaica sloops' carrying British goods to Spanish American ports. The Spanish authorities often fell foul of the sloops; and an incident with one of them led to the rupture between England and Spain in 1738.

Kingston profited by the contraband trade even more in war than in peace; and Kingston and Port Royal throve in wartime on the presence of warships, through the sale of supplies, furnishing services, and free spending of prize money. But this created a new menace to the 'Creole interest'.

The Kingston merchants, particularly the Scots, were now strong enough to persuade Governor Knowles to move the capital to Kingston. The 'Creole interest' saw its domination threatened if the business of government were transacted, and the sessions of the legislature held, in the merchant city. After a three years' struggle, the Scots were defeated, and Spanish Town became the capital once more (1758).

SECOND COROMANTEE WAR

Now a new storm broke over the island. The slavery system was wasteful to human life, and made difficult the successful rearing of slave families. By this time, 7,500 slaves were being imported every year, and once more there was a considerable proportion of Coromantees, who regarded with contempt the wretched white militia, and began revolts. A great rising in 1760 was suppressed with atrocious cruelty, and a slight revolt in 1766 was followed by thirty years of internal peace.

This was ended by a war in 1796 forced by the Governor (Lord Balcarres) on the Trelawny Town Maroons, who surrendered after a brave resistance against overwhelming odds, and were transported first to Halifax in Nova Scotia and then to Sierra Leone.

The war of American Independence had introduced changes (notably by forcing Jamaica to produce more local foodstuffs). The Revolutionary and Napoleonic Wars had still more important results. The Haitian revolution brought refugees as permanent settlers, while the Spanish American *entrepot* trade expanded, and the constant visits of warships to an ever-increasing ring of seaports brought disturbing news and disturbing thoughts which gradually penetrated the country.

EMANCIPATION AND FREE TRADE (1808-1846)

On March 1, 1808, the slave trade became illegal. About the same time the Duke of Manchester arrived in Jamaica as Governor and continued in office until 1827. No other Governor had so long a rule, and the Manchester régime was a prolonged experiment in conciliation and gradual reform, the home government endeavouring to mould the local governing class to its wishes.

Manchester effected numerous administrative reforms. He induced his third Assembly to pass a bill for the registration of all slaves—a measure desired by the home government, but regarded by the planters as the first step toward emancipation. The number of slaves was found to be over 345,000. Abolition of the slave trade had already produced a nearly normal balance of population—female slaves slightly outnumbered males, instead of being greatly outnumbered by them as formerly. A bill considerably ameliorating the condition of the slaves was also passed.

ABOLITION MOVEMENT AND THE MISSIONARIES

The shadow of emancipation already lay upon the estates. The Whigs in England were pressing for parliamentary reform. This meant abolition of 'pocket' and 'rotten' boroughs, redistribution of seats, and creation of a middle class electorate. Since rich absentee owners of West Indian estates kept a parliamentary 'lobby' by means of the existing corrupt system, the abolitionists were in the Whig ranks.

Unrest among the slaves increased in Jamaica, and this was often ascribed to the Nonconformist missionaries (particularly Baptists), who were now active. The Assembly decided to strengthen the Established Church, and provided for a bishop and archdeacon (1824).

Jews were now given the same status as other (non-Anglican) whites. But free people of colour, though now eligible for public employment, were still excluded from the franchise. They outnumbered the whites by two to one, and had an able leader in a printer named Edward Jordon, who was to play a conspicuous part in the island's life for forty years.

REBELLION OF 1831

In 1827 Manchester finally left the island. He had prevented any serious breach and steered the island through a difficult period economically. But conciliation had failed: the popularity of the Duke had been purchased in part by his connivance in oppressive measures gratifying the whites, who were deluded into thinking that Britain could be defied.

The lesson was lost on the British Government, and it was not till 1831 that the Earl of Belmore (then Governor) was able to take a firm line. The Assembly then passed a slightly better slave law and gave the vote to free people of colour.

Christmas of 1831 saw a sort of general strike in the west among the slaves, and when the authorities took steps to crush it, the rebellion of 1831-32 began. In St. James, the militia withdrew to Montego Bay, the rebels were thus left in control of the interior, white troops were rushed in; and the militia and the civil authorities began an orgy of repression. Minor disturbances occurred far and wide.

PERSECUTION OF NONCONFORMISTS

There followed one of the most remarkable episodes in Jamaican history. For over two years the island's peace was disturbed, not by the slaves, but by a section of the whites. The first step was the persecution of the missionaries, particularly the Baptists, four of whom were arrested on charges of inciting to rebellion. Next the Colonial Church Union was formed, theoretically to protect the Anglican and Presbyterian churches.

The trials of missionaries proved failures, but persecution continued on an unofficial plane, many chapels being burned by the 'populace'—that is, the poorer whites, incited by the Colonial Church Union. The governing class had in fact ceased to govern.

Trial and acquittal of Jordon on a charge of sedition—his newspaper had called for abolition—and an abolitionist campaign in England by the Baptist missionary Knibb, showed that the pro-slave party was building up opposition. Just as the Tories had forced various sections of British opinion into the Whig camp, so the anti-emancipation group in Jamaica had now forced slaves, free people of colour and missionaries into an alliance against slavery. The Colonial Church Union, dreaming of secession to the United States, was broken by the Earl of Mulgrave in 1833, and the Assembly, now representing Jews and people of colour as well as whites, co-operated, though not very graciously, in the work of emancipation.

Arawak kitchen, St. James　　　　　　　　　　　　　　*F. J. Vaculik*

An old slave house at Good Hope, Trelawny　　　　　*Pierre Chong*

EMANCIPATION

The British Government now decided to abolish slavery as from August 1, 1834, with compensation of £20,000,000 to the slave owners, a third of which went to Jamaica, mainly into the pockets of mortgage holders. Children born to slaves were now to be free, and children under six became free. House slaves were to be 'apprenticed' for four years, praedial slaves for six. The 'apprentices' were neither slaves nor freemen. They were bound to their masters and liable to be flogged, but received wages and certain privileges. The system did not work well. On August 1, 1838, the apprenticeship system ended. Emancipation was complete.

THE EXODUS FROM ESTATES

The property-owners now no longer had to feed, house, and clothe their labour, and they still controlled the legislative machinery. But payment of wages required more working capital, which was not available, and employers offered very low wages and charged high rentals for huts and allotments. The more enterprising freedmen left the estates and became squatters in the wooded highlands.

The Baptists resisted the oppression of the labourers, and property-owners retaliated by attempts to strengthen the Established Church and encourage white immigrants as labourers or peasants—Scots, Irish, Hanoverians, and Portuguese from Madeira. But the labourers were badly treated, and died or returned home, while the peasants had to accept Negro standards of living. Importation of East Indians (1845-46) was also unsuccessful as a means of obtaining a better supply of labour.

COMMERCIAL DECLINE AND END OF PROTECTION

The revolt of the Spanish American colonies killed the contraband trade. There was now a large market for British goods in Latin America, but steamers made it unnecessary to use Jamaica as an *entrepot*. The collapse of trade was as marked as that of agriculture.

The market for sugar in the United Kingdom was seriously affected when Free Trade was adopted there. The abolition of the differential duties on sugar (1846) meant that slave grown sugar could compete with that of Jamaica. All classes united in protest: but the old mercantilist system had passed away, and the old Jamaica with it.

VI

THE NEW OLIGARCHY (1846-1900)

In the new economic, social and political order, a new governing class emerged. But its character continually changed, principally in three directions. The white planters, while performing many public duties, increasingly disappeared from politics; they were replaced by coloured men and Jews; and the influence of the merchant class tended to increase, the seat of Government being at length transferred to Kingston.

For some years (1847-54) the Assembly sought to impose rigid retrenchment on Governor and Council. This contest, like that at the beginning of the eighteenth century, ended in a partial victory for the Assembly. It surrendered, indeed, its right to originate financial measures, but only to an Executive Committee advisory to the Governor, two members of which were appointed by the Assembly and one by the Legislative Council. (There were now two Councils—the Legislative Council and a separate Privy Council in which both Houses were represented.) A loan of £500,000 from Britain helped the local administration out of its immediate difficulties.

The experiment in semi-responsible Government was successful for some years. Jordon was usually on the Executive Committee, and the principal figure in the Assembly. But his position was increasingly difficult. Black and coloured Assemblymen were only about one-third of the total, and Jordon did not have the full confidence of the whites, while his public services embarrassed him financially. He retired from political life and accepted a Government post, becoming eventually Island Secretary, the chief official of the colony.

MORANT BAY REBELLION

The Colonial Office sent a well-known Australian explorer, Edward John Eyre, first as Lieutenant-Governor, then as Governor. Eyre took a bitterly personal view of political criticism, and a sharp critic of Eyre and his advisers appeared in George William Gordon. The Assembly found it difficult to cooperate with the Governor; and the vigorous mob-appeal of Gordon, the distress caused by the American Civil War, and the smouldering animosity of Eyre to his critics, drew the island toward a crisis.

In the parish of St. Thomas-in-the-East, of which Gordon was one of the Assemblymen, the Custos, Baron von Ketelhodt (a German by birth), was one of Eyre's supporters. There was strong class feeling in the parish; the Negroes had lost faith in the white-dominated law courts, while Gordon had attacked the parochial administration. The pot boiled over in October, 1865, when Gordon was out of the parish. A crowd demonstrated while the Vestry was meeting. The local volunteers fired, killing several persons; the mob rushed the volunteers, set fire to the court house, and eventually killed the Custos and some others.

St. Thomas was in the hands of the mob, but there was no further bloodshed except at one point. Little wanton destruction took place. Eyre poured white and African regulars, sailors, militia, and Maroons into the parish. He arrested Gordon, took him by sea to Morant Bay (where martial law had been proclaimed), and had him tried by a military court for high treason. Gordon was promptly found guilty on flimsy evidence, and hanged. Three hundred persons were shot down or executed, hundreds of huts burned, and hundreds of Negroes flogged. Eyre now induced the Assembly to surrender the constitution, but was himself recalled, a Royal Commission having condemned his severity and his hanging of Gordon, though it praised his promptitude and vigour.

West Indian Review

Church in Falmouth, Trelawny

REVOLUTION FROM ABOVE

Sir John Peter Grant, an experienced Indian administrator with a hatred of paper plans, ruled from 1866-1874 with an Executive Council (called, however, the Privy Council) and a Legislative Council with no elected element. Grant was a business-like despot whose reforms, unlike those of Manchester or Jordon, effected a revolution. As Jamaica's first Colonial Secretary, Jordon was Grant's lieutenant till his death in 1869.

In two years, financial stability had been restored by judicious increase in taxation; capital goods for estates and other commodities needed for production were freed from duty; an efficient constabulary was established; the number of parishes was reduced to fifteen and parochial administration remodelled; a reorganised judicial system commanded respect; free medical services were introduced; education was improved; and a successful beginning was made with East Indian Immigration. Americans started the banana export trade from Jamaica in the same period.

In 1870, the Anglican Church was disestablished and Government Savings Banks were initiated. In 1873 Kingston became the capital.

ELECTED MEMBERS

Without Grant, the great machine of benevolent despotism creaked ominously. Its material benefits restored the spirit of the new oligarchy, which charged the Government with extravagance and arbitrary conduct. From 1884 an elected element was introduced, and though in theory Government had a majority, the seats were not filled until 1899. There was a liberal franchise and there were nearly 23,000 voters on the roll in 1887. The 1884 constitution was the basis of Jamaica's political life for sixty years.

THE BANANA TRADE

The banana trade was now superseding sugar and bananas had become the leading export crop. The fruit grew quickly and commanded high prices, so that it attracted both large and small proprietors. A new middle class arose throughout the island, of small farmers and salaried employés of fruit companies and merchants; this class was potentially dominant with the new franchise, but was little interested in politics.

THE PROSPEROUS 'NINETIES

Jamaica's highest pitch of general well-being was probably reached in the 'nineties. The population had nearly doubled since 1834 (when it was 370,000), but the 640,000 of the 1891 census did not imply serious population pressure. East Indian immigration was still encouraged. Although the sugar industry, faced by competition from beet, was not flourishing, it was in better shape than that of some other colonies. The fruit trade had diffused prosperity without, as yet, drawing the people from the cultivating of food crops. The rural population was well-fed and well-clothed. There were still wide areas that could be brought under cultivation; and destructive land-use caused too little concern.

POLITICAL COLLAPSE

There existed in the constitution two unusual provisions. If all elected members voted one way, votes of Government members were not counted unless the Governor declared it of paramount importance to carry Government's proposals; and if nine voted together on a financial measure, the same applied.

In 1899, Governor Sir Augustus Hemming, being defeated on a financial measure, prorogued the Council, filled all the Government seats, re-introduced the measure, declared it of paramount importance, carried it, and dismissed the new members. But Joseph Chamberlain, then Secretary of State, instructed him (1900) to keep a permanent majority. This was the position for over forty years, and the country lost all grip on political realities.

FAILURE OF CROWN COLONY RULE (1900-1934)

The power of the Nine and the Power of the Fourteen (the unanimous vote) remained with the Elected Members. But they seldom exercised either. The ruling class had been crushed in 1900. Henceforward it preferred to work with the bureaucracy and influence it behind the scenes. This was easier for the merchants—now that Kingston was the capital—than for the planters. New politicians, with purely local programmes and appeals to class and colour sentiments, gained ground.

A great earthquake destroyed Kingston in 1907, and killed hundreds: but the insurance collected after prolonged litigation provided an immense fund of loose money, and Kingston rose from its ruins greater and stronger than before.

From 1907 to 1913 Sir Sydney (afterwards Lord) Olivier was Governor. Possessing the driving force of Grant, the tireless and versatile Olivier did much good, but failed to achieve radical change.

EMIGRATION

The construction of the Panama Canal drew thousands of Jamaican labourers to the Isthmus. Others went to Cuba and Costa Rica. The country was actually suffering from concealed population pressure. Olivier's solution was a Negro yeomanry and the opening up of unused land reserves.

WAR OF 1914

The war of 1914 brought new ideas to Jamaica, some thousands of men going on foreign service. These new ideas were not given direction: there was no one to perform a task parallel with that of the missionaries a century before. Some attempts at organisation of thought appeared amongst planters and a sugar boom and its catastrophic collapse gave them a good deal to think about.

INDIAN SUMMER

Sir Edward Stubbs was the most popular Governor with the educated classes since Manchester. Under his genial and tolerant sway, the country showed unexpected reserves of strength. The survival of the sugar industry and the rise of the co-operative movement owed much to him. The banana industry flourished, there was no financial crisis, and Stubbs had excellent relations with the elected members. But the economic position deteriorated after his departure (1932): and the governorship of the unimaginative Sir Ransford Slater (1932-34) was merely the prelude to the disasters of Sir Edward Denham (1934-38).

VIII
THE RETURN OF POLITICS (1934-49)

The outstanding feature of Denham's period of rule was the emergence of the proletariat as a militant force.

Emigration on any considerable scale was impossible: thousands of Jamaicans were being repatriated. The great banana co-operative was forced to reorganise without a co-operative basis. Wages were low, and widespread malnutrition was proved.

Denham applied the stock colonial remedies to a novel situation. He increased indirect taxation and raised a loan to expand the public works programme. With thousands of unemployed and underemployed persons in town and country, this meant that large masses of men felt that they would be given relief work and were entitled to it. The propertied classes were alienated and the proletariat was not conciliated. The small farmers were tied to the rural proletariat by kinship and habits—they themselves often worked for wages. The salaried and professional middle class had no rallying cry.

The 1938 disturbances (in which no one was killed except by the police) led to the rise of Alexander Bustamante as a trade union leader, the acceptance of unions as the spearhead of the proletarian movement, an upward trend of wages, a new social policy sanctioned and even imposed by the Colonial Office, and a revival of political activity.

The new social policy meant higher taxation. Soon after Denham's death, the acting Governor raised the income tax rates. The government was now acting against the advice and wishes of the propertied classes, which had shown marked failure of nerve. The war was to make further direct taxation necessary.

At the end of 1938, the People's National Party was formed by a group (including professional and business men) around Norman Manley, Jamaica's leading barrister and Bustamante's cousin. Its objects were self-government, shift from indirect to direct taxation, and adult suffrage. On the whole, Bustamante opposed it; the middle classes gave little support; the propertied classes were repelled; and the war seemed likely to destroy the Party, which damaged itself further by declaring for Socialism (1940).

The new Governor, Sir Arthur Richards (now Lord Milverton), interned Bustamante, but pressed hard on the propertied classes. His taxation policy was actually supported by the People's National Party, which, however, contrived to marshal all the discontent in the country; then, in 1942, when Britain seemed weakest, it suddenly showed a disposition to compromise and accept something less than full responsible government, with a wholly elected House of Representatives, a nominated Legislative Council, and an Executive Council of ten (and the Governor), five to be chosen by the Lower House.

Bustamante had been released and was opposing the P.N.P. Richards left and was succeeded by Sir John Huggins, who held the first election under adult suffrage (December, 1944) in which Bustamante's newly-formed Jamaica Labour Party gained a sweeping victory. The moderate Jamaica Democratic Party did not win a single seat.

The war, by stopping banana exports, had assisted plant diseases in almost killing the banana industry. Sugar had once more taken first place and Bustamante's Union dominated the sugar industry. But virtual cessation of capital investment during the war had increased unemployment; and Bustamante's lack of administrative and parliamentary experience exposed him to criticism over the most necessary measures of recovery. The People's National Party and their trade unions grew stronger on the discontent; a section of the Labour Party seceded and formed the Agricultural and Industrial Party; everywhere the farmers were organising as a new force; and from 1946 a series of disasters befell Bustamante—notably the breaking of his power on the Kingston waterfront, first nursery of his Union.

At the end of 1949, by concentrating on winning the support of the rural proletariat and small farmers in the areas of capitalist agriculture, Bustamante secured a small majority in the second general election. The People's National Party doubled its strength: the Agricultural and Industrial Party was as decisively rejected as the Democratic Party in 1944.

CHAPTER TWO

The Story of the Maroons

The Maroons are a remarkable phenomenon which have attracted much interest from historians and romanticists. Some day a fine novel will be written of these strange people against their wild and primitive background. None of the attempts yet made to depict the Maroons in fiction has succeeded to this extent.

It is estimated that there are about two thousand Maroons in Jamaica today. The official Maroon holdings are Moore Town in the little explored John Crow Mountains in the east; Charles Town in Portland; Scott's Hall in St. Mary; and Accompong and Maroon Town in St. Elizabeth, adjacent to the strange and weird Cockpit country of Trelawny. Here is a grotesque wilderness of rock, long barren stretches out of which rise fantastic pyramids and cones of limestone, thick forests of gigantic trees, awesome shapes jutting out from the rock face like prehistoric monsters, sink holes of unfathomable depth. This land, which seems to have been made by a god in terrible anguish and then forgotten, is the home of the Maroons.

They live a form of communal life under a chief who usually has the courtesy title of Colonel, by laws and regulations which they formulate themselves. Many are the strange tales of their past. As can be expected in a closed community, divorced from the main stream of a country's life, polygamy was common. Obeah in its worst form was rampant. Cruelty was a dominant characteristic. Head money was awarded for every slave returned alive or dead, and if it seemed too much trouble to take in one live or dead body, they simply cut off the ears and sent them with a demand for payment.

Today the Maroons pay no taxes but they do have votes. Both Accompong and Moore Town are in the mountain fastnesses of the weird mountain country and are difficult of access, so visitors are infrequent. In appearance the Maroons differ little from the rest of the Jamaican peasantry, though perhaps they are better physical specimens, probably because of the invigorating climate in which they live.

The original Maroons were doubtless slaves who ran away from their Spanish masters and established themselves in bands in the unexplored and unknown parts of the island. When the Spanish were finally driven from the island by the English, many of the Negro soldiers in their army joined these bands, which became a serious menace to the peaceful and successful settlement of the island. They became brigands, highwaymen, bandits, raiding the estates of the prosperous planters, stealing the cattle and destroying the crops.

Efforts were made to bring them under control or eradicate them. Various expeditions were organised and sent into the unmapped, unsurveyed, unknown interior. By and large, the final result was more or less equal. Many of the detachments of British troops, often fresh from England with little knowledge of the territory, had to retreat, if not defeated at least baffled. Posses of settlers, more familiar with the terrain and the men with whom they had to deal, were more successful.

The name of the first Maroon chief known to history is Juan de Bolas, who, in 1662, made peace with the English and secured lands and full rights of citizenship for the outlaws. The great body of Maroons, however, did not approve of him and in 1664 he was ambushed and killed while travelling into the Maroons' territory. The English were confronted with the fact that the Maroons were still unsubdued, and the trouble continued until it reached such proportions that in 1738 the Governor decided to deal with the insurgents.

By the treaty which begins:

'In the name of God Amen. Whereas Captain Cudjoe, Captain Accompong, Captain Johnny, Captain Cuffee, Captain Quaco and several other Negroes . . .'
and contains the clause:
'that they can enjoy and possess for themselves and posterity for ever all the lands situate and lying between Trelawny Town

and the Cockpits to the amount of 1500 acres bearing north
west from the said Trelawny Town . . .'
the Maroons secured the land (to which they subsequently
added another thousand acres, free of taxation) and a full
pardon. They undertook to return all runaway slaves, to cease
their depredations, and to support the Government in any war
or rebellion.

But it was an uneasy peace, and in 1795 the Trelawny Town
Maroons rose in rebellion. The reasons given—that two of their
number had been flogged for stealing, and that they did not
like the new English superintendent stationed in the settlement
—do not seem adequate. Probably the subsidiary reason—that
they were dissatisfied with the area of their grant of land and
wanted more—is nearer the truth. From the first outbreak, the
Island was put under martial law, and the Governor himself
headed the troops. Hostilities dragged on for eight or nine
months, the Governor bringing in bloodhounds from Cuba to
assist in tracking the almost invisible enemy. One of the English
officers of the time said, 'There was little chance of any but a
Maroon discovering a Maroon.' The news of the bloodhounds
had such a terrifying effect that the Maroons sued for peace,
stipulating that they were not to be executed or transported.
The Government agreed, specifying that they must all come in
and surrender within a few days. That was on January 1, 1796.
Probably because of the understandably suspicious nature of
the Maroons, probably because many of them lived scattered
in small settlements in inaccessible crannies of the eerie cockpit
country, this condition was not complied with and it was not
until March 21 that the last came in.

Claiming that the conditions of the treaty had been violated,
Governor Balcarres took six hundred Maroons, packed them
into ships, and instructed the Navy to accompany them to
Halifax, Nova Scotia. The Bluenoses were not very pleased to
see them and took them in with reluctance. With the hard-
headed business sense for which they are noted, they insisted
that the Jamaican Government support the Maroons who, not
liking the cold weather, refused to work. The sum of £47,000

was expended on their maintenance over a period of three years, when Jamaica suddenly refused to pay any more. The Nova Scotians thereupon sent a bill to London for £10,000 a year. After wearisome correspondence, they were removed to Sierra Leone, where their descendants are today among the most respected of the people of Freetown.

The Maroons who remained in Jamaica continued in peaceful obscurity, enjoying the privileges they had secured and honouring their obligations. In 1865, they assisted the Government to subdue the Morant Bay riots and were feted and afterwards thanked at a gigantic banquet at the Kingston Racecourse.

Today, although they retain their aloofness, they have been for all practical purposes absorbed into the life of the community. There are occasional disputes between the different settlements as to who is the authentic Chief; and sometimes the Colonel from Saint Elizabeth will come into Kingston, resplendently dressed and with the air of a celebrity. But it is still an adventure to travel to the remote hills in which the Maroons live and few people attempt it. In Saint Elizabeth there is a lady—Mrs. Earle—who works among the Maroons and serves as a go-between when visitors wish to be received, and they *are* received with the greatest hospitality and housed in separate huts. Katherine Dunham, the celebrated dancer, has written a fascinating book on the Maroons of Saint Elizabeth, called *Journey to Accompong*, and occasionally a writer in search of copy makes the arduous journey. But as a rule, they live their quiet remote lives undisturbed by the march of civilisation.

CHAPTER THREE

Old Tales Retold

THE PIRATE GOVERNOR—SIR HENRY MORGAN

Of all the filibustering scamps who swilled their wine in the wild haunts of Port Royal, none is better known to us than Henry Morgan. This strange individual began his life, as he ended it, in character. Running away from his Welsh home, where his father was a prosperous land-owner, he made his way to Bristol in search of adventure. From here he went to Barbados, some say as a member of the crew of a slave-trader. Eventually he travelled to Tortuga and joined the buccaneers, who used the island off Haiti as their hide-out and base.

At the age of thirty he was already a Captain, and we hear of him in the company of two other 'Brethren of the Coast' in a raid on Granada in Nicaragua. Having proved his capacity for leadership, he was appointed Vice-Admiral of the buccaneer fleet under Captain Edward Mansfield (or Mansvelt) and proceeded with him to an attack on Curaçao, in the year 1666. The defences here proved rather strong for Mansfield's liking, and he turned instead to the capture of the island of Catalina, or Providence, which belonged to the Spanish. Here we may see Morgan's hand, for this Welshman had as his ambition the reduction of Spanish dominion in the Caribbean, and the rise of English sea-power in its place (with himself in a leading role, no doubt).

Morgan returned to Jamaica to report the outcome of this raid. Thus began the unholy alliance of Governor Modyford and Morgan in which both their own and their country's interests were so skilfully served.

Hearing that the Spanish were intending to attack Jamaica, Modyford decided to send out a search party (perhaps with the idea of turning the position to account). Having no regular troops he appointed Morgan 'Admiral' of the buccaneer fleet.

Morgan chose Cuba for his first raid, but astutely avoided the well-fortified Havana (making only a demonstration there), and descended upon a small coastal town—Puerto del Principe (the present Camaguey)—sacking it with the customary barbarity. Later in the same year (1668) he turned his attention to Puerto Bello, on the Isthmus of Panama. Knowing that this town was well-defended on the seaward side he attacked it from the rear and forced the Governor and the diminished garrison to take shelter in the fortified Castle of Santa Gloria. Now Morgan showed his ingenuity and ruthlessness by forcing certain monks and nuns, whom he had made prisoners, to carry forward the great scaling ladders which were to be set against the walls of the castle preparatory to its capture. He hoped by this device to secure the town easily, believing the Spaniards would not fire upon these holy people, but the Governor refused to surrender, and they were mown down. Morgan and his men carried the fort. The Governor was eventually shot, with, it is said, regret on Morgan's part, who admired his courage. Followed the usual horror of theft, rape and torture of the civilian population that so pleasantly characterised these piratical raids. The takings here were put at two hundred and fifty thousand pieces of eight.

Next he sacked Gibraltar and Maracaibo in the Gulf of Maracaibo, now modern Colombia, at the latter place destroying or capturing three ships (appropriating valuable treasure from one) and demanding a heavy ransom for evacuating the port.

The political situation was becoming more delicate. In July, 1670, the Treaty of Madrid was signed whereby England and Spain mutually agreed to abandon official connivance at buccaneering in the Caribbean. Either Modyford had not received confirmation of the terms of the Treaty (they allowed of an eight-month stay before enforcement) or he pretended ignorance of them, for preparations for the raid on Panama continued. Morgan assembled his forces at the little Isle des Vaches (off Hispaniola), mustering twenty-eight sail English and eight sail French, with about two thousand men in all, and two hundred and thirty-nine guns.

The record of the crossing of the isthmus by Morgan and his wild men—now numbering twelve hundred—is an epic of its kind. Fighting the jungle, crocodiles, mosquitoes, jiggers, malaria and yellow fever, living off the country (to the extent of a little stolen maize) and sustaining themselves mainly by unlimited draughts of heavy red wine, this tough army presented itself at the gates of the richest city of Spanish America, still apparently fighting-fit. (But nobody has told us how many bleached skeletons were left along the way.)

The battle was joined on the plain outside the old city of Panama on January 19, 1671, and here Morgan apparently out-manoeuvred his opponents by skilful generalship. There is a strange tale of the Spaniards driving a herd of cattle into the enemy ranks to their confusion; but these, on being confronted with fire, immediately turned and charged their owners! The Governor of the town in desperation ordered the blowing-up of the powder magazines, and fair Panama went up in flame and smoke. The booty was estimated at around seven hundred and fifty thousand pieces of eight.

Madrid and the whole Spanish-speaking world broke into a seething rage of fury over this act of aggression, and Modyford and Morgan were both called home under arrest (not before the latter had received the official thanks of the Governor and Council of Jamaica for his 'noble deeds in defence of English freedom'). The English Government was very half-hearted in its condemnation, and both men were eventually rewarded with good appointments. Probably the King and his counsellors appreciated the value of Morgan's services in securing England's position in the Caribbean. What he had been fighting for had come about—the Treaty of Madrid recognised the right of the English to the places they held in Spanish America, and from this time the influence of Spain steadily declined in the Caribbean.

Morgan attained his own personal ambition—he was knighted and appointed Lieutenant-Governor of Jamaica. He held this position three times, but later Lord Vaughan censured him for dubious practices, and he was eventually deprived of most of his honours. He is pictured as ending his days in degradation. He was a hard-living man, but a product of a tough age. Perhaps he, as much as Rodney and Benbow, secured Jamaica for England. When he died in August, 1688, he received a salute of twenty-one guns.

Tradition says he left a variety of coloured progeny in and around the Yallahs Valley, whose descendants exhibit portraits of the old fire-eater, representing him as a man of their own race.

The visitor to Port Royal may see the set of communion silver that is claimed to have been a gift from Morgan to the Church of his time. It is very old and primitive in design but probably dates from the time of George II.

NELSON IN THE WEST INDIES

In all the biographies of Nelson, one senses a kind of shocked disapproval of the West Indies, since they nearly caused the death of the great man when he was yet in his twenties. But this dishonour is shared by the East Indies, and indeed by many parts of the world, for Nelson was a delicate man all his life.

His first trip to these waters was made in 1771 when his uncle, Captain Suckling, sent him out to the West Indies in a merchant vessel to learn the art of navigation. Six years later he returned in the frigate 'Lowestoffe' as Second Lieutenant in His Majesty's Navy, and was quickly promoted, becoming Post-Captain in the 'Hinchinbrooke' in 1779.

The arrival in Hispaniola of a powerful French fleet under Count d'Estaing constituted a serious threat to Jamaica at this time. Nelson offered his services to assist the Governor (General Dalling) and was immediately appointed to the command of the batteries at Port Royal. Here he cooled his heels impatiently, as the French showed no signs of fight. Instead, the Governor was inspired to carry out a project he fancied to capture the fort at San Juan in Nicaragua, and thus drive a wedge between the northern and southern dominions of the Spanish.

Nelson's part was only to convey the troops to the mainland, but on arrival he found no one with knowledge of the place or capacity for leadership and so took charge himself. History says little about the outcome of this expedition (national records tend to gloss over the failures) but the young Nelson very nearly died of poisoning and dysentery. He was recalled by Sir Peter Parker to take command of the 'Janus' and returned to Jamaica, but his health failed to improve and he was invalided home on the 'Lion' in September, 1800.

Though Nelson's sojourn in Jamaica was a short one he naturally occupies a place of honour in the island's history. A part of the old ruined fort at Port Royal (Fort Charles) is called 'Nelson's Quarterdeck'. Here he must have paced the old brick ramparts, scanning the sea for the French sail that never came, or dreaming the dreams of those who have greatness in them. Over a doorway is his coat-of-arms, and there is an inscription: 'In this Place dwelt Horatio Nelson. Ye who tread his footprints remember his glory.'

High above the harbour he could see the Great House at Flamstead, where perhaps he stayed in a desperate effort to recover his health. The house may have been used as a naval hill station. In one of the rooms is an old four-poster bed which is called 'Nelson's Bed'; he may well have slept in it, for it certainly dates back before his time. Perhaps Sir Peter Parker sent Horatio there from his own official residence, Admiral Pen (now the Poor House).[1]

When he first returned from Nicaragua he was faithfully and tenderly nursed by an old black nurse named Couba Cornwallis, who looked after the naval officers and was much loved; but later the Admiral and his wife took him to their own house. So sorry for himself was the young lieutenant that he could be persuaded to take food and medicine only from the hand of the little daughter of his hosts. Horatio was fond of children. On the occasion of his meeting his future wife, Fanny Nisbet, of Nevis, she came upon him playing with her small son under the table. This was when he was out in the island in the 'Boreas'. He

---

[1] Frank Cundall, however, places "Admiral's Mount" (the Admirals' hill residence) as unidentified, but suggests it may have been in the Red Hills.

Port Royal. The archway leading to Nelson's Quarterdeck
There are many legends of ghosts attached to this scene

married Mrs. Nisbet in 1787. Nelson's last appearance in West
Indian waters was in 1805 in pursuit of Villeneuve but he did
not come to Jamaica at that time.

PORT ROYAL

Port Royal, even more than Spanish Town, must look to the
past for its glories. It had a grand innings in its time, being the
richest (and the wildest and wickedest) city of the West Indies.
Nature dealt it a shattering blow by the earthquake of 1692,
and since then it has been shorn one by one of its lesser honours,
until today it is just a little neglected township, sunk in a certain
atmosphere of the past, and further despoiled by the hurricane
of August, 1951.

The Spaniards made their capital at Villa de la Vega (Spanish Town) and used the point at the end of the Palisadoes
merely as a careening depot for ships. It was the English, and
more especially the buccaneers of the seventeenth century, who
built Port Royal into a great city, with 'houses as good as some
of the best in London', and established it as an *entrepot* of all the
trade and treasure of the Caribbean. Here came the captured
galleons, the pride and glory of Spain—such as survived the
furious slaughter of the sea; here came the gold and silver, the
precious gems, the silks and jewels, the gold coin wrested in
ransom from the blood and torture of alien cities. Treasure of
Cartagena, Puerto Bello, Hispaniola (the names are music and
poetry) poured in to be exchanged, sold, fought over. Here
came, too, the 'black ivory' from Guinea, that cruel cargo of
human flesh, fore-runners of a new coloured race (how mys-
terious are the ways of God!). Here swaggered the buccaneers,
Morgan and his like, tough and brave and coarse, decked in
embroidered coats and jewelled swords, makers and breakers of
Empires.

So Port Royal wallowed in its wickedness (judged by the
standards of another age), unaware of the wrath to come. For
on a summer morning of June, 1692, four years after Morgan
had left the world and its vanities behind him, three shocks of

earthquake shook the city, and all the beauty and wealth of it tumbled into the sea like any toy knocked by a childish hand.

Fearful tales remain to us of this terrible experience. We are told that the earth opened and swallowed people going about their avocations; then closed again, burying some entirely and imprisoning others up to their necks, squeezing them in a cruel embrace. One such, a certain Lewis Galdy, was fortunate enough to be spewed forth again and thrown into the sea whence he was rescued by a boat. His harrowing experience is recorded on his tombstone at Green Bay near Port Henderson.

Dr. Hans Sloane, botanist and founder of the British Museum, who was in the employ of the Governor of the time, describes the horrid scene and the crowds of homeless and terror-stricken people who endeavoured to find some shelter and safety on the mainland, which was to become the site of Kingston.

Tradition and even recent records maintain that traces of the ruins of the city can be seen from the surface of the water in clear weather. The cracked Spanish bell in the Institute of Jamaica—one of the few Spanish relics left—probably hung in the old Church that was submerged on that June day. The legend persists that for years the note of the bell could be heard moaning with the movement of the tide. So was Debussy inspired to write 'La Cathedrale Engloutie'.

Port Royal never recovered from this disaster, and attempts to rebuild the city were frustrated by fire and hurricane. It was a naval station for many years, however. Nelson served here and his Quarter Deck at Fort Charles commemorates him. In 1782 Rodney brought in nine prize ships after his defeat and capture of de Grasse at the Battle of the Saints. Here the commanders licked their wounds and repaired their ships at the dockyard at Port Royal. Earlier still, in 1702, Old Benbow sailed in, dying from his wounds in the encounter with Ducasse, off Santa Marta. Port Royal, in common with other ports in the West Indies, must have been a valuable base for English ships during the American War of Independence and for the contraband trade during the Civil war.

The present church of St. Peter's is eighteenth century. It stands athwart the narrow spit of land, the sea on both its sides, brushed by the tall, sighing casuarinas, that willow which takes kindly to the salty air. It has (or had) an old wooden gallery, and its communion plate is very early Georgian in style. The craftsmanship is simple, and it was probably made by colonial silversmiths, of which there were a number in Jamaica. It is claimed by tradition as a gift from Sir Henry Morgan. Plenty of the raw material went through his hands in his buccaneering days! Morgan's funeral sermon was preached in the old church and he was buried on the Palisadoes. Time has lost note of his grave.

Only recently has Port Royal been connected to Kingston by road. Before that one travelled, romantically, by naval launch and so went rarely.

During the war an airfield was laid out on reclaimed land on the harbour side. There the Fleet-Air Arm trained, and flyers from many lands and nations came for rest and practice. Today the aerodrome is a busy *entrepot* for air services in the Caribbean, and so the Palisadoes have now a new, and different, importance.

THE LEGEND OF ROSE HALL

'Tis said that on a moonless night in the witching hours after midnight the white figure of a woman stands beckoning on the road near Montego Bay. She is the White Witch of Rose Hall, whose infamous life and death became a legendary tale of horror and bloodshed whispered in the nights under cover of the rustle of waving sugar cane, or the murmur of swaying coconut fronds.

In the days of the first great sugar empires, Rose Hall stood resplendent on its hill overlooking the Caribbean. Reputed to have been built at a cost of thirty thousand pounds in 1775, it was said to be the finest house in Jamaica, and perhaps in the West Indies. A double flight of massive stone steps led to an open portico and then to an entrance hall forty feet long. Great, solid, carved mahogany doors opened into a banqueting hall able to accommodate two hundred people. A magnificent mahogany staircase led to apartments on the second floor. The walls and ceilings were ablaze with gilt and paintings, tapestries and oils. Lavish and splendid was the entertaining, fabulous and costly the hospitality.

Into this mansion of fabulous luxury and elegance John Palmer brought his wife. For a while the social life continued but gradually fewer and fewer invitations were issued from Rose Hall, less and less was seen of the inmates. Strange stories began to circulate in the countryside. Tales were told of the continual whipping and lashing of slaves, prolonged shrieks were heard by those passing on the road, iron shackles and necklets were described, unmerciful floggings and beatings until death were rumoured. Mrs. Palmer became a figure of superstitious horror and terror.

Credence was given to the reports when Mrs. Palmer brought a servant into court at Montego Bay, accusing her of attempted murder by poison. The girl was convicted and beheaded. Mrs. Palmer ordered the head to be carried back to Rose Hall and stuck on a pike as a gruesome warning.

At nights, in their compound or under the thatched roofs of their cottages, the slaves muttered, a dull angry rumble. It was said that the murdered slaves were thrown into a vast kiln near the kitchen. But what of the white men who had died?

The Palmers owned the adjoining estate of Palmyra, and the story is told that one day, in a demoniac rage, Mrs. Palmer attacked a young Negro slave with her whip. The boy turned on her and seized her throat. Other slaves rushed in and, forcing her to the ground, threw a mattress on her, trampling on it until the breath had left her body.

Old folk tales relate that years later on his death bed a slave described the ghastly scene, recounting that the Negroes had to be tempted with bribes before they would bury the infamous Mrs. Palmer.

The story is based on legend and very few facts are available. For some time a great deal of confusion existed between the Rosa Palmer, a goodly and charitable woman, to whom there is a monument in the Montego Bay Church, and the Mrs. Palmer described above. They were certainly two different women. Some authorities maintain that there were two Rosa Palmers, the first being the Lady Bountiful, and the second the Mrs. Palmer of our story, and that it was merely a coincidence that John Palmer married two Rosas. Other investigators say that the infamous Mrs. Palmer was called Ann. A more likely theory is that, after the death of Rosa Palmer, her children adopted the surname of Rose Palmer in memory of this good woman and that the woman who became known as the White Witch of Rose Hall was Ann Rose Palmer, and thus the confusion arose.

The tale has become even more complicated by the old folk tales of Mrs. Palmer wearing a ring inscribed 'If I survive I shall have five'. The original Mrs. Palmer was married four times. The peasants will also tell you 'she killed three husbands and the fourth killed she'. It can only be surmised that the true story, gruesome as it undoubtedly was, became confused, exaggerated and elaborated in being repeated by word of mouth by simple and superstitious people. There is no substantial evidence that the evil Mrs. Palmer was married more than once. The story was told that some years after her death her husband was driving his horses along the road to Montego Bay when the animals were so terrified by the figure of a white woman beckoning that they bolted; and that John Palmer lost consciousness from the shock and died shortly afterward.

CHAPTER FOUR

Geographical Sketch

Jamaica is one of the Antilles, as the French called the West Indies. The Greater Antilles comprise Cuba, Haiti, the Dominican Republic, and Jamaica; the Lesser Antilles being Barbados, the Leewards (Antigua, Montserrat, St. Kitts and Nevis, Guadeloupe, Martinique, and the Virgins) and the Windwards (St. Lucia, St. Vincent, Grenada, Dominica). Trinidad is an island unto itself, belonging geographically to the South American mainland.

These islands are like a semi-circular ring of jewels, enclosing the Caribbean sea, and forming a broken land barrier between the Atlantic Ocean and the Panama Canal. Their strategic value has long been recognised, particularly by the United States, which has steadily increased her influence in the Caribbean. They give the appearance of a chain of mountain summits of a submerged range, and Jamaica may have been part of a land bridge which stretched from the mainland to Santo Domingo or Puerto Rico.

Jamaica suffered much from the early cartographers, being depicted in various shapes and sizes. In the Institute of Jamaica (*which see*) in Kingston there is a collection of old maps of Jamaica printed in many a European country (one by 'Bill Berry, at the Globe, betwixt Charing X and Whitehall'). They are the kind on which is displayed a fat and jolly little boy-god from whose mouth issue the four winds, streaming to the four corners of the world; and galleys and strange craft cross the parchment sea, and flying fish and dolphins skip for our amusement.

The earliest maps show Jamaica as a large lump of rock or a nugget (not, alas! of gold, for in this respect Jamaica was a sore disappointment to Spain). Gradually it assumed proportions more in keeping with its actual shape, and today the visitor studying it will see that it strangely resembles a turtle, the head being formed by the western parishes of Hanover and Westmoreland, and Portland Point being a most realistic flipper.

Jamaica is the only British island in the Greater Antilles. It lies ninety miles to the south of Cuba about two thousand miles from New York, and four thousand from England. It is the smallest island of the three forming the Greater Antilles, but quite sizeable by comparison with those in the Eastern group. It is 148 miles long and 52 broad at its widest part, but only $22\frac{1}{4}$ at its narrowest. It is a mountainous country, only a small proportion of its 4,450 square miles being flat. The high land runs mainly through the centre of the island, east and west, culminating in the east in the Blue Mountain range, Blue Mountain Peak being 7,402 feet high. There is no snow-line here; indeed the highest mountains are clad to their summits in forest, the upper heights being Forest Reserves.

To the south of the Blue Mountain range proper is the range of the Port Royal Mountains (so called as most of it was contained in the old parish of Port Royal as constituted in former days). They encircle the Liguanea Plain in which lie Kingston and St. Andrew, and include such places as Newcastle (the military hill station), Guava Ridge and Flamstead, all attractive places to visit.

The Red Hills, so called from the rust-red colour of their soil, raise their humped ridges to the west of the plain. In the gap between these hills and the Port Royal range, which forms a neck or pass to the North side, the towers of the Stony Hill wireless station rear gangling arms into the sky.

Roads to the north must all cross the great central range of the island; the main road to St. Ann and Montego Bay goes over one of the highest points of the range—Mount Diablo (2,300 feet at its summit). The highest road in the island is through Hardwar Gap at 4,000 feet.

The mountains of Manchester have long been a favourite resort for visitors and residents alike, the climate being a refreshing change from the heat of the lowlands. Mandeville

Where the river flows into the sea, Morant Bay   *F. J. Vaculik*

Hope Gardens   *Tourist Board*

and Christiana are two country towns of this parish, enjoying an altitude of between 2,000 and 3,000 feet.

No sooner does one drop off the Manchester Hills on to the plain below Spur Tree than one is rising again to the Santa Cruz Mountains, running north and south, with the little village of Malvern perched on the top, looking down on the town of Black River. All the Black River business folk of sense and discrimination are said to live in Malvern, and two of the chief schools in the island are there, owing to the healthy situation.

Again, in Hanover and St. James there is high land in the interior, falling away to a narrow coastline where the temperature registers at a higher level.

The variety of the terrain of the island is one of its amazing features. Dropping down off Mount Diablo, for instance, one comes upon the lovely rolling park lands of Moneague, almost English in character, and the pastures of St. Ann, where the Great Houses of pleasant country estates look down from their cool heights upon the coastal belt and the blue and jade of the sparkling Caribbean.

The low-lying areas are found mostly around the coast. On the north and east these form a narrow belt, but in the south they widen out to the plains which the Spanish used for their *hatos* or cattle ranches. The Liguanea Plain, around Kingston, was so used, as well as for the growing of sugar cane. It is fertile, rather dry, lying as it does in the lee of the great mountains which trap the rain brought by the north east trade winds; and it is healthy for this reason. These southern plains continue through the districts of Spanish Town, Old Harbour, May Pen and Vere, the latter now a great sugar-growing area. The Pedro Plains lie at the foot of the Malvern Hills, and the swamps around Black River, immediately to the west, are perhaps the hottest and least healthy part of the island. This flat coastal belt continues on to Savanna-la-Mar in Westmoreland. Though Montego Bay and the St. Ann and St. Mary coast are low, they derive the benefit of the cooler atmosphere of the hills close to them on their landward side, while the perpetual trade winds, blowing off the sea, temper the heat of the day.

The Arawaks (those gentle people who lived here before the Spaniards) called their tropical home 'Xaymaca', said to mean the Island of Springs, and generally speaking the island is well-watered, though periods of drought are suffered. There are many rivers, some of which have a continuous flow throughout the year—the Black River, the Rio Grande, the Rio Cobre, the Milk River. The smaller ones are apt to be floods in the rainy season and trickles during the dry weather. Several—the Hope River, the White River, the Roaring River, the Rio Cobre—are tapped to supply water and electric power.

A curious feature of some of the rivers of the island is their tendency to sink through the limestone, continuing as subterranean streams but reappearing above ground when their volume or the character of the soil demands it.

The largest river of all, the Black River, in the parish of St. Elizabeth, has this peculiarity. One may lean over a bridge, near Maggotty somewhere (odd names are a feature in Jamaica!) and see the young river gushing forth from a cave to begin its outdoor trip to the sea. It started life in the hills of Trelawny, but went to ground early in its existence . On the south coast it issues a fine broad stream, offering perhaps the largest source of water supply in the island. Yet parts of St. Elizabeth, the parish through which it runs, are the driest in the island. This is due to the honeycomb nature of the soil, which cannot retain moisture. Some day, no doubt, the Black River will be used to irrigate the neighbouring lands and make them blossom like the rose, but the expense of conservation has so far proved a barrier to such a scheme.

This river is one of the best fishing rivers of the island, especially at its mouth, and anyone filled with the ambition to shoot a crocodile should find good hunting here. The neighbouring marshes and the Pedro Plains give good bird shooting.

Many of the rivers are of the utmost beauty and of great variety; as a contrast there are rivers like the Yallahs, in its upper reaches a rushing mountain river cutting its way deep at the foot of precipices, or tumbling over great boulders like any trout stream, and the Rio Bueno (boundary of St. Ann and Tre-

lawny) flowing serenely to the sea through great forests of coconut palms. One longs to linger on the bridge where the White
River goes by, near Ocho Rios, to be lost in the frame of blue
sea and blue sky; or to idle along the gorge of the Cobre, that
'copper' river where the green water reflects the overhanging
trees, and where the blue or white gaulins or herons stand
motionless upon the rocks. The Flat Bridge here is unique—
built low on the river, its great stone buttresses pointed like
ships' bows to meet and breast the violence of the river in spate.
Often enough the water sweeps over it to submerge it completely
(but never to sweep it away). The high water mark here registers
thirty-three feet above the road, reached during the great rains
of 1933.

There are fifteen known mineral springs in Jamaica, many
containing valuable therapeutic properties. The best known are
the Milk River Bath in the parish of Clarendon, the Bath of St.
Thomas the Apostle, in the village of Bath, in the parish of St.
Thomas, and the Rockfort Bath in suburban Kingston.

Milk River bath probably has the most powerful radio-active
water of any mineral spring in the world. Competent scientific
authorites have found that it is fifty-four times as radio active as
Baden, fifty times more than Vichy and three times as powerful
as Karlsbad. Scientifically expressed, the water is equal to 160·2
× 10·10 curies per litre or 43·25 Mache Units.

The greater part of the island is limestone in geological
formation. The Blue Mountains are composed of shale and con-
glomerates, and are of an older age. There is a good deal of
erosion on these slopes, due to over-cultivation and the steep-
ness of the terrain. There are alluvial valleys of great fertility in
the lower-lying areas suited to the growing of sugar cane and
bananas. On the limestone uplands a great variety of crops can
be grown—corn (maize), cassava, ginger, pimento, cocoa,
groundnuts (pea-nuts), vegetables and fruits of all kinds, and
coffee (preferably at an elevation above two thousand feet).
Tobacco likes the lowlands, and rice is grown increasingly in the
swampier areas. There are fine pasture lands in St. Ann, Clarendon and the western parishes. In fact the variety of climate and

soil in the island permits of a wide diversity in its economic life, as well as in the delights it can offer the visitor.

There are two areas of which little is known—indeed they may be considered to be unexplored—the Cockpit Country in the Western end, and the John Crow (or Blake) Mountains in St. Thomas. They are both composed of honey-comb limestone, which makes them difficult and dangerous to traverse. In the Cockpit Country there are great 'sinks' or holes extending to enormous depths—often bottomless pits, according to legend. It is in this kind of country that whole rivers (if small ones) disappear, to reissue in what they presumably consider more reasonable and hospitable country! Man, too, finds his advances rejected, and even in a little island like Jamaica, short of land space, he cannot find here any scope for his husbandry. But the district yields timber, and is the last large source for this industry, though haulage presents difficulties.

The John Crow Mountains lie off the eastern end of the Blue Mountain range (running north and south), but are of a different geological age. They are little known, only a few enterprising naturalists having braved the forbidding ridges of sharp, pointed limestone and trackless rock.

CHAPTER FIVE

Climate

Jamaica lies round about the 18th degree parallel (the latitude of Kingston is 17·57 N.) and thus does not suffer from the worst equatorial heat. Being an island, it is milder in climate than the mainland of Central America (altitude for altitude); indeed, it is often cooler in the summer than New York or the Canadian cities. The variation between winter and summer temperatures is not great, being ten or fifteen degrees. There is a perceptible difference in the day and night temperatures, which is most marked in the winter and at high altitudes.

Statistics taken over several decades give the following mean annual temperatures (Fahrenheit):

Altitudes above sea-level	Mean Temperature	Mean Maximum Temperature	Mean Minimum Temperature
0	78·8	87·5	70·8
500	77·1	85·1	69·8
1000	75·3	82·8	68·6
2000	72·0	78·6	66·1
3000	68·7	74·9	63·3
4000	65·5	71·6	60·1
5000	62·4	68·8	56·8
6000	56·5	64·3	49·3

Jamaica is the land of eternal sunshine, but like all tropical islands, enjoys what the sailors call 'on-and-off shore' breezes. The day breeze comes in from the sea, and is locally called 'the doctor'. The night breeze comes from the mountains.

The north and north-east coasts are fanned by the trade winds, which blow throughout the day almost the year round. These winds bring the rain to Jamaica, the greater part of which is precipitated upon the high mountains of the east and

The Blue Lagoon, Portland

F. J. Vaculik

north-east. The rainfall there always exceeds one hundred inches and has been known to go as high as two hundred inches. The driest area is Kingston and the adjacent Liguanea Plain, which lie in the shelter of the mountains. The rainfall for Kingston is thirty to thirty-five inches, and in Montego Bay it ranges from fifty to seventy-seven inches.

Jamaica is an island of variety in scenery, in race, and in climate. Generally speaking, the higher you go, the cooler it is. The low lands along the coast, such as Kingston, the Liguanea Plain and Spanish Town, the plains of Vere, Black River and Savanna-la-Mar, are the hottest areas, but there are few days when the cooling sea-breeze cannot be felt. It becomes cooler and cooler as one climbs into the mountains to one, two and three thousand feet, and many people at four thousand feet enjoy the comfort of a fireplace in the chilly nights.

Normally, heavy rains occur in May and October, but this climatic factor is subject to wide variation and sometimes there is little or no rain and the island suffers from drought. The climate of Jamaica has shown considerable change in the last fifty years, due, it is thought, to deforestation which has created the dry seasons, and the fact that the soil, being porous, does not preserve moisture.

While the land may suffer at certain times from the lack of water, the air is nearly always damp, the humidity ranging between seventy-six and eighty-four. This is said to be the reason for the absence of sunstroke; unless one is spending several hours in the blazing sun, it is not necessary to wear a hat.

The Caribbean area, according to the meteorologist, is subject to hurricanes. These storms usually originate just north of the Equator and make their appearance at the eastern end of the Caribbean, somewhere north of Barbados, and blow north-west to the Bahamas and Florida. Jamaica, however, is apparently not in the path of these hurricanes, and really violent storms with winds blowing at a hundred miles an hour and upward are rare; prior to the hurricane of August 1951, which caused considerable damage in the Kingston area, the last two causing loss of life and property damage were in August 1880

and again in August 1903. In 1944 there was serious damage
to coconuts. Such storms as occur are usually confined to
certain months, as is evidenced by a piece of doggerel verse:

June—too soon,
July—stand by,
August—don't trust,
September—remember,
October—all over.

But generally speaking, heavy rain or strong winds are depar-
tures from the normal in Jamaican weather. Mostly, it is that
island of which Tennyson writes: the land where it is 'always
afternoon'.

CHAPTER SIX
Parishes, Towns and Villages

Jamaica is divided into three units known as Counties. They have borrowed the names of English counties and are called Surrey, Middlesex and Cornwall. They have only a nominal significance. For the purposes of administration, the island is divided into fourteen parishes. The old town of Port Royal, formerly a separate parish, is now part of Kingston, which is the smallest parish in the island with an area of only ten square miles. In this parish is the city of Kingston, which is the capital of Jamaica and the largest city in the British West Indies.

For purposes of municipal Government only, Kingston is united to the adjoining parish of St. Andrew, which has an area of 191 square miles. These two parishes extend from the sea in the south to the Port Royal and Blue Mountains in the north, and east and west from Bull Bay to Hunts Bay. The Port Royal Mountains are easily visible from the city and towering behind them is the Blue Mountain Range. The Port Royal Range is crossed at Hardwar Gap by an arterial road at an elevation of 4,380 feet. Nearby are the military cantonment of Newcastle and Catherine's Peak 5,056 feet high, a conspicuous sugar-loaf-shaped eminence. The mountains are also crossed by another arterial road leading from Kingston to Annotto Bay on the north coast by way of Stony Hill. This is the shortest artery for traffic across the island.

The parish of St. Thomas, adjoining St. Andrew on the east, has as its chief town Morant Bay. This parish takes in the eastern tip of the island and is divided on the north from Portland by the crest of the Blue Mountains. Prior to 1867, most of the present parish was called St. Thomas-in-the-East. The area of St. Thomas is 300 square miles.

Extending north from the slopes of the Blue Mountains to the north coast is Portland, which contains the John Crow

72

Mountains, a barren, inaccessible and unexplored region. Blue Mountain Peak (7,402 feet), the highest point in Jamaica, is on the dividing line between St. Thomas and Portland. The parish is 328 square miles and contains the towns of Port Antonio and Buff Bay.

West of Portland, extending along the north coast from Palmetto Bay to White River, lies St. Mary, 254 square miles, an area famous for its bananas. Its chief town is Port Maria.

Adjoining St. Mary lie the 481 square miles of St. Ann, known as 'the garden parish', and an important cattle-raising district. Its chief town is St. Ann's Bay, which is about a mile west of the site of the first capital of Jamaica established by the Spaniards, then called Sevilla Nueva, of which no trace remains.

This part of the coast, running through St. Mary and St. Ann, is fast becoming one of the largest tourist centres of the island.

Further west is Trelawny, comprising 352 square miles and having as its chief town Falmouth. The parish, called after a former Governor of Jamaica, Sir William Trelawny, who died here in 1772 and whose name is commemorated in an old song ('Shall Trelawny Die?'), is traditionally associated with sugar manufacture.

Continuing westward, the next parish is St. James, whose chief town is Montego Bay. St. James, named for King James the Second, has an area of 240 square miles.

Next is Hanover, with 177 square miles, named for the Royal House of England in the reign of George the Second. The charming chief town is Lucea.

Taking in the western end of the island are the 320 square miles of Westmoreland. The chief town is Savanna-la-Mar, near to which is the largest sugar-cane factory in the British Empire. This is Frome, which is owned by the West Indies Sugar Company, Limited, an associate of the world-famous Tate and Lyle group.

St. Elizabeth comes next, containing the town of Black River. The river at whose mouth it is situated is the largest in Jamaica and navigable by small craft for some miles. St. Elizabeth contains 474 square miles and is an important producer of logwood.

Manchester, east of St. Elizabeth and 339 square miles in area, is notable for possessing a considerable number of small independent peasants who live, for the most part, from the produce of their land; and also, near Mandeville, its chief town, for its citrus. There are also important bauxite deposits in this area.

Clarendon, named after the celebrated Lord Chancellor of England, is 467 square miles in area. Its chief town is May Pen. In Clarendon is Milk River Bath whose waters are among the most radio-active in the world.

The last parish is St. Catherine, lying between Clarendon and Kingston, and containing the old parish of St. Thomas-ye-Vale. The capital of the parish, Spanish Town, was known under the Spaniards as St. Jago de la Vega and was the capital of Jamaica until 1872.

TOWNS AND VILLAGES

The countryside abounds in villages and hamlets, but there are few large towns. There is no village system in the sense in which it is known in England, where the life of the community is concentrated in the village centre. Attempts have been made to introduce the village system, but it is doubtful if this can be done except spontaneously and by natural growth.

The towns and villages of Jamaica are chiefly centres for the collection and distribution of the agricultural products of the island. The coast is dotted with fishing villages and tourist centres, and a few shipping ports whose fortunes have fluctuated with the ups-and-downs of the banana and sugar trades.

Each village contains its Chinese grocery shop and its saloon or bar, often under the same Chinese ownership. On the piazza of the shop, the people gather in the evenings, and it is as much the 'club' of the villagers as the village inn of England.

There are only three towns of any real consequence.

Kingston

Kingston, with a population of approximately a quarter of a million, is the capital of Jamaica and its largest city. It is incorporated with the Parish of St. Andrew, the municipal

King Street, looking north

West Indian Review

Government Buildings

West Indian Review

government for the two areas being unified in the Kingston and
St. Andrew Corporation. The city was founded in 1692 but was
practically rebuilt after the 1907 earthquake. There have only
been two disastrous earthquakes in Jamaica, the last serious
one being in 1907 when the city of Kingston was practically
entirely destroyed. As with the San Francisco catastrophe in
the previous year, the earthquake was followed by fire which
gutted whatever buildings survived the shocks. About one
thousand people were killed and great loss sustained. In re-
building the city, the authorities insisted on reinforced concrete
construction. Some of the best examples of modern architecture
can be seen in the bank buildings. The Bank of Nova Scotia,
erected by a firm of Canadian architects, is built on the principle of a ship. The steel skeleton frame was riveted together.
The Royal Bank of Canada is also a fine structure and the black
marble pillars of Barclays Bank (Dominion, Colonial and Overseas) are impressive. The Holy Trinity Cathedral on North
Street is an interesting example of Byzantine architecture, with
its huge dome without pillars. It was built by the same firm of
Canadian architects.

The Parish Church near Victoria Park is worthy of a visit.
There are some old monuments and gravestones in the churchyard, notably that of Admiral Benbow, who died in Jamaica
after a disastrous engagement with the French in 1702. It is said
that

> *The Kingston town folk with sorrow did go*
> *To see the last of brave old Benbow.*

The shopping area is mostly confined to King and Harbour
Streets. The Public Buildings lie on both sides of King Street
and consist of the East Block containing the Law Courts, offices
of the Administrator General and Trustee in Bankruptcy, Sur-
veyor General, Registrar of Titles, and the West Block containing the offices of the Collector General and Collector of Customs, General Post Office, and Treasurer.

The Institute of Jamaica (*which see*) in East Street is a place of
great historic interest. Here are preserved the old minutes and
documents, slave contracts, portraits of past Governors and

men famous in the island's history. The West India Reference Library has the best collection of West Indiana in the world. In the Museum are Arawak relics, interesting old maps and natural history specimens.

William James Gardner, writer of the finest history of Jamaica and the foremost authority on the subject, is buried in the churchyard at the corner of North and Duke Streets.

The Airport is nine miles from Kingston on the Palisadoes Road, that narrow strip of land which embraces the far side of Kingston Harbour and leads at its end to Port Royal.

Port Royal

The old city of Port Royal has excited the imagination of generations of visitors. The remnants of the town, with the exception of the military quarters, are a few streets and lanes and broken-down hovels. This city of gold, the rendezvous of the swashbuckling gentry, the riff-raff of the seas, of pirates and gentlemen adventurers disappeared in the earthquake of 1692. (For the story of *Port Royal* see page 56.)

St. Andrew

St. Andrew, consisting largely of the residential area, offers a number of interesting places to the visitor. The Hope Botanical Gardens are within easy access and contain a fine tropical garden, and a collection of plants, trees and flowers. The Orchid House is well worth a visit. It is hoped that an aquarium and aviary will be available to visitors in the near future.

King's House, the official residence of the Governor of Jamaica, is also off the Hope Road and is set in rolling lands reminiscent of the great houses of England. Up Park Camp, abutting South Camp Road, is the home of the military garrison, housing whatever section of the British army is currently stationed in Jamaica. The military also have a hill station, Newcastle, far up in the mountains, which can be seen from St. Andrew on clear days.

The Parish Church at Half Way Tree has some interesting monuments, including those of Zachary Bayly, uncle of Bryan Edwards, historian of the West Indies, and one of the leading men of the mid-eighteenth century; and General Villettes, Lieutenant Governor of the Island, evidently a Huguenot.

At Mona is the University College of the West Indies, established in 1947. Modelled on the great English universities it specialises in medicine (see *Appendix*). Her Royal Highness Princess Alice, Countess of Athlone, is the Chancellor. The motto of the University is

ORIENS EX OCCIDENTE LUX
Light rising from the West

Spanish Town

Spanish Town, the ancient capital of St. Jago de la Vega, is but a ghost of its former magnificence. In the fine square can be seen the ruins of the old residence of the Governor, the one-time House of Assembly and the Court House, all eighteenth century buildings. The Rodney Memorial is by John Bacon, R.A., one of the foremost sculptors of his day. Many examples of his work can be seen in England, including the monument to William Pitt the elder in Westminster Abbey, and Dr. Johnson in St. Paul's Cathedral. The memorial was erected in honour of the celebrated admiral who crowned his three and a half years' service as Commander-in-Chief of the Jamaica Station with his famous victory over de Grasse in 1782. The original Cathedral was built by the Spaniards, taken by the English but rebuilt after the 1712 hurricane. The churchyard contains graves of many eminent early settlers but the flagstones of the Cathedral itself with their inscriptions of bygone men and women are impregnated with history. There are places where whole families have been buried. Many of them were victims of the dreaded yellow fever. Monuments of importance are those of the Earl and Countess of Effingham, Sir Thomas Modyford, Governor of Jamaica from 1664-71; and Sir Thomas Lynch, Governor from 1682-84. The earliest is that of Catherine, wife of Sir Charles Lyttleton who was deputy Governor of the island from 1662 to 1664.

The 'Eagle House' on King Street commonly known as John Crow House, once surrounded by a moat, is full of historic

St. James, Spanish Town

Drawing by M. Hepher

interest. It was originally the house of Sir James de Castello, who was agent in Jamaica for the Asiento Contract. This was the contract obtained by the English South Sea Company in 1713 to supply Spanish America with slaves. It was a condition of this contract that a royalty or duty on each slave was to be paid to the King of Spain and it was the non-payment of these royalties which led to war between England and Spain ending with the treaty of Aix-La-Chapelle in 1748. The contract was renewed but continued to be unprofitable to the English company and finally it ended in 1750 with the payment of £100,000 compensation by the Spaniards. In Spanish Town there is also a Tamarind Tree said to be that under which two colonels of the Army—Tyson and Raymond—were shot in 1660, convicted of endeavouring to effect a coup d'etat in favour of civil government for Jamaica as opposed to the military government then in operation.

Montego Bay

Montego Bay is the principal town in the western part of Jamaica in the Parish of St. James with a population of about eleven thousand. It is, in addition, the centre of the tourist trade. The town itself is the usual tropical town with a market and shopping centre. But it has an excellent natural harbour, from which a quantity of produce is shipped.

The name *Montego* is thought to come from the Spanish word *Manteca* meaning lard, the earlier commerce of the area being the making and shipping of lard derived from wild hogs in which the district abounded. There is little else left in Montego Bay of the one hundred and fifty years of Spanish rule except the monastery at Miranda Hill situated about half a mile from the Court House on the road to Falmouth. The garden wall and some of the building can still be seen.

In the Parish Church, the foundation stone for which was laid in 1775, is a monument to Rosa Palmer. This is not the famed 'White Witch of Rose Hall' but the first wife of the Honourable John Palmer who seems to have had a propensity for 'Rosas', his second wife also bearing the name. Local legend says she 'killed three husbands and the fourth killed she'.

Further details of the story can be found elsewhere in this book. There is a modern hospital a short distance outside the town and a number of sugar estates in the district, including Rose Hall, Catherine Hall, Ironshore and Hampden.

A mile and a half from the centre of the town are the White Sands of Doctor's Cave and the centre of the tourist colony. Behind the town overlooking the bay is the main residential section. There are also the residential suburbs of Fairfield and Reading, two and four miles from Montego Bay, the country club and race course being at the former.

Next in order of size is *May Pen*, named after a family which once owned a cattle estate (in Jamaica always called 'pen'). It is a town of considerable importance on the main road from Spanish Town to Mandeville. It is the chief town of the Parish of Clarendon and contains its law courts and administrative offices. It owes the acceleration in its growth during the last few years to the presence of an adjacent American base during the 1939-1945 War.

Port Antonio, although listed as a town, really has the air of a sleepy village. Its twin harbours made it a port of considerable importance in the past, and there is some revival of its importance in the restimulated banana industry. It is a tourist centre of great beauty and charm. It is the capital of the Parish of Portland and the terminus of the Jamaica Government Railway.

The only remaining town of over four thousand population is *Savanna-la-Mar*. It is the capital of the Parish of Westmoreland and is the centre of an important sugar district. Nearby is the West Indies Sugar Company's Frome estate, the largest in the British West Indies. It is a commodious little town with a wide main street. The outstanding year in its history was 1780. In the hurricane, the sea, breaking everything before it, overwhelmed the town and swept it to complete destruction leaving, as the historian said, 'not a vestige of land, bodies or habitation behind'.

Morant Bay is the chief town of the Parish of St. Thomas. It is a shipping port, especially for bananas. It is known in history as the scene of the Morant Bay riots (see *History*). It is an open

D   P.I.

roadstead with one danger point, Galatea Rock, which has only sixteen feet of water above it. Although small, it is of considerable importance in the parish, politically and economically . . . it has three banks!

Port Maria, the capital of St. Mary, is a busy little town amid some of the loveliest scenery in the island. It has a good harbour, somewhat protected from heavy winds by the little Cabaritta Isle. There is a good club and it is a popular centre for the many settlers from overseas, who include many distinguished persons, one of whom is Mr. Noel Coward. Not many miles away is the pretty little town of Annotto Bay, which is on the railway line.

St. Ann's Bay, though the population is little over three thousand, is the capital of the Parish of St. Ann and a town of considerable importance, being the commercial port for the surrounding country. St. Ann's Bay is another of those places which claim to have been Columbus' original landing spot . . . it was named by him *Santa Gloria*. It has an excellent water supply from the Roaring River. To the east of the town is the first Spanish road, running to Golden Spring. The St. Ann's Bay Fort, erected in 1777, is now used as a slaughter house.

Mandeville is a neat little town nestling in the hills between the Mocho and Carpenter Mountains. Two thousand feet high, it has an admirable climate and has become the centre of a large settlement of people from the United Kingdom, including many who have come to this excellent spot in order to spend their declining years. There is a first rate club (the Manchester Club), with perhaps the best golf course in the island and all the amenities. There is a limited town water supply, but the rainfall is plentiful and most householders supplement the town supply by catchment tanks. The nearby village of *Christiana* boldly calls itself a town, and indeed, it has an excellent market and a branch bank. It is set in magnificent scenery and is the centre of the ginger industry.

Falmouth, capital of Trelawny, is one of the few towns in Jamaica of any architectural interest. Its importance has de-

Brown's Town, St. Ann

F. J. Vaculik

Port Antonio

F. J. Vaculik

clined and its streets, though sleepy, have picturesque vistas. It
has a good harbour and one of the few partly-navigable rivers
in the island . . . the Martha Brae. William Knibb, who played
an important part in the emancipation of the slaves, is buried
in the Baptist Churchyard.

Lucea, the capital of Hanover, is enchantingly situated on an
arm of land which encloses a natural harbour. The drive from
Montego Bay to Lucea along the coast road is one of the most
beautiful in Jamaica. The fort, still in good repair, was built as
a defence against the French.

Black River is the capital of St. Elizabeth which, because of its
dryness and the difficulty of irrigation, is probably the poorest
parish in the island. The situation has been relieved in recent
years by the development of a tomato-growing industry, and
the unproductive soil does produce pineapples on a large scale.
Black River, at the mouth of the navigable river of the same
name, has a good water supply, the usual public buildings and
two branch banks. The town is the centre of the logwood industry, of the peasant industries of mat, hat and basket making
and of various other small undertakings.

Other small towns in the island include *Port Morant*, of considerable importance as a banana port, in St. Thomas; *Buff Bay*,
on the sea and railway line in Portland; *Brown's Town* and
Moneague in the hills of St. Ann; *Green Island* (the most westerly
town in the island) in Hanover; *Chapelton*, in Clarendon; *Linstead* (famous in song); *Old Harbour* (the most southerly town of
the island); *Bog Walk* and *Ewarton* in St. Catherine. *Spaldings*
has the distinction of being in two parishes—Clarendon and
Manchester.

Ocho Rios, regarded as a village, is destined for considerable
importance. It has a good harbour, and is becoming a bauxite
port. A large jetty is under construction by the bauxite interests
and, in addition, it is the centre of a new and important residential area which has become known as the 'Gold Coast'. Every
inch of the coast line is being developed, beaches utilised where
they exist or created where they did not, and hotels are springing up all along the shore. Although St. Ann's Bay and Port

Maria at present enjoy most of the trade from this developing area, Ocho Rios is bound to attract a good deal of it as soon as it has awakened to its own potentialities.

CHAPTER SEVEN

Jamaica's Dependencies

THE CAYMAN ISLANDS

If you would like to visit an enchanted island of great beauty and fascination you must make the two and a half hour air journey from Jamaica to Grand Cayman. A pinprick on the world's map, its seventy square miles seem at the quiet limit of the world. Here is the peace and serenity which Robinson Crusoe must have enjoyed set against a background which might have inspired Robert Louis Stevenson's *Treasure Island*.

Grand Cayman is the largest of the three Cayman Islands, dependencies of Jamaica, with a population of about seven thousand. Columbus discovered them in 1503 and called them Las Tortugas because of the large number of turtles in the sea. Later they became the hideout for pirates and buccaneers, some of whom, it is believed, left their treasure of gold and precious stones safely cached under the guard of ghostly pirate crews. Some say that after the sacking of Panama, Henry Morgan with four of his men came ashore at Grand Cayman and buried his plunder. The story goes that one of the men, named Bawden, deserted and could not be found. After killing the other three, Morgan sailed away to Port Royal. There are many Boddens in Cayman today doubtless descended from Morgan's truant gunner and most of them still hope to find the treasure—a hope which springs eternal in every Caymanian breast in this island where treasure maps are a frequent and exciting incident.

Certainly through the years some treasure has been found and, in heavy storms, pieces-of-eight and other ancient coins have been flung up on the beaches. In 1936, a fishing boat found some ingots of pure gold off Banner's Reef; and in 1939 Spanish coins were picked up on the beach at Gun Bay. Such names as Breaker Point, Half Moon Bay, Old Isaacs, Roger

Wreck Point, Old Man Bay and Rum Point still encourage even the most sophisticated moderns to continue the search.

The people of the Caymans, descendants of shipwrecked British sailors, Cromwellian soldiers, and buccaneers, are a friendly and hospitable people. The salt of the sea is in their blood and most of the men are seafarers or builders of ships. No finer sailor ever manned a ship of sail or steam and no boat-builder in the Western Atlantic can rival them. The main industry is the catching of turtles, which the Cayman fishermen catch off the coast of Nicaragua and adjacent waters. With the exception of the small number which go each year to make the famous soup for the Lord Mayor's Banquet in London, most are sold to the United States. Nowadays the Mayoral turtles are usually flown to England, being fed with champagne on the way, apparently to keep their spirits up! The Cayman schooners run mostly to Tampa or Miami . . . and most of the Cayman women wear American frocks and nylon stockings!

It is an interesting and sometimes strange community, with many quaint old customs. The clearance papers used for aero-planes are the same form as was used in the days of sail. Today they certify 'to all it doth concern that Captain Roberts Master or Commander of the aircraft . . . Burthen of 12½ tons navigated with 4 men built and bound for Jamaica having on board ten passengers hath here Entered and Cleared said vessel according to Law'. There is a strong Puritan flavour to the religion of the islands, and it is considered improper for young women to bathe in very modern swim suits. One may therefore be confronted from time to time with the rather startling vision of young women jumping in the sea in semi-Victorian attire.

This coral island, covered with dense luxurious vegetation ablaze with flowers, has a climate that makes one feel one is living through a day escaped from Eden. Near Georgetown is a four-mile beach of purest white and golden sand bordering a sea of indescribable beauty, with its varying and ever changing shades of blue, green, purple and mauve, in the lucid clearness of which one can see coral, fish, seafans and star fish of huge size of the most extravagant scarlet, crimson and orange. On the north side, there is a beach a mile long and countless small caves and inlets which seem untouched by man.

THE TURKS AND CAICOS ISLANDS

The Turks and Caicos Islands are a group of islets, which if not lost beyond the horizon, are at least but dimly perceived. They were given to Bermuda, then awarded to the Bahamas and finally handed to Jamaica, in whose possession they rest, except for the souls of the people, which remain with the Bahamas, the Bishop of Bahamas still undertaking their care.

The islands were discovered by Juan Ponce de Leon in 1512 and then forgotten for one hundred and sixty-six years. Geographically they are part of the Bahamas but were first settled by emigrants from Bermuda in 1678. The Bermudians spent each summer raking in the salt, but were not left undisturbed, being first harried by the Spanish and then by the French. They surpassed these hazards only to find themselves involved in further trouble and argument as to the jurisdiction of the territory. Their protests were overridden, and in 1799 the Turks and Caicos Islands became part of the Bahamas. This pleased no one, and the people petitioned the Crown. In 1848 the islands were formed into a separate government as a Crown Colony under the Governor-in-Chief of Jamaica. In 1873 the expenses of administration having proved too heavy, the islands were at the wish of the inhabitants annexed to Jamaica as a Dependency administered by a Commissioner, but retaining a separate legislature and local control of finance. The connection with Jamaica and the help given by Jamaica in very many ways have proved most beneficial to this small community.

The total population is about 6,500, although some of the Islands are uninhabited. The principal one, Grand Turk, is about ten miles long. It has a rather lonely and desolate atmosphere, probably because there are few trees. The vegetation consists of shrubs and a few rather tired Casuarina trees. The houses are all of wood, many two-storied, but they lack paint. All gardening is done in boxes, the soil being dug from rock interstices and pot holes. The island is very flat with a range of

Bodden Town, Grand Cayman

Stanley Couch

Lighthouse on the low, rocky coast of Grand Turk

Courtesy of His Honour the Commissioner

low hills along its east side. There are some lovely beaches around the coast, which is only slightly indented, but there are no hotels and no guest houses. There is a cable station and a small Government operated cinema.

The economy depends on the salt industry, which is entirely that of solar evaporation. The salt ponds are partitioned off into a series of basins with sufficient fall from one to another to cause the sea water to flow through. With the aid of the hot sun and strong winds the vegetable and mineral impurities are successfully precipitated before the brine reaches the last pond, which is called the fixing pond. The salt crystallises and is ready for raking. It is then put into small heaps by hand, taken out by mule cart and put into piles of three or four thousand bushels in pyramid shape. If left long enough it becomes very hard, but hardly the shape of Lot's wife, and when shipment has to be made it often has to be broken up with a pickaxe or a heavy mallet. It is shipped in bulk, being conveyed from shore to ship by lighter, in bags.

The Caicos Islands are rather more fortunate as far as agriculture is concerned and are able to grow their own produce. Generally speaking, the people live on fishing. The conch industry is a profitable one and two or three million a year are shipped to Haiti, where they are considered a delicacy. Lobsters (crawfish) and also conchs have their tails cut off, are cleaned, frozen and flown to the United States.

The people of the Turks and Caicos Islands live a quiet and uneventful life. They go to bed at eight o'clock and get up in the early morning to rake salt, to fish for lobster or to gather conchs. They are all literate—every fourteen-year-old child can read and write—but they are superstitious, perhaps being influenced by the elements of Voodoo which have leaked in because of their trade with Haiti. Most of them wear a little blue bag around the neck to ward off evil spirits. The population is predominantly Protestant and it is said that there is not one Roman Catholic on Grand Turk. The people are either Baptists, Anglicans or Methodists.

There is little more to say of these tiny spots on the world's surface. They are administered by a resident Commissioner who is selected by the Secretary of State for the Colonies and appointed by the Governor of Jamaica. The Commissioner is also President of the local Legislature.

CHAPTER EIGHT

Housekeeping

The newcomer who has suffered because of the servant shortage in the United States or Great Britain will be delighted to find that domestic help is plentiful and the quality reasonably high. Nevertheless, the situation is not without its difficulties; and forewarned is forearmed.

Wages will seem very low to those familiar with the high rates now obtaining in England and especially in the U.S.A. But the appearance is deceptive. Although there are households in which a maid-of-all work is employed, it is not usual in the better-class homes, and is indeed inconvenient, if not impossible, if a good deal of entertaining is contemplated. It might seem to the novice that it is better for everybody concerned to have one good maid well paid and well fed; but the habit of the country operates against this practice. After all, Jamaica is the tropics and hard and continuous physical labour is rough on anyone. It is easier to have a well-run and happy home if the custom of the country is observed.

The kind of home the new resident will occupy may be a bungalow in the plains or the foothills or a country house on an estate. In the latter case it may be one of the delightful old houses scattered around the island, and there will be hardwood floors to be cleaned and polished and a great deal of woodwork, in jalousies and perhaps ornamental carving, to be kept clean. Most country houses employ cleaners from the village, who do not live on the premises and are paid by the day or the week. The regular staff will consist of a gardener and a yardboy (in addition to the estate men), a butler or 'butleress'—his female equivalent—a laundress, a housemaid and, of course, a cook. The butleress does the work that a house-parlourmaid *used* to do in England; the housemaid may clean the floors (with a coconut 'brush' probably) and will certainly polish them. She or the butleress will substitute for the cook (and each other) on her days off. The cook is usually a woman; she will sometimes do the washing or some of the housework; but as a rule the best cooks do not wish to do any other work, and often are not competent to do so. Her work is not the sinecure it may seem, for probably she will cook on a wood fire, which produces a good deal of dirt. She will have to keep her kitchen clean, and she will have to cook for the staff (who usually provide their own food) and for any domestic animals you may have. And when there is entertaining to be done, she is kept busy enough; and she must be left free for such work if that is the kind of life you contemplate.

In the suburban bungalow, it is usually possible to manage with two women who divide the work of the house and the inevitable garden boy, who may literally be a boy or who may be a good gardener who can also wait at table. This, indeed, is the ideal staff for the small family without a great deal of heavy entertaining to do. A laundress could be employed on a part-time basis if necessary.

The wages vary from eighteen shillings to twenty-five shillings a week for the women, and from fifteen shillings to thirty shillings or more for the men, according to their age and ability. The servants 'feed themselves', although some employers provide 'findings', such as sugar and condensed milk. It is better, if you wish to contribute to the staff larder, to give something really nourishing, such as a few pounds of beef once a week. Some people prefer to feed their servants, in which case the wages are lower; but it rarely works, except with employers who like a Jamaican diet. The staff will probably tell you they 'don't like your food', and, like servants all over the world, they will develop very luxurious tastes if you are feeding them. It is much better to pay them the higher wages and to make them gifts of food from time to time if you feel like it.

If you think the wages low, and decide to pay more for a better type of servant, the probability is that you will pay more but will not get the better type of servant. The best plan is to engage your staff at the current rates; and if later on you find you can afford to pay more to a particularly good worker, you can raise the wages little by little.

Every humane employer will wish to treat his staff with kindness and consideration. In fact, only men and women who are naturally brutal can bring themselves to treat their dependents harshly. However, the reactions are not always what you would like and expect. It is a good plan to have a written agreement, setting out plainly the terms of employment and of dismissal. A servant who wishes to leave will very rarely give you notice, even though bound by law to do so—she just goes off and leaves you flat; but often they will make fantastic claims if dismissed. Whether you agree to one or two weeks' pay in lieu of notice, have it clearly stated and agreed to; when you discharge her, pay her off, do not give her notice and allow her to hang about your home. It is inadvisable anywhere, and particularly in Jamaica.

The best means of obtaining domestic help is through the Government Labour Exchange, but do your own investigating after the interview, and make sure the applicant has worked in a household similar to your own unless you wish for the heartbreaking task of doing your own training. There are plenty of well-trained, hard-working and civil girls and older women around, but they must be carefully selected, and you will probably have more than one disappointment before you settle down. You will be particularly lucky if you can find 'old time' servants, surviving from the days when manners were better and training was good. Do not expect perfection, for Jamaican servants have a habit either of remembering that you like a particular thing and giving it to you *ad nauseam* or of doing a task meticulously day after day for months and then forgetting how to do it. There are local characteristics, qualities and faults, which you will have to get used to. It is worth while, for the standard *under a good employer* on the whole is high.

FURNISHING THE HOUSE

We have given some advice on the renting or buying of a house (see also *Property Market*, Chapter 21) and we will now

Tourist Board

Two favourite methods of transporting food to market

West Indian Review

Left: The street corner 'higgler'. Right: The kerb tailor

offer a few suggestions as to furnishing it. Houses in Jamaica which are wholly or partly built of wood (concrete nog houses have a wooden framework) are subject to damage by the destructive ants known as termites, and so is any furniture of soft wood they may contain. (Books, also, are subject to damage by insects—they should be painted with a special preparation to be obtained from the drug store.) Very little imported furniture is made of solid hardwood—when hardwoods are used, it is usually as veneer—and most people prefer to buy such furniture locally. There are shops and cabinet-making establishments in plenty. Local taste is inclined to run to glossy French polishes and fanciful designs; but there are plenty of good craftsmen who can work to your instructions. There are also some unsatisfactory ones, so it is better to employ a recommended cabinet-maker or to order from a store which employs one. Agree on prices beforehand, and do not pay too large an advance—the small man will expect you to finance him for materials. Insist upon a time limit. You will avoid these difficulties if you order through an established dealer. There are beautiful native woods to choose from— go to the Natural History Museum of the Institute, where each cabinet is made of a different hardwood. (See *Institute.*)

Upholstered furniture is also subject to deterioration in the tropics, but some people will place comfort first, and there are all too few houses in Jamaica with comfortable chairs. Most people spend a large proportion of their lives on their verandahs and terraces, so comfortable furniture, in wood or metal, upholstered with loose cushions that can be taken in at night, is desirable. But we are among those who sometimes like to sit in a room, and we like that room to be comfortable; and if you share our taste, you will provide yourself with some upholstered (the Americans call it overstuffed) furniture. The best upholstered furniture must be imported; but quite good work is done by local men, and nobody need suffer from aching bones.

Curtains here, as elsewhere, are a matter of taste. Heavy draperies are seldom required and some people prefer to do without curtains entirely. It must be remembered that the windows are often jalousies—that is, movable shutters set into the

CLARK'S TOWN

In some remote country districts, water has to be transported by the time-honoured method.

F. J. Vaculik

A fine assortment of fruit at a street corner. The authorities frown on this method of marketing.

West Indian Review

usually very hot and peppery but the bountiful quantities of rum with which it is inevitably accompanied will probably make you think it more delectable than it is.

Pork is apt to be very fatty and without much lean flesh: so if you are accustomed to the delicious white loins of, say, Lincolnshire pork, you had better not challenge comparison. Attempts have been made to cure bacon and ham, but as there are plentiful importations of much better quality the embryo industry has practically disappeared.

Fish is not very interesting in Jamaica. For the most part it is coarse and without much taste. Snapper, kingfish and a fish called silk fish are about the best of the sea fish. The Jamaican cook makes delicious fish cutlets and this is usually the best method of using these varieties. The so-called lobster is really a giant crawfish and is a genuine delicacy. It is rather tough and indigestible when served plain. A delightful way of serving is to mince it and bake it in the shell. The recipe is given in the Appendix.

Old inhabitants like to tease newcomers with the information that oysters grow on trees, but this is very nearly true. The tiny oysters are found in the mangrove swamps and actually do cling to the sides of the mangroves. They are really too small for eating on the half shell but are delicious in cocktails, soups or for garnishing. Shrimps are very good; a favourite method of serving them is with fried rice and there is a so-called stew which is quite good, if you can persuade the cook to leave out the raw or nearly raw onions which ruin the delicate flavour.

River fish include mullet, which is very good when fresh from the mountain streams. There is also mudfish, well named because it tastes of mud. River shrimps and crayfish are very good if freshly caught. The former are hawked around the streets by men who catch them, cook them and pepper them so abundantly that you are unlikely to be able to eat them. If you find yourself in a river location, the boys will go out with torches at night and catch the shrimps by primitive means.

Novelty foods are the booby eggs from the islets called cays and land crabs, called black crabs (recipe in Appendix).

Turtle is a delicacy of the island. This was
caught between Falmouth and Montego Bay

West Indian Review

F. J. Vaculik

The fishing catch: off Rockfort

Salt fish is a favourite dietary constituent, both cod and salmon. When the salt has been soaked out, codfish forms an ingredient for a number of tasty local dishes, the most popular of which is described in the Appendix.

The vegetables include the starchy tuberous growths, such as the yam, sweet potato and ordinary potato, in Jamaica called 'Irish' potatoes. A delectable vegetable—probably the best starchy vegetable—is the yampie, a small, delicate-tasting tuber which has a haunting flavour of chestnuts. Rice, a great proportion of which is imported, is very expensive; its favourite form is in conjunction with the kidney bean, called 'red peas'. The conjunction of 'rice and peas' is so popular that it is sometimes called 'the Jamaica Coat of Arms'.

One of the staple 'vegetables', if it can so be called, is the breadfruit, which is really the fruit of a large and imposing tree. In a book called 'Orphan Island', which she wrote many years ago, Miss Rose Macaulay told of a young woman who 'pulls the breadfruit off the tree and bites into the luscious fruit'. The reader is not encouraged to attempt this, for the skin is as hard as iron and as unyielding, and it is sometimes as large as a baseball. It is much liked when cut into sections and roasted in the hot coals which, incidentally, is the best way to cook the more delicate yampie.

The green banana and the plantain are often served as vegetables but some people consider them too sweet as an accompaniment to meat. The ripe banana, of course, has many uses, which do not need cataloguing here.

Green Vegetables. There is a local variety of spinach which is practically a weed, called 'callalu'; it has thick but delicate stalks almost like asparagus, but because it is common and cheap it is not regarded as the delicacy it really is. Cabbages are plentiful. Cauliflower of inferior quality can be obtained, and broccoli grows with some ease but is not very much cultivated. Lettuce does not produce the firm hearts which need frost, and celery, although it can be grown and is useful for soups, is not crisp as in cold climates. Tomatoes are usually large and fleshy.

The fruits of Jamaica are delicious indeed. It is difficult to say which is the king of them. The pineapple, of which the best dessert varieties grow in Jamaica and which is at its best from June to September; or the juicy mango, which grows on magnificent umbrella shaped trees in great variety and profusion in the summer months . . . the Bombay mango is far and away the best, but there are other good varieties. Then there is the pawpaw (the papaya), a melon-like fruit containing pepsin, which is supposed to be good medicinally and is certainly good to eat. We need not mention the banana again. There are several varieties of the passion fruit, including the granadilla which makes excellent ice cream, and the starapple, which combined with the orange is known as 'matrimony' (see recipe); the soursop also makes good ice cream. Then there are a number of 'amusing' fruits—the naseberry which looks like a toffee apple and tastes very much like it too, the guinep, the sweetsop, the otaheite apple (a magnificent tree), the jackfruit (but beware of it, for its smell is worse and more penetrating than that of the skunk), the June plum and a host of other tropical products which the children like, you will wish to taste but probably will not want to add to your permanent diet.

Citrus fruits are plentiful and in good variety. The orange and tangerine, sweet and juicy, have also been merged into the ortanique, and there are other odd varieties. Grapefruit are sweet and good, and limes and Seville oranges are abundant.

DRINK

The 'wine of the country', of course, is rum. Beer is manufactured locally, and wines and spirits are imported. Those with particular tastes or drinking-habits will be able to indulge them. A guide to rum-drinking will be found in the Appendix, with recipes supplied by the manufacturers and blenders.

There are a few specific drinks native to the country. A liqueur with a fragrance and taste of its own is made from pimento berries; usually, it is over-sweet for those who have not the Jamaican sweet tooth. There are other liqueurs and ready-mixed cocktails, usually with a rum base.

Aerated waters of various kinds are manufactured by several firms. The juice of the green coconut, with or without rum, is very refreshing.

Fruit drinks are popular, as they should be, with pineapples, oranges, grapefruit, tangerines, limes and lemons plentiful and comparatively cheap in season.

The native who becomes merry (or morose) on one or two tots of rum is not drinking the refined varieties popular with visitors. He has probably imbibed 'white rum' or proof rum, which is practically pure (and crude) alcohol. It is not recommended to novices.

The manufacture of rum, with a note on some local varieties, is described elsewhere in this book. (See *Industries*.)

Home from market, Clarendon Hills

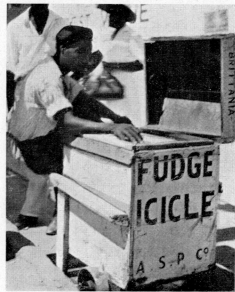

The itinerant ice cream man is as common in Jamaica as elsewhere. The home-made cart is called 'Brittania' with fine disregard for correct spelling.

CHAPTER NINE

Cultural Activities

Within recent years there has been a great quickening of the pulse of cultural activity in Jamaica. There is a definite art movement, although attempts to indicate that it is 'indigenous' or 'primitive' must be questioned. The theatre, deprived of professional companies since 1939, has in the following years been electrified from within until now there are amateur companies of outstanding merit. Literature, though lagging behind the other arts, has yet produced some interesting writers; and Jamaicans, always responsive to rhythm, have developed more and more exponents of serious music. In the middle of 1950, radio was commercialised and already there has been a burgeoning of local talent, in both writing and broadcasting.

The establishment of the University College (see *Appendix*) is giving a fresh impetus to intellectual life. A Film Society has been founded. The Musical Society has been in existence for several years, a Society for the study of French culture has recently been formed. An ambitious Library scheme is in process of translation into action.

Many of these activities used to circulate around the Institute of Jamaica. The Library was housed there for many years and inhabits the quarters in East Street, although this is one of the Departments of the Institute of Jamaica which eventually will pass to other hands. The Arts and Crafts Committee of the Institute was founded in February, 1941, under the directorship of Esther Chapman, editor of this book, who was also responsible for the idea of converting the daCosta Museum (bequest of a former Mayor of Kingston) into an Arts and Crafts Instruction Centre. Edna Manley, herself a sculptor of note, conducted an art class under the sponsorship of the Institute; and the Institute is the scene of lectures by celebrities, both local and from abroad,

West Indian Review

The Institute of Jamaica has been for many years the centre of culture in the island. The famous West India Reference Library is housed there and an interesting Museum is being developed.

on all kinds of subjects. The Lecture Hall has recently been air-conditioned.

The Institute of Jamaica was founded in 1879 ('for the encouragement of literature, science and art'). It is administered by a Board of Governors and its Director is Mr. Bernard Lewis. Its most famous Secretary, notable in West Indian scholarship, was the late Mr. Frank Cundall who, with the assistance of Miss Helena Morris, who carried on the tradition for many years after his death, built up the remarkable library of West Indian books, which is considered the best in the world.

The Institute comprises a General Lending and Reference Library, two Junior Centres, a West India Reference Library, a Natural History Museum and a Science Reference Library, History, Art and Exhibition galleries, a Lecture Hall, the Colonial Archives (situated at Spanish Town) and the daCosta Institute, already referred to.

The General Library is open from 9 a.m. to 8 p.m. on weekdays. There is a book stock of approximately twenty-eight thousand volumes. The membership fee is five shillings a year. Visitors to the island may borrow books for three months on payment of two shillings (membership fee) and a deposit of one pound.

The Library does excellent work in the island. It sends loan boxes of books free of charge to recommended small societies, especially in the interior country districts. These organisations are helped also with gifts of material withdrawn from the library.

Any visitor who desires to confer a genuine benefit upon the people of Jamaica might well present a gift of books in the certainty that the Institute will use them wisely.

The West India Reference Library, located on the upper floor of the Institute Building, is open from Monday to Friday, from 9 a.m. to 4 p.m. and on Saturdays from nine to one.

To quote from the Institute Report:

'The collection of books, pamphlets, newspapers, manuscripts, maps, plans, engravings, portraits and clippings, represents the devoted and untiring efforts of Mr. Frank Cundall, Secretary and Librarian of the Institute of Jamaica, from 1891 to 1937. In the library there are over 17,000 items dealing with Jamaica, other West Indian Islands, British Guiana, British Honduras, certain Central American countries, and West Africa. This reference library is now a recognised centre in the West Indies for historical research concerning the Caribbean area, more particularly Jamaica.

'Treasures from the manuscript collection include "The Letter Book of Roger Hope Elletson" (1737-1775) a Jamaican planter who became Lieutenant-Governor of Jamaica in 1766. Another item of interest is the original manuscript atlas, on vellum, relating to the occupation and sale of lands in Jamaica, from the commencement of British rule in 1655 to about the year 1760, prepared in connection with the estates belonging to the Dawkins family. These manuscripts have been placed in the custody of the Institute of Jamaica by the Sugar Manufacturers' Association (of Jamaica) Ltd., Kingston.

'The Nugent manuscripts comprise a collection of several hundred letters (including correspondence to and from General Sir George Nugent) written during his term of office as Governor of Jamaica (1801-06) a period of great activity of war and trade in the West Indies.

'The files of Jamaican newspapers occupy a considerable section of the Library, and are invaluable in matters of research. The collection of portraits and of maps is extensive and comprehensive.'

The Museum, which faces Tower Street, is open from Monday to Friday from 9 a.m. to 5 p.m. and on Saturdays from nine to four. The cabinets containing the exhibits are made of the beautiful native woods which abound in the island and these are an exhibition in themselves.

CHAPTER TEN
Obeah and Folk Lore

Obeah, Pocomania, or Voodooism as it is known in Haiti, has a religious as well as an African basis.

The island is predominantly Protestant; Anglican and Baptist being the strongest denominations. A small proportion of the population is Roman Catholic. As can be concluded, with a mixed population such religions as Confucianism, Hinduism and Buddhism appeared, but at the present time their adherents are few, practically all the people having been Christianised.

Most of the religious sects have been introduced into Jamaica by settlers and religious workers, each bringing his own peculiar belief or religion. In many cases the country from which immigrants came gave direction to their religious attitudes. This was conspicuously so in the case of the African slaves. Pocomania or revivalism can be traced back directly to the religious outlook of the first Africans. It was only natural that a people transferred by shiploads from their native land and their freedom in a country of large expanses to a place where their movement was restricted to the small confines of an estate in a small island, without any provision being made for their social or religious welfare, however primitive, would of necessity indulge with added fervour in the enjoyment of their natural customs. Their pent-up feelings thereby found a necessary outlet, for, while they were removed physically and geographically from their homeland, their innate sentiments and emotions could not be left behind.

Thus there have been woven into the religious fabric of Jamaica from earliest times, observances and practices which originated in Africa. In 1842, shortly after the abolition of slavery, Gardner in his *History of Jamaica* relates some of the religious activities of the emancipated slaves. He writes:

'They were accustomed to meet together after nightfall gen-

The beach

J. Dougall

The lonely cottage of a fisherman with its thatched roof in the mangroves

Paul Geddes

erally beneath the shadow of a cotton tree. Fowls were sacrificed, and wild songs sung in the chorus of which the multitude joined. Dancing then began, becoming more and more weird-like in character, until one and another fell exhausted to the ground, when their incoherent utterances were listened to as divine revelations. Half-demented creatures sat among the branches, or in the hollow of trunks of trees singing; while others with their heads bound in a fantastic fashion, ran about with arms outstretched and declared that they were flying.'

Some seventy years after this, H. G. deLisser writes in his *Twentieth Century Jamaica*:

'. . . Since the rise of Bedwardism there has been a recrudescence of what was known fifty years ago as "Myalism", a practice of cult which is nothing but a modified form and remnant of the old West African priest dance and divination.'

Bedwardism originated with a self-appointed prophet called Bedward who identified himself with the Holy Ghost, promised to fly to heaven but instead died in the mental hospital.

Another student of this trend said:

'Pocomania (a type of emotional religious expression derived from the African myal cult) derives from a suppression of emotion. It is the reaction from cold, formal religion. The Jamaican must express himself in motion and rhythm.'

In his *Psychic Phenomena of Jamaica*, Dr. Joseph J. Williams, S.J., identifies the modern practices of myalism (pocomania) and obeah with the old religious dance and ritual of the Ashanti race in West Africa and with the Ashanti practice of witchcraft.

He writes:

'. . . Strictly speaking, myalism, the direct antithesis of obeah, is the residue of the old religious dance of the Ashanti just as obeah itself is the continuation of the Ashanti witchcraft. Thus obeah is secretive, malicious, and has gradually taken on a form of devil worship. Myalism, on the contrary, is practised in the open. It is beneficent in its purposes, and it has developed into modern revivalism in Jamaica. In practice, however, the same individual is now frequently an obeah man by night and a myal-man by day, when he digs up the very obeah which he has planted while exercising the other role.'

There is a fundamental difference between myalism or poco-mania and obeah. Obeah is the propitiation of evil spirits; myalism is the supplication to good spirits for greater benefits.

It is impossible to say how much obeah exists in Jamaica at the present time. The practice was outlawed in 1898 and it is a criminal offence to accept money for the casting of spells to cure sickness or cause sickness, or other purposes.

It is said, however, that the Obeah Man is still available to the knowledgeable and while his services are less and less engaged for curing illness, he is still consulted in matters of the heart, whether it be to revive a fading love or assuage a broken heart or bring back the loved but lost one.

The theory is also advanced that he is a satisfactory source for the securing of rain or a good crop or a good price for yam, or the winning of a fortune in the Sweepstake, or the punishing of an enemy.

Pocomania, now rather mild and simple in form, is still prac-tised. The central figure is a shepherd who is the priest and directs his followers according to his particular inclination. Acti-vities usually consist of a whirling dance and continual chanting around a white draped table on which candles flicker in empty rum bottles, together with a calabash and a supply of rum, and perhaps some feathers. The dancing and the chanting are de-signed to bring on the 'spirit' and, it is hoped, a speaking in un-known tongues.

An interesting practice is the celebration of Nine Night. This is the holding of a religious meeting with the singing of many hymns on the ninth day after a person's death, by which it is supposed that the evil spirits are driven out and the soul is allowed to proceed on its way to peace and rest.

Annancy stories, those fairy-like tales of animals and birds, which were so often told by Nannies to the children in Jamaican nurseries, are African in derivation.

It is said that Brer Rabbit was born in Guinea, where some of the Negroes in the Southern United States originated. In the

Gold and the Ivory Coasts, there were Brer Annancy, Brer Tiger, Brer Snake, Brer Monkey and Brer Fowl. Brer Annancy became the central figure in Jamaican folk lore. In the earlier stories, he appears as a big black spider, and thus by inference a big black man. He was greedy, cunning and treacherous and brought trouble to his associates and animal companions. He lost most of his horror and vindictiveness through the years, and has become a sly, cunning character, with a certain amount of native wit and philosophy.

A specimen of the Annancy stories will be found in the Appendix.

CHAPTER ELEVEN
Jamaican Proverbs

Proverbs form a large part of the language of simple peoples, and Jamaicans of the older generation used to talk largely in proverbs and Biblical phrases. Some of these are falling out of use with the spread of education, but there are many that have become a part of the language. Like the people who use them, they show the most varying influences—English, Irish, Welsh, French and Spanish, but little African, apart from a word or two. Many of the Jamaican proverbs have counterparts in countries scattered all over the world. Often the Jamaican version is more witty or expressive.

The late Frank Cundall, who was Secretary and Curator of the Institute of Jamaica, for years collected these sayings and published them. There were 737 in his collection, and of them he says: 'They do more than show us our history; they also reveal the characteristics of the Jamaican people. Here is crystallised the wisdom of countless generations; here is enshrined the experience of the race; here are revealed their weaknesses and faults.' He admits that they have not the poignancy nor poetry of the Negro spirituals of the Southern United States, where the sufferings of the slaves were greater and more prolonged; moreover they had a different background.

Here are some of the proverbs, with English equivalents in some cases:

Darg (*dog*) hab liberty fe watch gubnor (*Governor*)
A cat may look at a King.

Neber buy puss in a bag.
Don't buy a pig in a poke.

Sof'ly riber run deep.
Still waters run deep.

No ebery ting wha' got sugar a sweet.
All is not gold that glitters.

Cuss-cuss no bore hole a me 'kin (*skin*).
Hard words break no bones.

Fisherman never say him fish 'tink (*stink*).
No man cries stinking fish.

Greedy choke puppy.
Enough is as good as a feast.

One daddy fe twenty picknie (*children*), but twenty picknie no
fe one daddy.
It's a wise child that knows its own father.

Coward man keep soun' bone.
He who fights and runs away may live to fight another day.

Darg don' nyam (*eat*) darg.
Honour among thieves.

(*Darg eat darg* [*often used*] *means the reverse.*)
Behind darg it is 'Darg'; before darg it is 'Mr. Darg'.

Others are:

Rock'tone (*stone*) in riber bottom neber know sun hot.

When cockroach gi' party, him no ax (*ask*) fowl.

No mine (*never mind*) how cockroach drunk, him no walk pas'
fowl-yard.

One which sounds very old runs:

Darg say sooner dan buy nakeen fe sixpence him wi' gi'
doubloon fe bone.

(*Nankeen is a species of cloth once much used in the West Indies,
and a doubloon an old Spanish coin. Thus: Spend your money
on what is of use to you.*)

Better belly bust than good food spoil.

Alligator lay egg but him no fowl.

Bad ting no hab owner.

You neber see empty bag 'tan' up.

Cheap bargain tek money.

No put youself in a barrel, when match box can hol' you.

Too much bed mek head dull.

Bottle no hab tapper belong to cockroach.

Mug no bruk coffee no t'row 'way.

If you put butter in a puss mout' him mus' lick i'.

Pack ob cards de debel's prayer book.

Chair fall down bench get up.

Darg bark neber frighten moon.

Two jackass can't bray one time.

Yaller snake an' fowl no companion.

Barrowed horse ride sweet.

When puss lay egg!

Ebery John Crow t'ink him pickney white.
   (The baby vulture *is* born white.)

When man drunk him walk an' 'tagger; when 'ooman drunk
    him si' down and consider.

Shut mout' no ketch fly.

When poor man owe debt eben darg and puss know.

Only shoe know ef 'tockin' hab hole.

Man wash often, him buy less clothes.

When you see ole lady run, no axe wha' de matter, run too.

Big wud bruk no man jawbone.

CHAPTER TWELVE

Songs and Dialect Verse

Calypsos are becoming well known in the Americas and England. They are stories of current events and opinions put to music. Their true home is Trinidad and the Eastern islands of the Caribbean, but Jamaica has some interesting folk songs. Amongst these are the 'Digging Songs', as they are called. There is a regular rhythm to these which makes the labourers' work go with a swing when they are 'picking' the roads or fields. There is a sort of 'aria' sung in a falsetto by the leader (he is often paid specially to do this job), and the men come in with a 'bobbin' or chorus, as they swing their picks in unison. The leader prides himself on varying his solo piece according to his personal inspiration, and the words are generally concerned with some current event, or domestic situation, or bit of scandal. The language is sometimes coarse!

There are also Ring Games, fashioned generally on old English nursery rhymes such as 'Little Sally Water', and dance tunes in plenty.

Some of the songs have gone round the world: 'Run, Mongoose', 'Mango Walk', 'Fan Me, Soldier Man, Fan Me', Linstead Market'.

Linstead is a village on the main road to Montego Bay from Kingston and most visitors will pass it. The song goes:

> Carry me ackee gone o' Linstead market,
> Not a quattie wort' sell;
> Carry me ackee gone o' Linstead market,
> Not a quattie wort' sell.
> Lard, what a night, not a bite,
> What a Saturday night!
> Lard, what a night, not a bite,
> What a Saturday night!

MANGO WALK

Mi brudder did a tell mi say y'u go Mango Walk,
 Y'u go Mango Walk,
 Y'u go Mango Walk,
Mi brudder did a tell mi say y'u go Mango Walk,
 An' tief all de Number 'leben.
Tell mi, Joe, do tell me fe true,
 Do tell me fe true,
 Do tell me,
Y'u nebba go to no Mango Walk
An' nebba tief Number 'leben!

A warra dat y'u peakin' Lilly lub o' mi heart,
 Lilly lub o' mi heart,
 Lilly lub o' mi heart,
Y'u brudder did a tell y'u say mi go Mango Walk
 An' tief all de Number 'leben.
An' y'u mean to say
Mi drop o' sunshine
Dat y'u really belieb dat liard,
Ah nebba go to no Mango Walk
An' nebba tief Number 'lebben.

SOJER MAN

Fan me, Sojer Man, fan me, fan me,
Fan me, Sojer Man, fan me, fan me;
Fan me, Sojer Man, fan me, fan me,
 Gal, you character gone!
Sake a pedlar man bangle, bangle,
Sake a pedlar man bangle, bangle,
Sake a pedlar man bangle, bangle
 Gal, you character gone!
What de use a you shawl up, shawl up?
What de use a you shawl up, shawl up?
What de use a you shawl up, shawl up
 When you character gone?

What de use a you lace up, stays up?
What de use a you lace up, stays up?
What de use a you lace up, stays up
 When you character gone?

WHEN YOU SEE A PRETTY GAL

When you see a ugly gal,
When you see a ugly gal,
When you see a ugly gal
 You cut you eye and pass him.
When you see a pretty gal,
When you see a pretty gal,
When you see a pretty gal
 You take you finger call him.
Marry the gal and take her away,
Marry the gal and take her away,
Marry the gal and take her away
 For kisses go by favour,
Favour, favour, kisses go by favour.
Marry the gal and put her away,
Marry the gal and put her away,
Marry the gal and put her away
 For puss and dog a neighbour,
Neighbour, neighbour, puss and dog a neighbour.

BIG SAMBO GAL

Big, big Sambo gal and 'im can't do a ting,
Sen' 'im home to 'im parents, oh!
Sen' 'im back to 'im mumu, oh!
'Im take ackee make soup, 'im take natta calar it';
 Gal, you want fe come kill me?

Refrain:

Gal, you want fe come kill me fe Dundus?
Gal, you want fe come kill me, oh!
'Im tak ackee make soup, 'im take natta calar it';
 Gal, you want fe come kill me?

Hand full a ring and 'im can't do a ting!
Sen' 'im home to 'im muma, oh!
Sen' 'im back to 'im muma, oh!
De gal can't wash and de gal can't cook;
 Sen' 'im home to 'im muma!

Rrefrain

MATTIE WALLA

Me no want, me no want wha' Mattie walla lef'!
Me no want, me no want wha' Mattie walla lef'!
Mattie run a mile and a half in a Gungo Walk,
Mattie run a mile and a half and 'im tumble down!
Mattie run, Mattie run, and 'im tumble down!
Mattie run, Mattie run, and 'im tumble down!
Mattie run a mile and a half and 'im tumble down!
Mattie run a mile and a half and 'im tumble down!

RUN, MONGOOSE

Chorus: Run, Mongoose, run,
  O, you name gone abroad (repeat)
  Mongoose go in a Bedward kitchen,
  Tief out one ob him righteous chicken,
  Put in a him weskit pocket
   Run gone hom.
  The righteous chicken him tief befo'
  Tek wey himself and gone out a doah;
  Lawd and Massa him get de blow,
   Slide, Mongoose.

CHAPTER THIRTEEN
The Jamaican Language

Most languages are a hotch-potch of many heritages. English is as mixed as others. The Gaelic was pushed west and north by the Anglo-Saxon tongue, which connects English with the Germanic languages. Grafted on to that was Norman French, derived from the Latin (what happened to their original Norse?). And that, with a few scattered modern words, is English as we know it.

Jamaican is not nearly as mixed as the language of other West Indian islands. St. Lucia is practically bi-lingual, the peasants for the most part talking French *patois*. The island was shuttle-cocked between French and English over the generations. Trinidad shows a strong French influence and there is a Spanish inheritance too.

The original inhabitants of Jamaica—the Arawaks—have left us a few words, which have indeed become international— hammock (*hamac*), hurricane (*ouracan*); and several place names, which live longer than ordinary language . . . until local authorities sacrifice the picturesque names of the past in deference to some current fancy.

The Spanish language practically disappeared. There was no one to carry on the tradition, save a few refugee slaves, and they may have had little enough of it. It is quite another case with Spanish place-names, of which there are scores, in the names of rivers and towns. Some family names remain; but they may have been introduced by immigrants from Central America, refugees from the Inquisition. The many Portuguese family names derive from merchant settlers seeking out profitable markets in the late seventeenth century.

The slaves brought African languages with them from West Africa, and some few words remain in Jamaican speech. But none of these languages was written down, and there were so

many varieties that the various tribes could not even understand each other. The common language therefore soon became
English, or a form of English influenced by certain factors. Thus
the English spoken by Quashie (the nickname of the peasant
class in the island) shows strong Irish characteristics, because
the field labour was supposed to have learnt the language from
the Irish indentured labourers, of whom there were a number
in the early years of English settlement. There seems no evidence that Irishmen came direct to Jamaica, but they may have
come from Barbados, where numbers were sent. Thus the construction of sentences is said to show Gaelic influence, in the
transfer of the subject: as—'Is what kin' of a man yu'?' Another
reversal occurs in the expression: 'What it is?' (for 'What is it?').

The insertion of a vowel as in 'cyan' for 'can', and 'cyard' for
'card' is supposed to derive from Gaelic and there are other
Anglo-Irish influences, for instance the use of 'd' for 'th', as in
'mudder' (mother), 'de' (the), 'dat' (that). Confusion of case is
common. 'Me no know she' and 'Let I go'; also 'Mek I see' (Let
me see), which may however derive from 'Make it so that I see'.
'Me' used in the nominative is common on the Gold Coast. In
fact it seems to pervade 'pidgin' English. Emphasis may be conveyed by repetition: 'plenty-plenty money', or by the expression
'for true', as 'It rain for true'.

Many people think that there is a suggestion of Welsh influence in the Jamaican language, especially in intonation, in the
'lilt' of sentences. No one seems to have traced any Welsh tradition, but the dropping of the 'w' as in 'ooman' for 'woman' may
be a case in point; also the sound 'likkle' for little, 'Myrkle' for
Myrtle . . . 'a likkle pickle bokkle'!

There is a good deal of Elizabethan English, or eighteenth
century English, in the Jamaican language. 'Vial' for bottle,
'goblet' for jug and 'kerchief' for handkerchief are everyday
words. Married women are always referred to as 'Mistress', not
'Mrs.' ('Missus' is the form of courtesy address to an employer).
Jamaicans use the term 'nayger' as a term of abuse; that, or
'neager', was the way the eighteenth century spelt 'nigger' or
Negro. (It occurs in Pepys' diary.) This tendency to use archaic

English is even more marked in remoter islands. It has a correlation in the Shakespearean expressions still current in the American language ('gotten' being perhaps the most common example).

The Jamaican working-class people seem to have two languages at their command, one which they use among themselves, and which the visitor will hardly be able to understand (such as in the folk-songs and the dialect poems of Louise Bennett and 'Quashie') and another which they will use in speaking to their employers, and which is quite good English. Calypsos, transplanted from Trinidad, are understandable enough in their tourist form. Middle class Jamaicans, especially of the towns, such as civil servants, and those trained in secondary schools often speak what is known as 'Oxford' or B.B.C. English. Many have been educated at English Universities. It was a fairly common sight in the last war to see coloured and black N.C.Os. (or aircraftsmen) of the R.A.F. enquiring their direction in perfect clipped English from burly policemen who had accents varying from broad Wiltshire, or a Devonshire 'burr', to cheeky Cockney or Lancashire.

The small amount of German immigration into Jamaica does not seem to have left much, if any, trace in language. Refugees from Haiti, around 1802, brought in a few words of French. 'Leggins', the name for a small bunch of soup vegetables, must surely derive from 'legumes', but whether from that immigration or from more distant French influence, can hardly be determined. Again there is a fair number of French family names representing good class families—mainly people who fled before the black wrath of Haiti during one or other of the revolutions in that Republic.

The African words include *nyam* (eat), *duppe* or *duppy* (ghost), *myal* (white magic), *duckonoo* (a dish of boiled corn) and perhaps *pickni*, or *pickney* (child). Persons' names often coincided with African days of the week—*Quashie* (Sunday), *Cudjoe* (Monday), *Quaco*, or for a girl, *Cooba* (Wednesday). Not that these are much heard now. Parents favour the most 'elegant' names today for their girl children: Retinella, Icilda, Francella—the newspapers present endless varieties. (Do these hark back to the flowery eighteenth century?)

The word 'quattie' (three halfpence) may derive from a 'quarter' of sixpence (or from *cuarto*, the quarter of a *real*). Sixpence seemed a standard for division—into a 'threepence', a 'quattie' (three halfpence) and a 'gill' (three farthings). A 'big gill' is a liquid measure (as a gill still is in England) equalling a quarter of a pint, and a 'half-gill' is an eighth of a pint.

Recent history has brought a number of American words and expressions into the language, but that is truc of many countries beside Jamaica.

CHAPTER FOURTEEN
Place Names

One of the most fascinating things in visiting a new country is the names of its places, what they mean or where they came from. It is the type of mental enquiry that the most indolent of us enjoy. With little effort one can become a private detective pursuing an investigation of unending possibilities where one's conclusions need only be of consequence or interest to one's self.

In Jamaica the most interesting case is certainly that of the name of the island itself, about which much has been written—erudite and otherwise. It must be remembered first that it is the Spanish pronunciation of the name the Arawak Indians told them, and second, the English pronunciation of the Spanish version. On the earliest maps it appears as Jamaicha, Jamaiqua, Jamaiana, although the Spanish historians wrote Xaymaca. In a script now in the British Museum the derivation is given as originally Jamajaco—Jamo being Indian for country—Jaco for water. It is not stated, however, if the Indian referred to is Arawak. In the Spanish histories it is written that 'Xaymaca is said to have signified in the language of the natives, a country abounding in springs'. This has become the commonly accepted version, although it can probably be more correctly said that the Arawaks themselves had probably forgotten the meaning of the word by the time the Spaniards came.

There are few other Indian names left. Mammee Bay, Mammee Ridge, etc., probably came from Maima . . . the name of an Arawak settlement on the north shore. An interesting sidelight on Mammee Ridge is that close by is a place with the odd name of Johnnie Spring, the site of an Arawak village from which many stone implements have been obtained.

Guanaboa in St. Catherine is certainly Arawak and means 'House of Gold' in the Arawak of Haiti from where it was probably imported. The Liguanea Plain no doubt obtained its name from the iguana lizard, the Spaniards adding the 'l'. Wareika also seems to be Arawak and appears in various forms in other parts of the West Indies.

Nearly the only evidence of the Spanish Occupation which remains is in the names they left behind them, particularly the rivers. We have the

Rio Alto	deep river
Rio Cobre	copper river
Rio Grande	great river
Rio Bueno	good river

The village of Ocho Rios was originally Cheireras—the Bay of the Waterfalls most appropriately. The lovely name Lacovia may have been the Spanish Lago-Via, the way by the lake. Montego Bay or Manteca Bahia—lard or butter bay. The area abounded in wild hogs and the Spaniards developed a considerable export trade in lard. Yallahs is obviously the Spanish deAyala, a name celebrated in Spanish history, being borne by a celebrated poet as well as an envoy to the Court of St. James's in 1498, said to have advised Henry VII to cut off the head of the Earl of Warwick.

With the advent of the English, kings, queens, statesmen, saints, public men, soldiers and sailors lent their names for towns, parishes, streets and roads and being obvious provoke little curiosity except to the historically minded. There is much more fascination and interest in the lesser names.

Wait-a-bit.

Come-see.

Shoe-myself Gate, because of the custom of people going to church to stop there and put on their shoes.

Buck-up, a sharp angle where two roads join.

Blow Fire, a steep fern-clad hill a few miles from St. Ann's Bay which often takes fire mysteriously. Peasants attribute the cause to duppies (ghosts).

Rest-and-be-Thankful.

Cook's Bottom.

Red Gal Ring, which may mean what it implies or may be a corruption of Red Gallery.

The Martha Brae River has an interesting legend that Martha Brae was a witch who knew the secret of the Spaniards' gold mines. The river is said to have changed its course during a storm, drowning her and obliterating the entrance to the mine.

Accompong and Cudjoe were the names of rebel Maroons and are African in derivation. Most visitors wonder about Half Way Tree. It was so called as being half-way between the barracks at Stony Hill and the harbour. One of the strangest names in Jamaica is undoubtedly the Y.S. River. Two explanations have been advanced. One that it is the Welsh word Ys, meaning crooked or winding: or that the name of the property was Wyess and that its commercial marks for shipping were Y. S. God Almighty's Cut Stones is the name given to a pile of laminated rock in St. Ann. Hell Below is a rather dangerous corner near Dunn's River where there is a deep fall to the sea.

Jamaica is full of fascinating names such as these—a delight to the appreciative mind.

CHAPTER FIFTEEN
Jamaica as a Tourist Resort

Whatever may be said by the people of Jamaica in regard to their political and economic difficulties, there has never been any question about the superb qualities which make the island so admirable a tourist resort. Not so many years ago, there were two hotels in the island, both owned by the United Fruit Company: the Myrtle Bank, and the Titchfield. The latter hotel was destroyed by fire, but the annexe survived, and this, with modern additions, is the present hotel. These two hotels were lordly establishments run less for profit than to provide suitable accommodation for the pampered passengers of the company.

Then Mrs. Ewen, a well-known resident of St. James, bought a charming little house on the cliffs at Montego Bay called Casa Blanca; she opened it for guests, and from this beginning the tourist trade of Jamaica has stemmed. Dr. Barker, the famous osteopath, spread far and wide the medicinal and invigorating qualities of the bathing at Doctor's Cave (which, incidentally, does not owe its name to him . . . see photograph on page 135).

Casa Blanca spread its wings on either side of the original house. It added and improved year by year, without detracting from the original character. It built and acquired cottages on the land side of the road which, in the cause of progress, it has again torn down, to replace them by its new and luxurious annexe; it has diverted the road for straightness and garden space. It began as the centre of the tourist industry and it has remained its hub. Around it has sprung a true resort, with enormous charm, of which its terrace remains the focussing point. At this writing, Sunset Lodge is the newest—as it is the most fashionable—hotel and has helped to add to the celebrity of a centre to which all its units have contributed. The life of the fashionable Montego Bay resort gravitates to the Casa Blanca

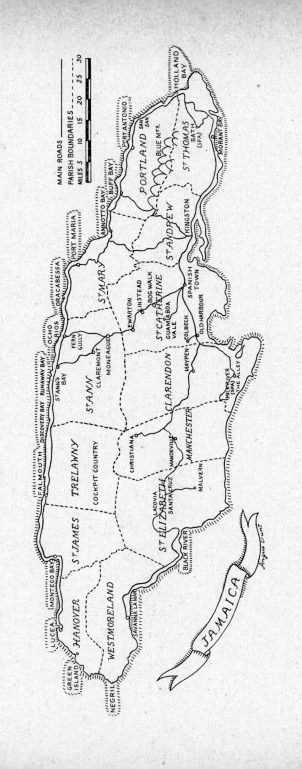

terrace, Doctor's Cave Beach, the Beach View bar, and the Fairfield Country Club. A number of admirable establishments of varying character, which cater to visitors with variable purses, together combine with its lovely sunshine, its incomparable bathing, and its flavour of fashion and enjoyment, to create a holiday centre unsurpassed in the world.

Montego Bay is the only resort of its kind in Jamaica and perhaps on the earth, for it is a smart Continental-type holiday spot in the loveliest of tropical islands surrounded by the most beautiful of seas—the delightful Caribbean—astonishing those who see it by its changing and ever-deepening beauty. But all along the coasts of Jamaica, and up in its hills, there are hotels, or clusters of hotels, which offer equal though different delights. In the last few years, a colony of winter visitors or settlers from colder and more austere climes has dotted what is called the North Shore with delightful villas, has bought country properties perched on the hillsides overlooking the tree-fringed coast, and has been helping to support a chain of new hotels, small and large. Tower Isle, the finest and largest hotel in the British West Indies and one of the most luxurious in the hemisphere, was completed in January, 1949, and immediately became the centre of the life of the area. In its shadow nestles the tiny Fern Brae hotel; and along to the west stretches a chain of new hotels, all described in detail in the next chapter. Here, as well as at Montego Bay, the roster of the winter residents includes names famous in the world of art, theatre, fashion, and affairs. These distinguished residents, or semi-residents, are part of the life of the country during its tourist months, which are becoming increasingly numerous and soon will stretch from end to end of the year.

The North Shore and Montego Bay attract most of the visitors, winter and summer; but there are people who never want to leave Port Antonio, where the Titchfield and the San San Beach Club are their gathering points. There are those who seek more secluded places, for there are beaches with good bathing all round the island, with the exception of the metropolis, around which the sea bathing is far from perfect. In the hotels of Kingston and its attractive suburbs, however, most hotels have their own fresh-water pools (Myrtle Bank has a salt-water one); and some people prefer to stay at Manor House, Courtleigh Manor, Mona or another of the comfortable hotels around the capital, from which they may tour the country and see its natural life.

The whole island is tourist material; for everywhere there is beauty, everywhere the sun shines, everywhere there is richness of scenery and softness of air. The breezes blow by day and night to temper the hot sun; but that sun is grateful indeed to skins roughened by the winds of the northlands.

Jamaica, most delectable of tourist lands, is accessible by sea and by air. Visitors from Britain used to consider that only a prolonged stay justified the long sea-voyage; now the distance can be spanned in a day or two. The cost is as variable as the accommodation; luxury hotels can command high rates, and, indeed, cannot afford not to charge them. But there are all kinds of places, from the finest hotels to modest guest houses at reasonable rates. There is a place for the honeymoon or other couple who regards this as the holiday of a lifetime and will spare no money to make it perfect; and there is a welcome for the school teacher who wishes, by travel through the island at moderate cost, to enlarge his travel experience. There are variations in climate, choice of food, degrees of luxury, means of recreation to suit everyone . . . and always, everywhere, the bounties of Nature in her most generous mood.

Details of communication by land and sea, together with current fares, will be found in the *Appendix*. The hotels and their location are described in the following pages.

WHAT TO SEE—WHERE TO GO—WHAT TO DO

Jamaica can offer the visitor the unparalleled beauty and superb scenery of one of the world's enchanted islands. There is little or no industrialisation to mar the breath-taking beauty of this lovely land, with the exuberance and richness of its tropical foliage, set in majestic mountains.

There is much to see, many places to visit and great beauty to discover. From Kingston, one can take the interior road to the North Shore. The thirteen miles to Spanish Town take one through the flat land of large sugar estates, the tall cane waving rather untidily in the breeze. At Ferry, the road crosses the river of that name. Generations passing here before us paid a toll and were ferried over, not the least of whom must have been Lady Nugent, wife of a Governor of the island. She wrote an interesting and fascinating diary of her four years in Jamaica from 1801 to 1804, and often made the journey from Spanish Town to Kingston. A little way off the side of the road, the stone ruins are all that remain of the Ferry Inn, a frequent house of call in the days of horse-drawn carriages.

On the left of the road is an enormous cotton tree of great age, called 'Tom Cringle's Cotton Tree', after the story of Tom Cringle's Log, another record of Jamaican life in the eighteenth century.

In Spanish Town, the road goes past the old Cathedral, where so many of the victims of the yellow fever are buried. Tread lightly on the flagstones, for here in the inscriptions is a chapter of the island's history and those who made it. Growing profusely in the neighbourhood of Spanish Town is the *Tribulus Cistoides*, a buttercup-like flower called locally 'kill backra' because its appearance denoted the presence of the particular kind of mosquito which carries yellow fever and killed off so many of the white population. Yellow fever has now been eradicated.

In the square are the ruins of the old King's House, the House of Assembly, and the Court House in the days when Spanish Town was the capital of the island. It is not difficult to imagine what the square must have looked like in the days when Spanish Town still bore its original name St. Jago de la Vega. The business of government was conducted there, proclamations read from the stone steps, soldiers, politicians, statesmen, men of affairs hurried across its paving stones.

A few miles further on we cross the Rio Cobre at the Flat Bridge and go by the beautiful, narrow gorge of the river. Bog Walk is said to be a corruption of 'Boca del Agua'—'Mouth of the Water'. The mountains tower up to the sky and it is easy to believe a contemporary account of the 1692 earthquake which says 'the mountains on each side of the river road were thrown down'. In the township of Bog Walk, on the left, is a milk condensery owned and operated by the world-famous firm of Nestle's. We are now in the district of Saint Thomas in Ye Vale (to distinguish it from St. Thomas in the East), one of those fertile alluvial valleys with which Jamaica is blessed and which are so suitable to the growing of cane. Here is another sugar estate, Bybrook, and if it is the cutting season, one can see in the grounds the teams of quiet, patient bullocks, with their carts laden with stripped cane.

The next village is Linstead, celebrated in the folk song, 'Linstead Market', which, as the visitor may know, occurs on a Saturday night:

> Carry me ackee gone a Linstead market,
> Not a quattie wort' sell;
> Lard, what a night, not a bite,
> What a Saturday night!
> Lard, what a night, not a bite,
> What a Saturday night!

A few miles further on is Ewarton and here we are at the foot of the great pile of Mount Diablo, and as the grade rises, there are the spectacular views over the valley and toward the Blue Mountains in the far distance. Near the summit of the pass, small boys are usually to be found on the side of the road selling fruit or wild orchids and exotic lilies.

Soon the road drops away to the pleasant pastures of Moneague, so different from the tropical seacoast or the high mountains as to make one think one might be travelling through English park land. There is a delightful and well-furnished hotel at Moneague, where one might stop for luncheon and then resume one's journey. There are two roads from here to Montego Bay, one going via Claremont, where we keep to the high land and reach the coast near St. Ann's Bay, or through the Fern Gully to the coast at Ocho Rios. The way through Clare-

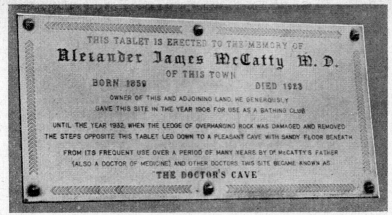

Plaque at Doctor's Cave showing its origin. It reads:

'This Tablet is Erected to the Memory of Alexander James McCatty, M.D. of this Town. Born 1859 Died 1923. Owner of this and adjoining land, he generously gave this site in the year 1906 for use as a bathing club until the year 1932, when the ledge of overhanging rock was damaged and removed. The steps opposite this tablet led down to a pleasant cave with sandy floor beneath. From its frequent use over a period of years by Dr. McCatty's father, (also a Doctor of Medicine) and other Doctors, this site became known as The Doctor's Cave'

From a charming ornamental pool, Shaw Park looks down upon lovely Ocho Rios Ba

mont takes us by country estates, where cattle feed in the shade
of quiet spreading trees. Many of the fences are made of pink
flowering *Gliricidia* (St. Vincent Plum), locally called 'Quick
Stick'. The trees are used as stakes for the fences, but the flower
is so anxious to bloom that it lends its beauty to the countryside.
Through Fern Gully, we can see the giant tree ferns towering
above, sometimes eclipsing the sun, and at its end, the whole
beauty of the coast bursts upon us, the synthesis of jade and
sapphire sea and silver sands, with coconut palms bowing in the
trade wind and the breakers creaming upon the reefs.

There are many hotels in the area. Just above Ocho Rios is
the lovely Great House of Shaw Park, a private home converted
into a luxury hotel. A few miles away, right on the coast, are
Tower Isle, Silver Seas and Jamaica Inn.

If one is going on to Montego Bay, one follows the coast as the
road winds in and out around the little coves and bays, fraught
with the history of the Caribbean. Here the Spaniards and English fought by sea and land; here Columbus brought his ships.
And so to St. Ann's Bay, thought to be the Santa Gloria Harbour where Columbus sheltered; Dunn's River, with its wide
stretch of glistening sand and the waterfall cascading into the
sea; Runaway Bay, where the retreating Spaniards had their
last sight of Jamaica; Discovery Bay is said to be Columbus' first
landfall. There is a fine beach at Columbus Inn. Falmouth,
breathing the history of the eighteenth century, founded by the
Barrett family (the family of Elizabeth Barrett-Browning) is a
sugar port; and finally to Montego Bay, a hundred and eighteen
miles from Kingston.

The fame of Montego Bay has spread around the world. It is
a paradise of sunshine, blue sky and green water, a quiet and
lovely place for the tired and jaded in spirit or for those who are
wearied with the noise and bustle of great cities. Doctor's Cave
is a stretch of fine, pure white sand and the quality of the water
is such that it is said to have healing properties, as the name implies. In the mornings, gay umbrellas and beach chairs make the
scene colourful, and one may sun and lie on the sand or take a
boat to the reef to gaze unbelievingly at its undersea wonders.

Immediately adjoining the beach is the Casa Blanca Hotel, built on the rock overlooking the sea, where one may have an aperitif on the terrace before luncheon, or dine and dance in the open dining room to the sound of the waves against the seawall. To sit on the terrace and watch the moon and the evening star —the great lamp of Venus—slip down the velvet sky to the darkening hills is a moment of loveliness one will often remember.

There are many hotels in Montego Bay to offer many different types of accommodation to suit the personal requirements of every visitor. A golf course and a race track are within a few miles of the town.

At Montego Bay one is almost at the farthest end of the island, but its tip is twenty miles farther on in the little town of Lucea. It is a delightful drive along the coast and one passes enchanting little coves, which seem to be untouched by man. Here, too, is the Tryall coconut plantation. Its great house, perched on a breezy hill, is a hotel. Lucea is a sleepy little town with an old stone fort with the eighteenth century guns looking out to sea. It was built with a number of others around the coast of Jamaica as defence against the French. The road of course goes on to return to its beginning, as it would on any island, but such places as Green Island, Negril, Savanna-la-Mar and Black River are usually approached from the southern route.

We may therefore return to Montego Bay, where ten miles to the east there is the sugar estate of Rose Hall. This was one of the most magnificent estate houses of its day, having cost, it is said, thirty thousand pounds in 1775. It is now a ruin, but the solid mahogany staircase was removed to one of St. Andrew's large houses. (See *The Legend of Rose Hall*.)

Further details of Montego Bay can be found under the chapter on 'Towns and Cities', as well as of Falmouth, twenty-two miles away. Good Hope, a Jamaican Great House converted into a beautiful hotel, is a short distance from Falmouth; and so is the delightful Silver Sands residential beach club.

Finishing our time in Montego Bay, we can now retrace our steps to Ocho Rios, and turning right follow the beautiful St. Mary coast, passing by or stopping at the Silver Seas Hotel, almost tumbling into the Caribbean, then Jamaica Inn, Sans Souci, then Tower Isle, Jamaica's most luxurious hotel. The road winds along a coast of breath-taking beauty. Here we find the winter home of Noel Coward, Blue Harbour, clinging to the cliff side. In Oracabessa is the house of Ian Fleming of England's powerful Kemsley Press, and another house belonging to the famous flyer, Jean Batten. Close to Port Maria overlooking the bay, where a little wooded island is set in the aquamarine sea below the azure blue sky, is Castle Gordon. Its hillside is swept by the trade winds, and it forms a centre for one of the loveliest spots on the island.

On we go through coconut properties, through estates of bananas and, reaching the Wag Water River, turn south to cut through the mountains on the way back to Kingston. We are now on the Junction Road, which twists and turns, running snakily through a narrow valley soft and beautiful with the lush vegetation of large alluvial pockets, climbing the edges of mountains beside the towering rock face of the cliffs, running beside the river bed, gazing down from the mountain heights. Having crossed the range of great mountains, we come to Castleton, where the public gardens draw travellers from many countries. There are most interesting trees, shrubs and plants, which the visitor should not fail to see. One spectacular tree is the *Amherstia Nobilis*, noble indeed with its drooping scarlet flowers. Further on is Stony Hill, one of the most exclusive residential districts, and a few miles further downhill we are back in Kingston.

Eastward from Kingston the first fifteen miles is through dry and arid country, over a sand-dusted road, where grow innumerable varieties of cacti: the Dildo, looking like green palisades, is frequently used for fences, the Prickly Pear has tiny red blossoms on its edges, the Jerusalem Candlestick, with its spined candelabra branches, the Turks Hat Cactus, with its red fez and long spikes (see *Flora*).

There are a number of lagoons and marshes along this road, which at certain seasons of the year abound in wild bird life.

Waves break against the cliffs on which the Casa Blanca is built, but bathing is in miraculously calm and translucent water

One of the attractive cottages at Glitter Beach which can be rented by the week or month

Many strange and beautiful birds, such as the white and blue heron, the reddish egret, the black and white stilt, migrate here and breed. (See *Fauna*.) Along the road the traveller may notice a high mountain with a sheer granite face. The 1692 upheaval dislodged its other portion to completely submerge a plantation. At White Horses, the tropical beauty of palm tree and cane field again appears, and we go on to the small town of Morant Bay. Most of the land through which we have passed was originally composed of two large estates at the time of the Spaniards, the Hato deAyala and the Morante Estates. Thus Morant Bay and the Yallahs River acquired their names. The great Spanish family of deAyala's holdings extended from Bull Bay to Morant Bay. Here we are in the lee of the highest of the Blue Mountains and the views of the river valleys are impressive. In the morning and evening one may look at the giant hills with their shades of green and blue, but usually by midday the highest peaks have wrapped themselves in white clouds.

The village of Bath lies close to the eastern spur of the ridge. Here is a hot and cold mineral bath of high medicinal properties. There is a small guest house for those who wish to take the waters. Around the corner of the island by Holland Bay, we turn north and travel parallel with the John Crow Mountains, that wild, unexplored range on the western slope of which is the Maroon village of Moore Town settled by escaped slaves long years ago. Along the way are some beauty spots as lovely as anything one could wish to see, including Priestman's River, Hector's River and the Blue Hole, or Blue Lagoon, in the east, the intense colour of the water giving it its name. The banks are densely clothed with palms, bread-fruit trees and many other tropical trees and plants. As we approach Port Antonio, we reach Boston Beach with its surf, the delightful Frenchman's Cove and the San San Estate.

Port Antonio is a town of great charm. Ella Wheeler Wilcox called it 'the most exquisite harbour on earth'. Small islands just off the shore complete the picture of a tropical paradise, and the Titchfield Hotel is a delightful hostelry. From Port Antonio, you may go rafting down the Rio Grande, one of the most pleasant things to do in Jamaica, for here there is the scenery of a great tropical waterway and were it not for the Jamaican accent of the boatman, one could imagine oneself on the mighty jungle-clad rivers of South America. There is excellent fishing in the river and the Portland Fishing Club at its mouth can introduce you to the best deep-sea fishing in the West Indies. (See *Sport*.)

One can return to Kingston from Port Antonio by continuing east and reaching the Junction Road by which we travelled on our way home from Montego Bay.

Mandeville is sixty miles from Kingston on an excellent road and we go through Spanish Town, Old Harbour and May Pen to reach it. The country is flat and perhaps less fascinating than other parts of Jamaica. Some of it is pastoral land, in which cattle stand knee-deep in the guinea grass, under the huge spreading guango trees. The bean of this tree makes good cattle fodder and in the spring its umbrella-like branches are decorated with delicate pale pink blossoms. If one has the time, there are a number of side excursions one can make. From Spanish Town one can leave the main road and travel ten miles to Guanaboa Vale, where there is one of the oldest churches in the island. The structure itself is probably little more than a century old, but no doubt embodies some work of a much older date. There is a tombstone of a man who landed with Venables in 1655 and died in 1681, but the church must be much older than that. It has an air of permanence and quiet as though it were reaching back into the distant past. The name Guanaboa is doubtless Arawak, and is said to mean 'House of Gold'. There was certainly a Spanish ranch called Guanaboa, with wild horses and cattle, when the English arrived in the island, and it was one of the English strongholds during their fighting with the Spaniards, as it guarded one of the approaches to Spanish Town and threatened communications across the island. It was from Guanaboa that Colonel Tyson and his Regiment penetrated beyond the mountains into Saint Ann and inflicted the final defeat on the Spaniards, and it was in Guanaboa in 1660, after the news of Oliver Cromwell's death, that Colonel Tyson and Colonel Raymond hatched a plot to overthrow the then existing military government of Jamaica and replace it with civil administration. They were supported by a number of soldiers who, not having been paid for some time, had decided that they would prefer to become planters and give up soldiering. The plot ended ignominiously, for when Tyson and Raymond marched to Spanish Town and met the Governor with his army, many of their adherents deserted them, and the two leaders were subsequently tried and shot for treason under the famous tamarind tree.

From Old Harbour, one may take a short journey of one and a half miles to see the ruins of Colbeck Castle, which probably dates from the seventeenth century and must have been the most imposing building of its kind in Jamaica. It was evidently over a hundred feet long by about ninety feet wide and consisted of four three-storied square tower-like buildings at each corner with connecting arcades. There was a square of some size and dungeons in the corner buildings of the outer wall.

It belonged to Colonel John Colbeck. His black marble gravestone in the Spanish Town Cathedral reads:

'Collnel John Colbeck of Colbeck in St. Dorothyes was born ye 30th of May 1630 and came with ye army that conquered this island ye 10th day of May 1655, where having discharged several honble. offices both civill and military with great applause he departed this life ye 22nd day of February 1682.'

Coming with the army of Venables, Colbeck apparently settled in the country and took part in and led at least one expedition to quell the Maroons. He was a member of the first House of Assembly, acted as Speaker of the House and was finally elected to the Council, but died before the appointment reached Jamaica. Nothing is known of his life before and no mention was made in his will of relatives or family. He left his fortune to his executors with a number of smaller bequests including the gift of a ring to a number of his contemporaries, one being Sir Henry Morgan. There is a tradition in the Colbeck family in Lincolnshire that one of their members was transported to the West Indies for cutting down an elm tree and that he acquired

Sunset Lodge, with its own private beach, was formerly a Club.
A fashionable modern hotel has been built on this site

The old Great House at Good Hope

a fortune. These are the only fascinating glimpses we have of the owner of this stone-walled fortress.

We can also cut away from the main road beyond Old Harbour and go to Vere, where there is St. Peter's Church, another of the old churches of the island, at The Alley. The original structure was Spanish and appears to have been rebuilt by the English about 1671, and again, after destruction in the 1692 earthquake, and in 1872. The walls of the church are rich with tablets in memory of those who served their day and generation with distinction. Milk River Bath, with its fine mineral springs, is reached from this road. There is accommodation for guests, but it is far from luxurious and proposals have been made for its improvement.

Returning to the main road, we journey on to Porus, where the road begins to rise and at the top of Melrose Hill is Williamsfield, the railway station for Mandeville, which is five miles further on. Mandeville is often compared to an English village, with its stone, square-towered church and village green. There are comfortable hotels and a popular club, with tennis courts and a golf course. The south coast is about a two-hour drive from Mandeville and at Treasure Beach there is a hotel and sea-bathing.

From Mandeville, one can travel to Black River, through beautiful country. On the top of Spur Tree is a panoramic view of the island, which should not be missed. Dropping off this tremendous but well-graded hill, one can see, across the valley, the gigantic thatch palms of Malvern Great House silhouetted against the sky line of the distant range. The small village of Malvern, so high in the mountains, is the home of two schools.

In the plain are pasture lands thickly dotted with logwood trees, once a substantial source of wealth to Jamaica, and still providing a lucrative trade in dye. These trees are also valuable for their bloom, which provides honey for bees. The cashew tree, which provides the delicious nut, which oddly enough grows outside the fruit, is prevalent here too.

Along this road one will pass through Bamboo Walk, where the lovely lace-like bamboos form an avenue like the nave of some great cathedral, through Santa Cruz, Lacovia, to Black River, the chief town of the parish. The town has a certain charm, with its stone church and sea-wall, where the fish come in and the sandpipers and pelicans hover around the break-water. Black River itself provides the best sport in the island as far as fishing and crocodile hunting are concerned, and despite the fact that most people do not consider mangroves beautiful, their colourful copper-green and gold on the river at sundown, with a flight of wild duck against the sky and the mullet jump-ing in midstream, is a quiet moment of loveliness. There is a guest house for visitors.

We can now follow the south coast to Savanna-la-Mar, where we are only about forty-five miles from Montego Bay. The coast is attractive, perhaps because it is comparatively un-discovered. There are many charming small coves around Blue-fields and near Savanna-la-Mar is the Frome Sugar Estate.

Back in Kingston, there is a drive over the high ridge of the Port Royal Mountains. One leaves Kingston and St. Andrew at Papine and starts to climb hills down which the Hope River rushes on the right, spluttering over its dams and buttresses. We climb up and around the towering hills through what must be some of the loveliest mountain scenery in the world to the fairy-like town of Newcastle, a military hill station. With its red roofs mounting in tiers up the side of the mountain, it looks like a village from the Land of Oz.

Three miles further on, at Hardwar Gap, the range is actually crossed and one looks down a beautiful valley which runs north-ward to the coast. Here we are four thousand and seventy-nine feet up, the highest altitude on any road in the island and Catherine's Peak, five thousand and sixty feet, is just behind us. This is a land of glistening fern and ginger lilies, of running streams and wild begonia. There may be masses of white mist drifting through the gap or spirals of spent cloud rising from the valleys.

The road from the Gap down to Buff Bay is one of the most precipitous in the island. It is, however, well engineered and protected by masonry walls. To go down is like stepping down the staircase of the seasons, for in a few miles one passes from the cool zone of mist and fern to the hot tropical plane of cane and bananas.

The highest mountain is Blue Mountain Peak, its elevation being seven thousand four hundred and two feet. No road runs to the summit. One can drive via Gordon Town to Mavis Bank and from that point the remainder of the journey is made on foot, or on horse or mule back. The distance from Mavis Bank to the Peak is approximately thirteen miles. It is an interesting climb, which can be made by any good walker, there being a bridle path all the way.

For long or short trips, cars and chauffeurs can be hired or one can rent a car to drive oneself. Excursions and tours can be arranged through Travel Bureaux: the John Crook Travel Bureau, Martin's Tropical Tours, and Jamaica Tours.

WHERE TO STAY

Jamaica is a diadem sparkling with jewels. Its beauty spots gleam in their lovely settings.

Some are remote; but most of them are easily reached by good roads; and at each of these a comfortable hotel or guest-house invites the visitor to stay.

The hotels of Jamaica are mostly unconventional. There are few glittering caravanserais. The hotels are modern, well-equipped and comfortable; but they are not the orthodox centres which grow up artificially in a man-made tourist resort. The hotels of Jamaica have sprung up naturally at places where there are special attractions and lovely scenery, fine bathing, and delectable climate. In many cases they began as the mansions—Great Houses as they are called in Jamaica—of the well-to-do planters. We have already described the evolution of the famous Casa Blanca Hotel. Other hotels are highly-modernised old houses on fine estates, which have grown from other beginnings.

Shaw Park, set in most romantic scenery, was built by Sir John Pringle, who selected hill tops and built houses on them from which to look down upon the rolling plains and the shining

In the Blue Mountains

Tourist Board

Caribbean Sea. Royal princes and dukes have made it their headquarters and it still retains the charm of a country estate.

Good Hope is a handsome eighteenth century country house which has expanded into a resort unique in the West Indies and perhaps anywhere, in which visitors can live the genuine plantation life of the island under conditions of luxury.

AROUND THE CAPITAL

The visitor who arrives in Kingston usually spends his first night or two at the Myrtle Bank Hotel. Some like to make it the centre for their entire stay. This hotel is famous wherever the West Indies are known. Its slogan is 'Life begins at Myrtle Bank'. It will be the visitor's first introduction to the charms of the tropics, and very lovely he will find it with its palm trees swaying and whispering above the swimming pool, its green lawns and its gay life. Everyone comes and goes at Myrtle Bank. It is a social centre for visitors and residents alike; and how many business deals have been settled over its lunch tables! It has been called 'the best club in Jamaica'. For shopping in Kingston it is the imperative centre.

The Issa family, who own Myrtle Bank, are also the owners of Tower Isle Hotel on the North Shore (of which more later) and the two luxurious establishments attract visitors all through the year.

For those who would like to look around the outskirts of Kingston before following the crowd northward, there is a choice of many pleasant places.

Manor House Hotel, which is one of those which began life as a Great House, is one of the foremost of Kingston's hotels. Beautifully appointed, it has the air of gracious living usually associated with a more leisurely age. Situated in the foothills of the mountains, about six miles from the centre of the city, it is surrounded by tropical gardens of outstanding beauty and interest. The area was once part of the Constant Spring Sugar Estate, the abandoned chimney of which can be seen near the front gate. The hotel has forty rooms, most with private bath. There is an attractive bar, tennis and badminton courts, a swimming pool. Three cottages for prolonged visits are available and more are planned. The cuisine and service are notable. Hotel transport to town is provided—taxis and buses are easily procurable. The hotel grows its own fruit, specialising in the famous Bombay or Freestone Mango. Constant Spring Golf Course adjoins the hotel.

Mona Hotel is another old Great House of a former sugar estate with the special charm of history around it. One may have a room in the hotel or a bungalow and perfect privacy. Here, too, one is at the very foothills of the mountains, and the great range is spread before one, high land from which blows the cool light evening breeze that refreshes after the heat of the day. It is about six miles from town but arrangements for transport can be made. It has a good bar and a swimming pool.

Courtleigh Manor, the new and delightful hotel on the outskirts of Kingston, has become a favourite rendezvous for discriminating travellers who enjoy the graciousness and charm of this lovely English Manor House in its delightful tropical setting, its pleasant verandahs and patios, spacious lawns and landscaped grounds. Although only ten minutes from the centre of Kingston, Courtleigh Manor has a delightful resort atmosphere. There is a magnificent view of the nearby Blue Mountains and from the Roof Garden racing and polo may be watched at the Knutsford Park Course. Courtleigh has its own swimming pool and sun decks. For golf and tennis, a short walk across the lawn leads to the Liguanea Country Club, where temporary membership can be arranged. The hotel is luxuriously appointed, the rooms are large and designed for through ventilation and all have private baths. Courtleigh's cuisine is exceptional. Nearby are the beautiful Hope Gardens.

Quite near is Abbey Court, another converted private residence which caters for guests both temporary and permanent. It has an excellent bar and good food. Rates are very moderate. It is under the same management as Clifton House in Montego Bay (*which see*).

On the Hope Road, in one of the best residential areas, is the Liguanea Terrace Hotel. It is on the way to Hope Botanical

Gardens, and is called after the plain on which Kingston and Lower St. Andrew lie. Flats are available, with part service, as well as ordinary hotel accommodation.

Mount Mansfield, one thousand feet up in the foothills of the Blue Mountains, is the nearest to an English country inn Jamaica can offer. A river runs through the property and guests can sleep to the beguiling sound of water cascading over rocks in its downward plunge to the valley. There is a charming open-air bar where one may sit and gaze on the grandeur of the surrounding mountains and listen to soft music. This terrace bar is a popular after-dinner rendezvous. Accommodation is simple, but food is good, with an English chef.

Higher still, in the true mountains, there are a number of pleasant small hotels and guest houses, with breath-taking views and an altitude that gives them a climate—brilliant days and cool nights—perfect of its kind. Such is Bamboo Lodge at two thousand feet, yet only thirteen miles from Kingston. Through the feathery bamboos, Kingston Harbour and the Liguanea Plain lie far below, laid out like an aerial map, the car lights flashing and fading, like errant fireflies. And to the west the great mountains pile up into the blue of distance. Bamboo Lodge is under English management and ownership, has a delightful swimming pool for guests, and a badminton court.

THE NORTH SHORE

Beautiful as the mountains are, the visitor will be impatient to see the North Shore, of which he has heard so much. Here is the tropical beauty of golden sunshine and azure sea, blue sky and white cumulus cloud . . . velvet sky of night sown with stars, whispering palm and murmuring wave, and the Trade Wind blowing.

The motorist who crosses the Junction Road, the shortest route across the island, reaches the coast at Port Maria, the bay where history declares Christopher Columbus first sighted the island of Jamaica. (There are other claims!) A mile or so to the west is a new luxury hotel which overlooks the inimitable Port Maria Bay. This is one of the most beautiful coast views in the

ierre Chong
Packer

Kingston's celebrated hotel. Above: From the rear
Below: The Swimming Pool

island. Castle Gordon was built, to her own design, but with the assistance of a well-known architect, by Mrs. Hardy-Barrett, widow of an English Naval Officer. It is decorated with Continental taste and Mrs. Hardy-Barrett has placed her own personal treasures within it. She has also inaugurated a standard of Continental cooking with a Swiss chef, which is hard to surpass. There is a swimming pool with sea-water pumped up from the shore below or visitors may swim in the sea. The rooms are charming and comfortable and the entire frontage is terraced, with resting places on various levels to sip the drinks of the country or sun-bathe under the sky.

The most splendid and elaborate hotel in the island is Tower Isle, which, built only recently at a cost of a quarter million pounds, is the highlight and apogee of tourist accommodation. It is situated on a long stretch of white sand, with a small island in the Bay. Here, every marine sport is available—bathing, fishing, boating—in the incomparable Caribbean waters. The hotel itself is spacious and designed to catch every breeze in its particularly fortuitous situation. The rooms are large. Each has its own private balcony and its own luxuriously fitted bathroom. In the lounge there is a mural panel by Hector Whistler, the dining room murals are by John Pike, both outstanding artists from abroad, and the gay native scenes in the bars are by Rhoda Jackson, a talented Jamaican artist with a light-hearted style of her own. (The dust jacket of this book and most of the black-and-white drawings are her work.) There are terraces overlooking the sea which nightly are the scene of calypsos and floor shows and where a Jamaican band plays at lunchtime and in the evening. And there is a roof where guests dance under the stars to music which sets the pulse throbbing to a tropical tempo.

Nearby is the small but well-equipped Fern Brae Hotel, situated right on its own beach, within sight of its neighbour, Tower Isle.

On top of the cliff, with a breath-taking view of the Caribbean, is the charming Sans Souci Hotel. Terraced gardens take one down the hillside to a circular swimming pool which is fed by a mineral spring and whose stone wall encloses it from the sea. It also has a private beach and a delightful sunken bar, and an open-air terrace built on the second level and guarded by a stone tower. The accommodation is comfortable (mostly in cottages, which sometimes can be rented) and the food good. This hotel usually imports a pianist from abroad for the season.

Two miles from Ocho Rios on a delightful small bay is Glitter Beach. Here are beautifully built completely furnished beach bungalows. The houses are ideal for a week or a month or a year. They have all the comforts of the modern furnished service flat of the North, complete with servants and janitor service, with the addition of tropical beauty and bathing on a private beach. The sea is right outside the front door. Being within the hotel area, it is a short distance from some of Jamaica's finest hotels, where the glittering and colourful international society of the world's most popular tropical island resort meets for cocktails or dinner.

Jamaica Inn, at Ocho Rios, is newly built and delightfully situated right on its own magnificent white-sands beach. Small but exclusive, it accommodates fewer than forty guests in its luxury suites. Run by the well-known couple, Gloria and Cy Elkins, it specialises in good food and wines. It is within easy reach of the other North Coast hotels and offers a luncheon and dinner service for epicures. It is one of Jamaica's best hotels.

Over White River one must idle a minute to take in the beauty of palm and sea and white breakers. A short distance further on is the new Silver Seas Hotel, a well equipped and well appointed hotel with luxury cottage type accommodation. Each bedroom is actually a private suite, consisting of bedroom, bathroom, and a large verandah, and most of them overlook the blue Caribbean. The sparkling white sand beach is enclosed by a reef and there is a mineral spring flowing into the sea beside the hotel. Silver Seas supplies the visitor with sport and entertainment. The swimming is of course excellent and there is deep-sea fishing in a 42-foot Chris-craft Diesel cruiser or off-shore fishing with a small outboard motor boat. Enthusiastic spear-fishermen will find good sport and there are miles of reef where fish abound.

These hotels adjoin the village of Ocho Rios; and on up the hill above is Shaw Park. A former Great House, it retains the atmosphere of elegance and charm. Situated at an elevation of five hundred feet, in spacious grounds amid terraced gardens, Shaw Park commands magnificent views of the Caribbean and the surrounding country. Lawn tennis, putting, croquet, badminton and riding may all be enjoyed in the hotel grounds, and ten minutes' drive along the coast is the charming private beach where you will laze in the sun or on the sands and later sip cool drinks in the bar patio. With its own home farm and six hundred acre estate, the traditions of gracious living and unexcelled personalised service have been jealously guarded at Shaw Park.

St. Ann's Bay is a few miles away and here there is a small, comfortable hotel, the Windsor, situated on a hill a short distance from the main road with a magnificent view of the sea. The hotel's private beach is only five minutes' drive from the hotel and guests are taken down by car each morning. The Windsor has a mineral spring, the waters of which have excellent curative properties for skin diseases. Polo is played half a mile away each Saturday and there is excellent fishing in nearby rivers.

A few miles further on is Runaway Bay, where the last of the Spaniards are said to have embarked for Cuba, leaving the island to the English—and our eternal delectation. Eaton Hall Hotel is here, its stone foundations speaking of another age. It is the site of an English fort three hundred years old and has now been turned into a modern hotel, but retains its lovely old lines. It is right on the sea, with its own private beach.

Along the coast, a mile or two, is Discovery Bay, a large property which has been developed and sub-divided into residential sites. Already houses are springing up. On the same site, on a rise above the Bay, is Columbus Inn, a pleasant hotel with accommodation in separate cottages. The dining room and bar are well run and the food is good. This is one of the places where Columbus is said to have landed and Mr. Harold Peat, who has

Tower Isle, one of the newest and finest hotels in the Western Hemisphere, has its own private beach and salt water swimming pool

developed both housing scheme and hotel, has made the most of this circumstance. The hotel and cottages share a superb private beach, where dressing rooms with showers have been erected.

Silver Sands Beach Club is a novel resort, which deserves particular notice. The owner, Mr. 'Bob' Huggins, took a stretch of silver sand near Duncans in Trelawny and made it a background for a group of bungalows where guests can be assured of privacy and comfort without the disadvantages of housekeeping. The club membership list includes names famous in England, in the United States and on the Continent. There are writers, artists, men of affairs, big business men and men outstanding in the learned professions, and they come to relax in the delightful informality of this charming club. The beach is one of the best in the West Indies (which is to say anywhere!) and the sea bathing is of the most marvellous. It is midway between Tower Isle and Montego Bay with Good Hope within easy distance, so there are plenty of interesting trips, and the club itself provides all kinds of entertainment (including fishing and shooting in season) by day and by night.

At Falmouth, town of the eighteenth century with marks of the old Colonial times still upon it, the Martha Brae comes down from its beginnings in the 'Cockpit Country'. For seven miles of its course, it runs through the property of Good Hope. This old Great House bears many souvenirs of slave days and there are picturesque ruins of several Great Houses and sugar works on the various estates. Good Hope, with its surrounding cottages, has been thoroughly modernised and is one of the most comfortable places in the island. It still has the air of spacious times and the old luxurious way of living without any of the uncomfortable features of the early days. Sea-bathing on its own private beach, riding, tennis, fishing are part of the routine and even the predinner cocktails are in the all-inclusive rate.

MONTEGO BAY

Montego Bay is the only place in Jamaica which can genuinely be regarded as a tourist resort rather than as a particular beauty spot on whose site a hotel has grown. Doctor's Cave Bathing Beach is famous throughout the world. It is a mile or so east of the town and about it congregate hotels with a Continental atmosphere and charm but with the peculiar Caribbean graces that no Continental resort can achieve.

As we have said, the Casa Blanca Hotel is not only the pioneer hotel of Montego Bay but it is the foundation stone of the entire tourist trade of Jamaica. Its reputation is based on years of steadfast tradition. Built on the solid rock, its terraces and the balconies of its bedrooms lean over the crystal-clear water, where the parrot fish flash their kingfisher blue scales among the rocks. Breakfast on your own balcony overlooking all this tropical life is a notable experience.

The original house, which crouched on the cliff above the water, is still discernible. But year by year the Ewen family have added to this delightful hotel without in the least affecting its charm. It now stretches for a considerable distance along the shore, hugging the cliffs the whole way. Its terraces and patios overhang the water and additions now being made or planned preserve this hotel's charming tradition of creating intimacy between the visitor and the fascinating Caribbean sea.

There were formerly several cottages on the far side of the road but these have been pulled down in order to improve the garden frontage and new accommodation has been built adjacent to the Coral Cliff Hotel with exposures to both sea and hills. It is unthinkable to come to Jamaica without visiting the Casa Blanca Hotel. It is unique.

The Coral Cliff Hotel is small, and well situated for family parties. It accommodates thirty-five guests and is owned and operated by the Casa Blanca on the basis of bed and breakfast there with lunch and dinner in the main dining-room or terrace. Free admission to the bathing club is also included in the Coral Cliff rates.

Right beside the Casa Blanca is the Doctor's Cave Bathing Club. To reach it you need only walk from the hotel, through a gate, in your swim suit, a convenience cherished by visitors. The translucent and stimulating water is famous throughout the world. Club facilities are granted to visitors at all the adjacent hotels.

Sunset Lodge is undoubtedly the most fashionable resort in the West Indies. It was built a few years ago by Mr. H. G. deLisser but his daughter, Mrs. Carmen Pringle, was the inspiration behind it. She is well known in international sets, fashionable and artistic, and Sunset Lodge bears evidence of this. Great names are found in its register. The holders of fabulous titles brush shoulders with the no less fabulous figures of the literary and artistic scene. You can read as much about Sunset Lodge and its celebrities in the writings of the New York columnists as in the *West Indian Review*, for the doings of these people make news in the big world.

Sunset Lodge has its own beach. Although there is a conventional dining-room, it is the frequent habit of guests to eat their dinner on the terrace or even on the sands adjacent to the sea, with the white-capped chef presiding at the barbecue from which grilled chickens and other delicious dainties are served. The note is informality except on special dance nights when the dinner jackets and evening gowns are brought out to give the ballroom the air of a smart international rendezvous.

The Beach View Hotel, which accommodates fifty, is situated directly opposite Doctor's Cave Bathing Beach and all guests have the privilege of using the Club free of charge. The hotel is most comfortable and the food excellent. The service is known to be as good as any in Montego Bay and it has the gayest and most amusing bar. The rates are somewhat lower than the 'luxury' hotels. The Beach View includes everything (except drinks!) in its rates and there are no extras whatsoever. It is operated by the owners and is a most delightful place to spend a holiday.

The Fairfield Hotel is adjacent to the Country Club. It is owned by the Custos (Chief Magistrate) of the Parish of St. James, the Honourable Mr. F. M. Kerr-Jarrett, and is run by his family. Its location makes it particularly pleasant for sportsmen and sportswomen. Transportation to the beach is easy and is arranged by the hotel.

Doctor's Cave, the famous bathing beach, with a sprinkling of fashionable winter visitors

The promenade near Montego Bay

Richmond Hill Inn is another charmingly situated hotel with buildings of the cottage type. Located on a low hill, it receives freshening breezes yet is not far from the beach, to which transport is provided. It is particularly liked by those seeking rest and quiet.

Nearer town on a hill is the Ethelhart Hotel. Miss Ethel Hart —who founded it—precedes even Mrs. Ewen as a pioneer in hotel-keeping in Montego Bay. It is now owned by Mr. James Marzouca. The Ethelhart Hotel has much of the charm of an old-time tropical house, with its deep verandahs. It is always popular and the table is especially good. They say that you haven't seen sundown till you see it from Ethelhart. The food has a high reputation and the rates are moderate. The view is superb.

The Chatham, east of the cluster around Doctor's Cave, has its own beach, and Clifton House is a very comfortable Guest House at moderate rates. It faces the sea.

Gloucester House has long had the reputation of a small, well-run luxury hotel. It has now been enlarged and, while retaining its character of quietness and exclusiveness, has become one of the finest hotels in the island. It has a private entrance to the famous Doctor's Cave.

MONEAGUE

The main road to Montego Bay from Kingston goes through the gorge of the Rio Cobre, over Mount Diablo, and passes through Moneague. But one must *not* pass the Moneague Hotel. It is an English country house, run on country house lines, in the proper setting of English parkland which the slopes of Moneague resemble. Here are great spreading trees and pasture lands for the grazing of cattle, and here, in the hotel, in the great rooms, there is traditional English furniture—Chippendale by the master cabinet maker—tables with pedestals carved in the famous pineapple pattern, four-poster beds, with head-boards showing the Prince of Wales' Feathers. Here are Persian carpets and tapestries, beautiful pictures, Crown Derby and Ming China, Bristol glasses, lovely things to delight the eye. There is a golf course; there are tennis and riding; there is a swimming

The original Titchfield Hotel was burnt down many years ago.   F. J. Vaculik
On a beautiful adjacent site is the present Titchfield

One of the pleasures of Port Antonio is rafting on the Rio Grande   D. C. Corinaldi

pool. The table is excellent. It is a good stopping place on a cross-island journey.

PORT ANTONIO

On the north-east corner of the island, in the parish of Portland, Port Antonio and the surrounding coast are increasingly popular. The Titchfield Hotel is very comfortable, its rates are moderate and it is open all the year round. It is delightfully situated on the peninsula between the East and West Harbours, and has its own swimming pool. It is difficult to imagine a lovelier scene, with the double lagoon, and Navy Island across the way. Rafting down the Rio Grande is a delightful experience.

Another coming resort is San San Estate, covering over twelve hundred acres and ranging from sea level to eight hundred feet. The property has bananas, coconuts, pastures and some fine bathing beaches. Frenchman's Cove, an unspoiled inlet between the cliffs, with acres of white sand, has a fresh water river running into the Bay. San San Bay is shut in by an enchanting small island and a coral reef, and here is the San San Beach Club with bar lounge and dressing rooms.

There is no hotel, but bungalows are built on the cliff overlooking the translucent waters and writers and artists are among those who have already bought houses. A part of the property has been divided into house sites with driving roads, water mains and electricity. It is only sixty-five miles from Kingston on a main paved highway and five miles east of Port Antonio.

MANDEVILLE

For an inland trip to cool latitudes the visitor will want to see Mandeville, called the English village, with its old stone church and the 'green' in the square. The leading place to stay is the Hotel Manchester, modern, spacious, with outstanding cuisine. The Mandeville Hotel is old-fashioned but comfortable. There is golf and tennis.

CHAPTER SIXTEEN
Sports and Pastimes

Jamaica has fifty-two weeks of sunshine and it is an ideal spot for the person who likes to spend his time in the open air. Here one can participate in or watch practically every sport. Cricket is perhaps the favourite game, but there are softball and football as well as horse racing, polo, shooting, fishing, and yachting.

RACING AND BREEDING

Each year, there are twenty-four days of racing in Jamaica organised by the three racing Associations—Knutsford Park Ltd., who have fourteen days at beautiful Knutsford Park in St. Andrew; Jamaica Turf Club Ltd., who have seven racing days, some at Knutsford Park and some at Marlie, which is twenty-five miles from Kingston at Old Harbour (which track they own); and the St. Ann Racing Association, who have two days of racing at Fairfield in Montego Bay, generally in February. In these races are included many two and three year old futurities and the Knutsford Park meetings are well attended.

Jamaica is one of the few British countries which operate a Sweepstake, which provides more funds for purses. This has encouraged owners to raise and breed more horses, and to import English stallions for improving the stock. Three outstanding thoroughbreds have been produced, Sun Hunter, Mark Twain and All Smiles, each of which predominated in its own year in the two-year-old field. The highest racing authority in Jamaica is the Jockey Club, which controls racing and whose rules are based more or less on those of the English Jockey Club.

BREEDING

There are four or five reputable stud farms in the island, with mares which are either offspring or descendants of English importations. Outstanding English stallions which have been imported are:

Massif, who ran in the Airborne Derby in 1946; bred at the National Stud, owned by the Government of England, by Mieuxce out of Snowberry, by Cameronian.

Merry Mark by Precipitation out of Mary Vixen, by Sir Galahad III. Merry Mark was bred by William Woodward, until recently Chairman of the New York Jockey Club and one of the leading race horse owners in the United States.

Fair Tip by Fair Trial out of Tip the Wink, by Tetratema. This horse was bred in Ireland by Major Giles Loder.

Watchlight by Signal Light out of Nuit de Noce, by the same sire as Big Dipper, Champion two-year-old of England in 1950.

Phenomene by Hyperion out of Wafer, by Sansovino—a very valuable horse, as he is the only entire son of Hyperion in the West Indies.

The supply from the stud farms is still inadequate to keep the sport at a proper level, and it therefore continues to be necessary to import regularly from abroad. Jamaica cannot bring in horses from America or the other West Indian islands, and has to depend almost entirely on England and Ireland for her requirements.

GOLF

There are a number of interesting golf courses in Jamaica, although because of the extremes of drought and rain the greens are perhaps not of the standard attained in the North. There is only one eighteen hole course, at Constant Spring, adjoining the Manor House Hotel. It is set in beautiful country with the mountains towering in the distance. Liguanea, adjoining Knutsford Park Race Course, is a twelve hole course. Probably the best course in the island is the nine-hole course at the Manchester Club in Mandeville, where the greens are good because of the cooler and wetter climate. There are what can be described as 'knock-about courses' in Malvern (in the very high hills beyond Mandeville), at Paradise near Savanna-la-Mar, and at the

Moneague Hotel. These are all nine-hole courses. In Montego Bay, the Fairfield Club has a nine-hole course.

All clubs welcome visitors and green fees can be arranged by day, week, or month, and are very reasonable. The Jamaica Golf Association arranges tournaments from time to time and Liguanea and Constant Spring each brings a professional from abroad for the winter season.

CRICKET

The standard of cricket in the West Indies and in Jamaica is high, although average cricket is not up to the standard of County Cricket in Britain. The game is well supported in Jamaica and there are many clubs.

The season usually begins on the last Saturday in February and continues to the end of August. Games are always played on Saturday, play begins at 1.30 and continues until about six according to the light. Jamaica's short twilight forbids long-drawn-out games. There are regular inter-colonial tournaments, teams from the various West Indian colonies exchanging visits and usually playing two five-day matches. Such cricket is of a very high standard. Tournaments of this kind have been made possible in recent years because of the increased facilities for air travel in the Caribbean.

All the wickets in Jamaica are turf, which provides a hard and very fast wicket. The balls are Wisdom's Special Colonial, which are found to keep their shape best in the heat.

Jamaica has produced some outstanding cricketers. The fine and celebrated batsman, George Headley, is the only cricketer to have made a century in each innings of a Test Match at Lord's. Alfred Valentine is a top-notch bowler. There are other first-rate names on the roster. In the past, Ivan Barrow, Frank Martin and Karl Nunes were among the men of Test Match quality.

Tours proposed for the future are:

India in the West Indies   (1952-53)
England in the West Indies   (1953-54)

FOOTBALL

Association football is a favourite game in Jamaica and the standard of play is high. The season extends from about October to the end of February, when three or four games a week are played. There are many flourishing clubs and the Army always has a strong team. There are occasional International matches when countries such as Haiti and Cuba send teams to Jamaica.

FISHING

Some fine river fishing and excellent deep-sea fishing are procurable in Jamaica. Black River attracts the river fishermen and Kingston and Port Antonio offer excellent facilities for deep-sea fishing. Under-water spearing is also becoming popular in the shallow waters of north shore coves.

About fourteen to fifteen miles south of Plum Point Lighthouse near the Palisadoes Airport lies the California Bank, a high ridge on the ocean floor, probably a submerged range of hills, approximately four miles in length.

Here in late April, May, June and July abound kingfish up to ninety pounds in weight, tarpon, Spanish mackerel and barracuda. The depth of water on the actual bank is thirty-two to thirty-five fathoms, and if the fisher is accompanied by an experienced guide there should be excellent sport. The bank is clearly marked on marine charts, which can be procured from the Harbour Master's office. For small tuna and sailfish of medium weight (fifty to eighty pounds) the fisherman should go a mile farther south by east to the one hundred fathom mark.

These fish will take a troll with a linen or monel wire line of thirty pounds breaking strength and at least three hundred yards in length, which may on occasions be taken up to the last twenty-five yards. Rods of eight to ten ounce tips are advisable and a number four or five reel, according to the angler's taste. A good gaff is also necessary.

In Kingston Harbour, particularly around the mouth, it is sometimes possible to get a good catch of kingfish. In June and July, these run to fifteen or twenty pounds and sometimes there

Moonlight fishing in Montego
Bay

F. J. Vaculik

Paul Geddes

Looking across the bay, Port Antonio—Folly Lighthouse in the background

are schools of jack up to seventeen pounds, which are easily caught on troll. Small tarpon also come into the harbour on occasions.

In Kingston, the visitor would be well advised to go to the Royal Jamaica Yacht Club or get in touch with the Jamaica Angling Association with regard to boats, guides and so on.

In the late summer the fish in and around Kingston seem to migrate along the south coast and settle in the waters off Savanna-la-Mar, Black River, and the little village of White House, ten miles east of Black River. The fishing there is excellent and, although taken with hand lines, provides fine sport, with fish weighing up to seventy or eighty pounds. The catch is usually kingfish or jack, with an occasional barracuda or Spanish mackerel. There is a small Fisherman's Inn at Black River and at White House the local fishing experts offer simple accommodation to the sportsman.

The Black River itself is navigable for some distance and mullet and snook can be caught with hand line or rod with a small dry fly or moss bait. Mullet is used as bait at the mouth of the river where tarpon up to one hundred and fifty pounds have been caught. Spear fishing is also available.

At Port Antonio, there is also excellent fishing and the Portland Fishing Club offers all facilities to visitors. The headquarters of the Club is the Titchfield Hotel, but there is an attractive bamboo camp house with a bar lounge and changing rooms at the mouth of the Rio Grande. In the upper reaches of the river, mountain mullet and calipoeva can be had on shrimp or avocado bait with a fly or plug casting light rod and Colorado spinners and miniature plugs. In the lower reaches, ninety pound tarpon, forty pound snook and jack rise to sprat, mullet, shrimp, spoon, fly or spinner on a fly rod, plug casting rod or light trolling rod.

Within a radius of about fifteen miles off Port Antonio there is excellent deep sea fishing. There is the Henry Holmes Bank, eighteen miles north-east and a bank off Buff Bay, approximately about half a mile off-shore. Fish awaiting the angler are blue and white marlin, blue fin tuna, sailfish, dolphin, bonito and barracuda. A white marlin of tremendous size was caught a mere half a mile off the Titchfield Hotel. The usual types of light and heavy salt water tackle are used with mullet, mackerel and bonito bait. The Portland Fishing Club offers every facility to the visitor as to boats, bait and guides. Temporary membership is inexpensive. (See *Appendix*.)

YACHTING

Kingston Harbour, one of the finest in the world, with the long arm of the Palisadoes protecting it from the open sea, is an ideal place for yachts. The harbour, fourteen miles long by two miles wide, is always swept by fresh breezes. There are sailing and cruising outside the harbour, made delightful by the number of tiny coral islands which are locally called cays, which are popular bathing spots. The Royal Jamaica Yacht Club on the north side of the harbour is easily reached from Kingston, and has wharf and docking facilities for small boats. Visiting yachtsmen are always welcome.

The ideal craft for sailing under tropical conditions is the popular eighteen foot O Class boat designed by John Alden, the American designer. This is closely followed in popularity by an island-built sixteen foot centre board boat, locally called the 'Snapper Class'. It can be purchased at a very reasonable cost. There are also one or two large cruisers which once a year participate in round the island races.

The Yacht Club Fleet has steadily increased since the end of the last war and three or four regattas are held annually in Kingston and one at Montego Bay, where there is also a Yacht Club. Port Antonio is also forming a club. The Royal Jamaica Yacht Club is the oldest Royal Charter Club in the West Indies, its charter having been granted by Queen Victoria in 1885, giving its members the privilege of flying the Blue Ensign (defaced).

Appropriately enough, there is a boat building yard at Port Royal where those masters of the craft, the Caymanians, build boats of native lumber to their own or American and English design both for sail and motor. These boats can be favourably compared with the finest built anywhere and are ideally suited to the conditions under which they sail.

TENNIS

Tennis players should certainly include a brace of racquets in their luggage, for they will find plenty of opportunity for play. St. Andrew Club, near Cross Roads, has always been the classic home of tennis in the island, but Liguanea Club (by Knutsford Park Race Course, Half Way Tree Road) has eight or more good courts. Both Clubs have annual tournaments, generally held between January and March, and a Jamaican Lawn Tennis Championship is run at St. Andrew in the early months of the year. There are a number of other tennis clubs in Kingston, including the Melbourne, Kingston and Wembley Clubs.

Tennis Week at Mandeville (followed by Golf Week) is a very popular annual event in August, and the Northern Championships are held on the courts at the Fairfield Club, Montego Bay, in January or February. Tower Isle has its courts, and so have several of the hotels in Montego Bay and elsewhere. There are smaller clubs in many of the rural centres.

Courts in Kingston and St. Andrew are generally of grass, but one or two hard ones have been laid down in recent years at the Clubs. There are hard courts at Mandeville and Malvern.

The average standard of play in Jamaica is good but in tournament and international games (which are becoming an annual institution) perhaps it is less high than it should be, considering the all-year-round facilities for practice. Many famous tennis players from abroad have visited the island, and, though they can be sure of a good game, no Jamaican team has yet won an international victory.

SHOOTING

During the winter months, Jamaica is visited by large quantities of migratory duck, principally the blue-wing teal, the pin-

Tourist Board

*Constant Spring Golf Club, just outside Kingston, with the foothills of the
Blue Mountains in the background*

Cleary & Elliott

The attractive lounge of Castle Gordon Hotel

tail, the scorp, and occasionally the mallard. There is no closed season for water fowl and bags are not limited. In January, February and March, the birds are plentiful and bags of twenty-five teal or fifteen pin-tail are not unusual. The birds confine themselves to the swamps.

The only other shooting in Jamaica is for pigeons and doves, included in which are baldpates, white wings, peadoves and white bellies. The season opens on August 12th and closes on January 31st, but during the rainy months of October, November and December, there is practically no shooting of this type. In January, however, in Westmoreland, when the rice is being reaped, there may be a fair supply of white wings.

Dogs are not generally used, the birds being retrieved by young boys of the district, who are very keen to go out and in addition are of great assistance as guides and for carrying equipment. There are three gun clubs in the island but the gun man will be well advised to see Andrew Aguilar at 93 Harbour Street (a short walk from the Myrtle Bank Hotel), an outstanding sportsman who is always willing to supply information and to give assistance in the securing of licences and equipment.

Crocodile (incorrectly called alligator locally) shooting can be obtained in the swamps all along the south coast of the island. Strangely enough, no crocodiles have ever been found along the north coast. A number of local tanners specialise in curing the leather. There is a certain amount of shooting for commercial purposes. As far as local memory goes, no alligators have been found in or around Alligator Pond, although the name would indicate that they were there at some time.

There are a number of rifle clubs and Jamaica has produced some front-rank contestants for the Bisley team.

OTHER RECREATIONS

There is excellent POLO in Jamaica, at the military camp in Kingston, in St. Ann and at Montego Bay. There are good ponies and several flourishing clubs.

Good RIDING can be enjoyed in the foothills of the mountains of St. Andrew and in the country. Good Hope particularly caters to the horseman and delightful hours can be spent riding on the estate.

WALKING is not a favourite pastime in the plains but at higher altitudes there are delightful paths and tracks winding through wooded valleys and over the hills. Blue Mountain Peak must be reached on foot or by mule from Mavis Bank, the end of the driving road. It is usual to spend the night at a nearby guest house and start for the Peak early in the morning in order to see the sunrise and the view, as by eight o'clock the mountain is often enshrouded in cloud. From the Peak, a panoramic view of Jamaica is obtained. To the north is Port Antonio, to the east the Morant Bay light house, to the south, looking over the range of the Port Royal Mountains, is Kingston. The sea and the surf in the distance look like a frozen white line or like icing on a cake. To the east, one can see the hills around Mandeville and Mount Diablo, and beyond, range after range of hills melting into the indiscernible blue.

On the lower levels there are innumerable walks around Guava Ridge, Content, Flamstead, Cinchona and along the upper Yallahs valley. On the Newcastle side, there is a delightful walk through Fairy Glade, around Catherine's Peak and through the forest reserves. For those who dislike walking, there is always the mule. Sturdy, if obstinate, it is the most surefooted of beasts. The animal knows its country well and it is usually best to let it pick its own way. If it stops frequently to eat a mango on the path, do not be impatient but use the time to look at the scenery. There is no trick in riding hill trails; one leans back on the steep down-hill grade, and forward when climbing. A little difficult to emulate is the seat of the country people, who take up a position on the extreme stern end of the beast.

A unique pastime is RAFTING down the Rio Grande, which no one can fail to enjoy. The Titchfield Hotel in Port Antonio is the centre from which to arrange this delightful outing. You are driven to the starting point, to be met by a local boatman, and embarking on your bamboo craft you start down the river, sometimes running swiftly on the current, sometimes being guided expertly by your bargeman with his long pole. Your journey takes you through wooded country of tall tropical trees, past flat reaches of the river where peasants are washing clothes, through rapids and into quiet pools. One may tie up the raft and slip off for a cool swim or the fisherman may take advantage of the excellent fishing the river provides. At the end of the trip your taxi will be found waiting to whisk you back to the Titchfield.

NIGHT LIFE

The seaports of Jamaica, like those of other places, offer a type of night-life which is designed to lure the visitor—sailor, soldier or civilian—into establishments which are scarcely material for this book! There is also plenty of healthy amusement.

The leading hotels arrange periodical dances so as not to conflict with others nearby . . . for instance, Sunset Lodge (on Wednesdays and Fridays), Casa Blanca (on Saturdays).

There are several night-clubs, where dancing can be enjoyed to excellent native bands, in the environs of Kingston, and in some other centres. Most clubs offer floor shows, native or otherwise, on certain nights.

Kingston has a number of excellent cinemas. The Ward Theatre, intended by its philanthropist donor as a playhouse, is now mainly used for motion pictures. There is a good motion picture theatre in Montego Bay and most towns have a cinema of more or less merit. The chain-theatre system is controlled by the Rank organisation, but many American films are shown. There is Cycle Racing at night occasionally.

On the road

West Indian Review

CHAPTER SEVENTEEN
What to Wear

Don't pack your New York or London clothes. They will be useless to you.

There is a great temptation when surveying your wardrobe to select gowns because they are attractive and they suit you, but the coats and skirts, however light, and the smart black town frocks that you are accustomed to wearing have no place in your tropical outfit.

How To Travel. If you are coming direct from New York or some other cold place by air, there is a definite problem, because you will be wrongly attired either in New York or in Jamaica. Recently, we saw a woman step on the plane at Idlewild dressed in a cotton frock, with white shoes and a light straw hat. This was in mid November and she certainly did not look properly dressed for New York. On the other hand, you cannot arrive in heavy woollen clothes. The obvious solution is to wear a light suit or dress with a warm coat, which can be discarded en route.

If you are travelling by sea from England, you will need some warm clothes for the first few days of the voyage; but unless you are travelling in a luxury ship (and few of them go to the West Indies), don't take your best things to wear on board. The banana boats are informal and you will find it very comfortable to longe about the deck or to play games in a sweater and skirt, or slacks. After a few days, the climate changes, and you are soon in the Tropics. You will find slacks useful all through the voyage and, in the latter days, shorts and cotton frocks are appropriate. Pack an evening dress or two for use on the voyage, but not over-elaborate gowns.

In Jamaica, if you are spending the usual holiday, you will probably breakfast in shorts and shirt or a cotton frock. You will change immediately afterward into a swim suit and, later in the morning, will fling on a wrap or change back into shorts to have your pre-luncheon drink at the bar or on the terrace of your favourite hotel. For lunch you should change into something smart but very simple. The afternoon you will probably spend lounging and reading in your room. In the late afternoon you may take another swim, so it is obviously wise to have at least two swim suits. Let them be as smart and attractive as possible, for—if you are a woman—you are going to meet a lot of competition on these fashionable beaches.

Men like to disport themselves in fancy resort clothes, too. Shorts and shirts are favourites. Bathing shorts can be very fancy indeed, and so can the shirts worn in the morning or afternoon. The bandana cloth which is the headwear of the native women is a favourite material for shirts for both men and women and there are many other colourful prints obtainable in Jamaica.

It is wise to have a light cocktail frock or two; but very often you will find that your cocktail engagement extends right up to dinner time, so you can keep this appointment in a dinner dress, short or long. At Sunset Lodge, the smartest hotel in Jamaica, it is fashionable not to wear evening clothes except for dance evenings. Men and women go to the beach picnics and barbecue dinners in slacks or other informal attire. At other hotels, many people wear evening clothes. For men, a white dinner jacket is the lightest and coolest wear, although a black dinner jacket is quite correct. Tails are rarely worn, except for formal occasions at Government House, to which you will only be asked if there is some special reason for inviting you to a kind of function that is only rarely held.

Some women never wear stockings during the whole of the season and hats are seldom worn. You should have a big straw hat for beach wear, but you can buy that in Jamaica. You should have sun glasses, too. The climate is so delectable that you may not realise that the sun is hot. You should take precautions against sun-burn, as well as against a glare that may hurt your eyes.

Every kind of garment that you will wish to wear, whether

you are a man or a woman, can be bought in Jamaica; but you may want that New York or London cut, in which case you might like to bring at least some of your own things. There are dresses in the shops which are moderately priced and also others which are in the higher-priced category. There are also 'little dressmakers' if you happen to know someone who can recommend you to a good one, who will run up the attractive materials that can be bought locally at trifling cost. You will have to supply the taste and judgment.

As for the men, there are tailors in Kingston, Montego Bay and elsewhere, who will make a tropical suit in twenty-four hours; and very well, too. There are also stores for all kinds of ready-made men's clothes.

There are good shoes for men and women, but not in the variety in which they are found in large Northern cities.

As for underwear, especially girdles and bras, better bring your own . . . particularly if you are an American!

Visitors are very fond of the hand-embroidered linen dresses to be found ready-made in several of the shops. Beautiful linens, both dress and household, abound in the stores; and Americans will look at materials such as doeskin, tweeds, and other woollen fabrics, with great pleasure.

Coats and furs are not really necessary, but summer ermine, for instance, looks handsome with an evening dress; and in the hills a light wrap is really required in the winter. Your mink and sable coats, however, would be an embarrassment to you. Better leave them at home.

CHAPTER EIGHTEEN
Shopping in Jamaica

The first requisite of the shopper is the money to shop with. This book cannot offer any suggestions for the acquisition of the necessary funds, but it can reassure the traveller who is worried about currency.

Jamaica is a British possession and the normal currency is sterling; but dollars are equally—or perhaps we should say more —acceptable. As rates of exchange vary, it is impossible to give an equation here, but this will be provided by any bank or by such reputable hotels as Myrtle Bank, Courtleigh Manor, and Manor House in the Kingston area, and any of the good hotels in the country. The traveller need not be afraid of advantage being taken of his possible ignorance in such reputable places or in the big stores. He is advised to arm himself with the necessary information before spending dollars too freely elsewhere.

The greater number of good stores are in Kingston, but the town of Montego Bay, which is about a mile from the hotel district, has very good shops, too. Myrtle Bank Hotel, Tower Isle, Sunset Lodge, Shaw Park, Jamaica Inn, Titchfield and some other hotels have shops of their own, where the special articles dear to visitors can be obtained.

The visitor from the United States would be particularly interested in woollen fabrics, linens, perfumes, leather goods and jewellery, all of which can be obtained at lower prices than in his own country, and often in a quality that cannot be secured there. English china and silverware are also liberally displayed.

The visitor, of course, will also wish to accumulate a few souvenirs of the island to take back to his friends and to remind him of his own pleasant visit. Special industries in Jamaica include hat and basket making and charming examples of these can be obtained in such stores as Chamberlin's, and Jamaica Cottage Industries. There are street vendors, too, and such charming mementoes as little Negro figures carrying baskets of fruit on their heads will be found in the streets and market places.

Jamaica grows some very lovely timber woods, but these are not found in large quantities and so each article made of these delightful woods has an individual appeal. The woods include the beautiful gray-green of Mahoe, the golden Satinwood, the Yellow Saunders, which is really yellow, Jackfruit and Yacca, as well as the hard Bullet Wood, which is used for ships' propellers. Gift articles of these woods, used individually or in conjunction, are to be found in many of the stores. Some firms, such as Jackson on King Street or Lacy on Water Lane, specialise in such items and all the stores that offer tourist articles have them on show in more or less variety.

Another type of souvenir, easily packed and of extremely high quality, is the product of the Jamaica Embroidery League, where linen embroidered in gay and characteristic Jamaican style is made into various articles such as guest towels and table mats and handbags. A charming type of summer bag which is shown in several of the shops is in white embroidered linen, and there are beach bags lined with rubber and gaily embroidered with Jamaican scenes.

P. A. Benjamin, Ltd. manufacture a highly characteristic perfume, known as Khus Khus, which has a unique scent and is liked by a great many visitors. French perfumes are in all the shops at a lower price than at home. There are a number of Indian and Chinese shops which import silk goods from the Far East. Made in Jamaica are beautiful hand-worked Indian silver bracelets and these are to be found in several of the large stores, as well as in the Indian shops.

Everywhere in the Island will be found street vendors with native articles such as baskets, rattles and necklaces of dried seeds. These are amusing, but the visitor should not pay too much for them, neither should he allow himself to be pestered if he does not want them.

Orchids are inexpensive in Jamaica, but they are not easily located. There is an Orchid Society from which information can be obtained. The hotels will also assist.

West Indian Review

Visitors like to buy hats and baskets at attractive street markets

Shopping for Food

Hints on marketing will be found under *Housekeeping*.

There are numerous items bottled, packaged or canned, some of them in attractive form for gifts. Guava Jelly is a famous product of Jamaica and marmalade made of local oranges and sugar and various other kinds of preserves are to be found in specialty shops. Mangoes are now being canned.

One article which is always popular is Picka Peppa Sauce, an aromatic sauce of unique flavour.

Visitors can buy rum in bond—that is to say, duty free—to take or send abroad. It would be invidious to advise on a particular brand, as this is a matter of taste, but the selection may well be made between Myers', Wray & Nephew, The Rum Company, and Ehrenstein, all of whom produce first-rate varieties. (See *Rum*.)

Cigars and Cigarettes

Jamaican cigars, too, are famous throughout the world. An article on this subject also appears in this volume. Not all makes of cigars can be bought in Jamaica, for some manufacturers export their entire output, but visitors will find their enquiries welcomed by all the first-class manufacturers, including Machado's, Temple Hall and the Jamaica Tobacco Co.

There are several brands of locally made cigarettes, all manufactured of imported Virginia Tobacco. All the hotels, however, also import American or English brands.

CHAPTER NINETEEN
The Property Market

To advise on this question is to assume a great responsibility. The available agricultural properties frequently come into the market, but it is not everyone—even a trained farmer in the United Kingdom or the United States—who can take over the management of a Jamaican property and make an immediate success.

Full investigation should be made, not only into the unique farming conditions of Jamaica, but also into the labour situation. Some remarks on this will be found in another chapter. (See *Industries*.)

There can be no finer life anywhere in the world than to own and manage a property in Jamaica. It is almost certain, wherever it is situated, to contain some hill land, and the finest houses—whether they be ancient great houses or more modern buildings—are built on the crown of a hill, commanding beautiful views of the surrounding country, and perhaps of the lovely Caribbean Sea.

Properties in Jamaica divide themselves broadly into two classes. Cattle properties are called Pens. There is no finer cattle in the tropical world than that which has been bred and developed from the finest imported stock, in Jamaica. The Government has taken a deep interest in this question and is continually working to improve breeds, both of Dairy and Beef Cattle. The active or semi-retired man, who wishes to lead a delightful life in the world's best climate, might well consider investing his capital in such a property.

Cattle properties are never exclusively used for breeding cattle and horses. There is always some portion on which certain crops are cultivated and this gives interest and diversity to the work of management.

Large property owners in Jamaica are usually inclined to concentrate upon one major crop, whether it be sugar cane, coconuts, or bananas. Market gardens (called truck gardens in the United States) are a rather difficult proposition, as the climate is not always suitable to the growing of vegetables and similar produce. Nevertheless, there is a shortage of green vegetables in Jamaica and an expert, prepared to allow for the vagaries of the climate and to specialise in this field, ought to find a ready market in the hotels and other consumers.

Poultry farming is another occupation which has never been expanded to its fullest extent. Pig rearing is another minor industry, which has never been developed to its full scope. We have heard of optimists who wished to raise sheep on the Jamaican hills, but this is not considered an economic proposition. Good cultivable land is too valuable and natural food too sparse.

There are several very reliable Estate Agents, who will investigate a proposition, and there is an extremely good body of solicitors who will look after the legal aspects. Some investors have bought properties without seeing them first, and have been fully satisfied.

There is one piece of advice that should be given to everyone who wishes to embark upon a venture of this kind. Use all the influence you possess to obtain a first-rate Manager (or Attorney), who has been born and reared under Jamaican farming conditions.

Buying for Building

A good modern house, built of one of a number of excellent materials—whether native stone, concrete, Bellrock or some such patented product—can be erected in Jamaica in a matter of a few months on completely modern lines, with all modern amenities. The man who wishes to build in the country may not be able to obtain a pipe water supply and electric light, and will probably be out of reach of the telephone, although the telephone system is becoming island-wide. Obviously, however, it is not carried to isolated spots. If he wishes to build in the Kingston area, he will certainly choose a site outside the city.

Hunting Aero Surveys, Ltd.

Cold Harbour from the air. Situated near Port Antonio, this beautiful estate is part of an important development project. House sites are available

'Everybody' lives in the foothills, or higher up in the nearby mountains. Stony Hill, the favourite residential section of the upper classes, is only nine miles from the city, is twelve to sixteen hundred feet high, according to location, and enjoys the most delicious climatic conditions, bearable when the sun is hot and delightfully cool at night. There are very few building sites left in this highly desirable district, where most houses have their two or three acres of land, where, nowadays, many people are equipping their homes with swimming pools. A few sites remain, but land values are not low and the intending resident will be fortunate if he can buy a half acre site in a pleasant location for six or seven hundred pounds. There are still a few larger sites, but they will have to be searched for, and if a sea view is expected, the price is likely to be high.

Other hill districts within easy reach of Kingston are being developed, but they do not yet possess the amenities, in the form of first-class roads, electric light, telephone and water supply, which are enjoyed by Stony Hill residents.

Spreading out all around the congested city area, there are pleasant suburban roads. There are not many good building sites available, but diligent search will find a few. Although these districts are pleasantly wind-swept in the daytime and reasonably cool at night—for the mountain breeze blows as regularly by night as the sea breeze by day—the resident cannot expect the ideal conditions enjoyed at Stony Hill. Having acquired a site, the novice will do well to place his building project in the hands of a reliable and recommended builder.

BUYING A HOUSE

In Jamaica, as elsewhere, desirable houses are continually coming into the market for one reason or another. Prices vary, but here, as elsewhere, the newcomer will find that he must pay more for a house in an exclusive and superior location than for one in a congested district. Prices, for the type of house in which the reader of this book will be interested, vary from as little as £1,000 or so, for a cottage in the country, to as much as eight or ten thousand pounds or more for a luxurious modern house in a

*High up in the Blue Mountains, the Owl Rock commands
a breath-taking view of half the island*

special situation. Prices compare more or less favourably with those in northern countries. As there, it is a matter of the capital available and luck in finding just what you require. Here again, the services of a reliable agent are invaluable. Prices in favourite coast resorts are high. Here, competition and scarcity dictate the price. There are not very many coast locations in districts where tourists flock, and the man who wants his own private beach in such a location will have to pay quite dearly for it. There are sites available in new developments at reasonable cost. Examples are the San San development in a beauteous situation near Port Antonio; Boscobel, a few miles from Tower Isle, and the attractive hill sites at Discovery Bay. A favourite spot for retired English and American residents is Mandeville, situated two thousand feet up in the hills. It is supposed to resemble an English village and it really has the peace and charm of one. It is as popular as Cheltenham or Connecticut with retired people living on their income and it is liked by such individuals, not only for its climate and attractiveness, but also because they may hope to find congenial society there. Younger people, who like gaiety, will probably prefer Ocho Rios or Montego Bay. San San is a happy compromise and is much liked by writers and artists.

People with business interests are likely to wish to settle near the metropolis. They are warned to investigate carefully, or they may find they have bought a house which is a sun-trap in the hot months. Coolness by day and night is quite feasible if care is taken in selecting the location and the house has been properly designed.

CHAPTER TWENTY

Flora and Fauna

In the time of Columbus, Jamaica was covered in primeval forest, except for the small clearings of Arawak Indians. There were no banana, logwood, ackee, tamarind, or bread-fruit trees. In the forest grew magnificent timber trees such as mahogany, West Indian cedar, bulletwood, mahoe and *lignum vitae*, all of which are in general use today. When in bloom, the lignum vitae is one of Jamaica's loveliest and most shapely trees with its mass of violet blue flowers, which colour is replaced by orange when the fruits are formed.

Since those days, a great variety of trees has been brought in. The logwood, which is found in pastures, was introduced in 1715, and provided an important industry in the production of a commercial dye for which it is still used.

The ackee introduced by slave ship from West Africa is a beautiful tree with decorative hanging clusters of bright red capsular fruits which hold the yellow edible flesh and the black seed. Ackees form part of Jamaica's national dish, codfish and ackee. (See *Appendix*.)

King of the countryside is the huge cotton tree, which stands out in stately dignity, with low spreading branches on heavy buttress roots. Although the Jamaican cotton tree does not produce the cotton of commerce, its pods contain seeds covered with a silky down which is sometimes used for similar purposes. The fishermen construct their canoes of trunks of cotton trees; the cutting down of a cotton tree for contriving a boat by a crude method of burning and chipping is an elaborate ceremony. First, the duppies have to be chased away and this requires a long ritual and a lot of rum!

In the country after rain, the hillsides are dotted with a glorious profusion of yellow—the blossoms of the West Indian ebony tree.

One of the glories of the landscape is the magnificent poinciana. Originally a native of Madagascar, it is now widely used as an ornamental tree throughout the tropics. Cassias, of which

The night blooming Cereus

there are several kinds, can be seen in many gardens and bordering sidewalks. The most attractive is that called Golden Shower, which during early summer displays long hanging sprays of golden yellow flowers, reminiscent of the laburnum of colder climes. Fringing the coast, and also in plantations inland, are the graceful coconut palms with their numerous uses. Jamaica has many other varieties of palms, the Cuban royal palm with swollen trunk is widely used as an ornamental tree. The leaves of several palms are used for thatching peasants' cottages and making mats. The yippa yappa, which is used for making attractive hats (of the 'Panama' type) and bags, is generally considered a palm, but actually belongs to a different family.

The famous Gros Michel banana was introduced from Martinique by Jean François Pouyat in 1835, for which he was awarded the prize of One Doubloon. From this humble beginning sprang the great banana trade, which has brought many thousands of pounds to the island.

Another interesting story is related of the introduction of the mango. In 1782, the corvette *Flora* of Lord Rodney's squadron captured a French Merchantman bound from the Indian Ocean to Santo Domingo. The French ship had on board a number of plants including the mango, jack fruit and woman's tongue, all of which have become common trees in Jamaica. The plants were all numbered, and the one numbered eleven was the variety of mango now known as 'number eleven'. In later years, many other varieties of mango were introduced, the most important being the Bombay, imported in 1869 by Sir Peter Grant, then Governor of the island.

The breadfruit was brought by Captain Bligh in his second attempt from Timor and Tahiti in 1793. His first voyage was disastrous and resulted in the Mutiny of the *Bounty*. He also brought the otaheite apple (a lovely tree) and the Jew plum.

Sugar cane was first known in the Far East and came steadily westward to the West Indies, appearing in Santo Domingo in 1520, and we may conjecture, must have spread throughout the Caribbean Islands during the next century. The Spaniards apparently made little effort to cultivate it in Jamaica, and the first regular plantations were not started until 1660 under the English.

Coffee was introduced in 1728 and is entirely the Arabian variety. Special mention must be made of the Pimento, the Allspice of commerce, which is native to Jamaica. Jamaica provides almost the entire world's supply.

Travelling throughout the country, one will look with delight at the 'flame-of-the-forest' Spathodea, another African tree, with its orange-red blossoms bursting out magnificently against the landscape. Farther afield, the native mountain pride can be seen with its summit crowned by a dense pyramid of mauve flowers several feet in diameter and height. In April and May there is also the maypole, an agave with its tall sentinel-like spike of yellow blossoms rising from a cluster of dark green leaves, usually on the rocky hillsides.

The grasses in the island are many in number, including the well known khus khus which is used for making perfume, as a repellant against moths and, most important, as a most valuable anti-erosion agent for binding hillside terracing. Guinea grass, the most widely used animal feed, was accidentally introduced as a bird food in 1745. 'Seymour' grass grows abundantly in the lowlands. It is *Andropogon pertusus* and was introduced some years

ago. Another introduced grass is Wynne grass, now spreading
rapidly over the Blue Mountains, and growing in dense mats
over three feet in thickness. Because of its stickiness, it is also called
molasses grass. In addition to its usefulness as fodder, it is said
to be an aid against ticks—in Jamaica a serious pest—which will
not live in it. Bamboos grow in profusion in the damper parts
and there is beautiful Bamboo Walk near Lacovia, where the
lacy arms of the trees meet overhead like the elongated dome of
a cathedral, for a distance of over a mile.

For the many beautiful and charming gardens, a great many
flowers have been imported from abroad. It is these introduced
flowers which make the gardens in Jamaica riot with colour,
with hedges of hibiscus and bougainvillea in every conceivable
shade. The single red hibiscus is locally called shoe black because
it is excellent for cleaning shoes. There are flaming red poinset-
tias and bright yellow allamandas. The nights are made fragrant
with the heavy scent of the night flowering jasmine and once in
a while the eye is entranced by the cool white beauty of the
night blooming cereus, a flower which blooms at long intervals
and lasts only a few hours. The fragrant honeysuckle grows in
the mountains and there also are grown fine Agapanthus lilies,
which are brought down to the towns and sold in the street
markets with many other flowers.

In Jamaica wild flowers do not riot in ravishing colour as
in northern countries. The black-eyed Susan is common.
Interesting is the mimosa or sensitive plant locally called
'shamer' because of its ability to fold itself up and hide at the
slightest touch. However, it recovers in a few minutes. Dodder
called love bush is a common sight, with its trailing pale yellow
branches spreading over other plants. It is not a welcome sight,
because it is a parasite which steals food from the plants to
which it clings. In the forests, especially at higher altitudes, the
trees are festooned with old man's beard and also serve as host
to many other plants such as wild pines, mistletoe and orchids.
The more spectacular varieties of orchids are not native to
Jamaica and the beautiful specimens in greenhouses and on
shaded verandahs are imported, mostly from South America or

Example of a rare orchid from the Far East (Vanda Sanderiana) successfully grown in Jamaica by Dr. Gabriel Machado. The specimen shown carries seventy three-inch blossoms on seven spikes.

Lambert

Castleton Gardens, on the Junction Road, nineteen miles from Kingston

F. J. Vaculik

the East Indies. There is one small species of wild pine which visitors will see growing on the telegraph wires.

Jamaica, for its size, has perhaps the richest fern flora in the world, ranging from the tiny delicate filmies to the large and attractive tree ferns with trunks often twenty feet in height. There are gold and silver ferns, maidenhair ferns and tropical brackens. One common fern in Jamaica, the sword fern, was taken many years ago to the United States, where a new variety sprang up in a greenhouse near Boston, and was called the Boston fern. Since then, many new varieties have been developed. The Boston fern, a favourite in many gardens, will be familiar to most visitors.

Native Orchid, *Epidendrum Fragrans*

Mangroves are to be found in many places along the sea coast. The black mangrove produces rootlets which stand up like fingers. Their function is to absorb oxygen from the air and thus facilitate breathing, which is always difficult when roots are in mud. The red mangrove is easily recognised by the aerial or 'stilt' roots, which come off from the lower part of the trunk and curve down through the muddy water to the soil below. The bark of the red mangrove is very rich in tannin and when mixed with divi-divi pods is used for tanning leather, including the skins of crocodiles. The Jamaican mangrove makes excellent firewood and many bakeries prefer it to any other wood.

Silk cotton tree on main road about two miles west of Albany, St. Mary.   F. J. Vaculik
Covered with epiphytes it is a most spectacular tree

Giant guango tree, probably the largest in the island, on the main road   F. J. Vaculik
east of Bath in St. Thomas

Along the sea coast there are dense areas of sea grapes, a shrub with roundish leaves and edible berries often eaten by birds and children.

Jamaica grows excellent citrus. Oranges and grapefruit are plentiful and of good quality, and limes are abundant. Lemons are less common. There are some types of crossed fruits including the Ugli which in appearance lives up to its name but tastes better. It is a cross between the bitter orange and tangerine orang . The ortanique, as its name implies, is a cross between the orange and the tangerine, and is a tasty and juicy delicacy. The mango has already been described. Other fruits are the naseberry, star apple, passion fruit (of which the granadilla and sweet cup are two), custard apple, guinep, soursop and sweetsop, of which probably only the last two are native fruits. Pineapples are grown throughout the island, perhaps the best known varieties being the sugar loaf and cowboy. Paw-paw is a usual breakfast fruit. (See also *Food.*)

In dry regions, particularly along the south coast, the outstanding feature of the landscape is the cactus growth. One of the tallest and most common is the dildo, which reaches a height of over twenty feet and is particularly prevalent on the Morant Bay road near Kingston. It makes excellent hedges which are virtually impenetrable. The prickly pear also makes a good fence and its roasted stem is applied to wounds to draw out inflammation. The mistletoe cactus is a trailing kind, usually seen on tree trunks and rocks. The seed is sticky like that of the true mistletoe and is also spread by birds. Other cacti are the Turk's head cactus and the torchwood, the latter being a variety of the dildo. Jerusalem candlestick, which is fairly common, is often considered a cactus but in fact belongs to quite a different family of plants. Unlike the cactus, it contains a white milky juice which is a poisonous irritant especially dangerous to the eyes.

In an article of this length, it is not possible to mention every flower, plant and tree which grows in Jamaica. We have endeavoured to give in this chapter a general description of some of the most frequently seen varieties.

FAUNA

There are no particularly spectacular animals in Jamaica and certainly no dangerous ones. Apart from the domestic rats and mice, the only mammals are the Jamaican or Indian Coney, which is not a true coney, but a large tree rat with the appearance of a gigantic brown guinea pig. There is also the Mongoose, introduced in 1872 to kill the rats in the cane-fields. They have multiplied mightily and can often be seen dashing across the road. They prey on all types of life and are a danger to bird life, including the domestic fowl.

There are a great many bats in Jamaica, which the local people call rat-bats to distinguish them from moths, which strangely enough they call bats. Of the forty to fifty different kinds, some are fruit-eating, some insectivorous, but no vampires. A great many caves can be found where thousands, if not hundreds of thousands, of bats hang in the daytime. One interesting species is the fish-eating bat which can occasionally be seen in Kingston Harbour around sundown. It is a large bat with a wing spread of about three feet.

The Manatee, undoubtedly Columbus' mermaid, and probably responsible for the original idea of mermaids, is occasionally seen in Jamaican waters, particularly in the vicinity of Portland Bight, as the name Manatee Bay signifies. The face of the Manatee is cow-like, from which arose its other name, Sea Cow. Short white bristles project from its snout and the nostrils are closed by valves. The four limbs are paddle-shaped and bear rudimentary nails, but strangely enough the creature does not use these limbs for swimming, locomotion being entirely through the use of the powerful transverse tail. Manatees are vegetarians, feeding mostly on seagrass for which they have an enormous appetite. The female usually gives birth to a single offspring.

BIRDS

There are many birds in the island, some being found only in Jamaica. The four types of humming bird include the Doctor

Bird, which can be frequently seen and is probably the most beautiful and the most interesting. There is also the little Bee humming bird, or the Vervain, which is next-to-the-smallest bird in the world, the smallest being the Bee humming bird of Cuba. This bird is very fond of the shrub called Japanese Hat and also of the Tamarind tree and can be seen in gardens where these are present. The Mango humming bird has a very long beak and is of a rather dark mottled colour, but when the tail is spread, there is a play of beautiful violet and orange colours.

Of the Jamaican song birds, the Mocking Bird is perhaps the most interesting. The local people call this the Nightingale. Song birds unique to Jamaica are the Solitaire and the Glass-eye, both thrushes. These are rarely seen, but the plaintive, lonely whistle of the Solitaire can frequently be heard in the high mountains.

There are innumerable grass quits, some exclusive to Jamaica. The small olive-green quits with yellow or black faces are particularly delightful birds. The birds locally called canaries are mostly Saffron Finches and were introduced into Jamaica about a hundred years ago. There is another bird locally called the Canary, which inhabits the mangrove swamps. This is the Golden Warbler.

The Tody, which most Jamaicans call Robin Red Breast, is a diminutive and brilliant relative of the Kingfisher. It has a bright emerald green back and a striking red throat.

The Jamaican macaw has long been extinct, but the island has two green parrots—the black-billed and the yellow-billed. They can be found in the interior, often in large flocks. In captivity they can be taught to talk, but in their wild state they are noisy birds, being excellent ventriloquists. When eating, they usually station one of their number as a sentinel to give warning of the approach of danger. The Parakeet is very similar, of the same deep green, with a pronounced tail. They are abundant and very destructive, particularly liking corn. An interesting member of the parrot family is the Parrotlet, which is a native of the Guianas and was introduced to Jamaica about 1918, although it is not known precisely how it arrived. There is a local

Washing Day   *Tourist Board*

story that someone attempted to import a number as cage birds for an aviary, but that the crew of the ship allowed them to get away. They are mostly found around Old Harbour, where they appear in great numbers, but have recently been reported as far east as Spanish Town and Stony Hill, and as high as Mandeville. They are particularly destructive in the rice fields. They are light green in colour, appearing like short-tailed budgerigars.

Doves and pigeons and migratory ducks comprise most of the game birds of Jamaica and include the Baldpate or White Crowned Pigeon. Those which reside in Jamaica are joined around the first of September by many migrants. The Ringtailed Pigeon is only found in Jamaica, as is also the Jamaican Blue Pigeon, which unfortunately is on the point of extinction. The Mountain Witch is the most attractive of Jamaica's doves; it is confined to the mountainous regions as is also the Partridge; they are both protected by law.

Although Jamaica is not on the main migration routes, the enormous coastal swamps attract thousands of migratory birds during the latter part of September and October, particularly Herons, called Gaulings by Jamaicans. The White Ibis, with its striking orange beak, can occasionally be seen. The Brown Pelican lives here, nesting on the cays around the coast, as does also the Frigate or Man-of-War Bird. These strange birds, with a wing-spread of eight to nine feet and weighing only about two-and-a-half pounds, are spectacular during the mating season, when the male develops a huge red goitre. The feet of this bird are so little developed that he cannot take off on a flat surface.

The gull-like bird with a yellow beak, which can be seen fishing from pilings and from buoys in the harbours, is a Royal Tern, and is called the Sprat Bird by the fishermen. During the winter, large flocks of Laughing Gulls can be seen. This is the only gull which breeds in the West Indies. Its winter plumage is uniformly gray, but in summer it develops a black head.

The booby eggs which can be bought along the streets of Kingston from March to June, and are considered a delicacy, are brought from the cays lying to the south. The eggs are not laid by boobies, but by terns, mostly the Sotty Tern, but the eggs with the speckles concentrated at the end come from the Noddy.

Nobody who comes to Jamaica can miss the John Crow. He is a vulture or buzzard, and acts as the scavenger of the island. In the air the bird is beautiful, as with taut wings outspread he moves apparently without effort. On land he seems sinister and almost obscene. They are usually quite unafraid of human beings and will remain sitting on a post while people pass close by them. The birds are large, blue black, with a strong hooked bill, pierced by large nostrils, and have a head which is bare of feathers. The sinister appearance is produced by the dirty, ragged wings and the ugly head.

The name 'John Crow' is said to have been given to the bird some time around 1690. The legend is that a clergyman named John Crow, preaching to a congregation largely made up of prisoners from the Monmouth and Argyll Rebellion, exhorted them not to complain of their ill-treatment. In contempt, they named the bird, whose black plumage reminded them of the preacher, 'John Crow'.

All along the north shore can be seen handsome blue black birds, locally called Cling Clings. They are Grackles, bold and mischievous and tame enough to come to the breakfast table for crumbs. When no suitable human providers are available, the birds follow the cattle and eat any ticks lurking on their backs.

LIZARDS

Lizards, which abound in Jamaica, are beneficial reptiles, most of them eating insects, and none of them, in this island at least, harmful to man. The largest and possibly the most interesting Jamaican lizard is the Iguana, now almost extinct. They attain a length of four feet and are rather sluggish in movement. Many years ago these giant lizards roamed the dry hills of the southern coast, but the introduction of the Mongoose in 1872 signed the iguana's death warrant. The mongoose is particularly fond of iguana eggs and the slow-moving lizard is an easy prey to this swift rat-like enemy.

Iguanas at the Institute

The harmless Galliwasp is wrongly thought to be poisonous. A curious superstition exists among the country people. If a Galliwasp bites you, you must run to water, for the one (you or the Galliwasp) which reaches the water first will live, the other will die.

The Croaking Lizard is the most annoying variety. Having no eyelids, it rarely comes out in the day to expose its eyes to the sun but at night it comes forth stealthily to look for unwary insects. It will come into the house and, stationing itself in an inaccessible spot, will emit the rasping croak. Having sucker pads on its feet, it can run with ease on smooth surfaces such as window panes or even upside down on the ceiling.

The Tree Lizards are the gay members of Jamaican lizard society, dashing about after their favourite insect, the males undergoing marked colour changes from brilliant green to dark brown. The males also have brilliant throat fans which they can blow out at will. These fans are differently coloured in various species, and like the peacock's tail are for showing off before females. When you see a male exhibiting, you will usually be

Examining the glass bottom boat at Silver Seas Hotel

West Indian Review

Cleary & Elliott

Tobacco growing at Temple Hall estate, St. Andrew

A Crocodile at the little Institute Zoo

fined to the Orinoco River, one to Cuba, another to the Yucatan
Peninsula. The fourth, *Crocodilus acutus*, is the one found in
Florida, Jamaica and the West Indies generally, and in Central
America and the north part of South America.

The simplest distinction between the crocodile and the alligator lies in the shape of the head. The head of the crocodile is
long and pointed, whilst that of the alligator is short with the
snout flat and blunt. More detailed differences are that the four
long teeth of the under jaw of the crocodile fit into notches between the teeth of the upper jaw. In the alligator these long
teeth fit into pits in the upper jaw—if you are prepared to get
close enough to make this examination. The feet of the crocodile are also more webbed than the feet of the alligator.

From earliest times the crocodile has been called alligator in
Jamaica, by legislators, historians, high men, low men. Despite
this, the fact remains that it is the crocodile who establishes himself in the mangrove swamps and can be frequently found with
his mouth open basking in the sun. In dry weather, the routes
of his trips to the water are clearly discernible. Early in the year,
the female crocodile lays eggs in the earth on the landward side
of the mangroves, and sometimes along a sandy beach, but
always in the sun. The eggs are laid about a foot beneath the
surface and no vegetation is piled on top, as is the practice

among alligators. The mother crocodile visits the site only occasionally. Actually, the young crocodile breaks through the strong shell by means of an egg tooth which projects from the tip of the snout and which he loses shortly afterward. The newly hatched (and ferocious) young crocodile usually measures at least three times the length of the shell from which he has emerged. In Jamaica, the crocodile usually grows to fifteen feet. There is no record of one ever having been captured or even seen on the north coast, although suitable swamps exist. They confine themselves to the south coast. Crocodile shooting is a popular pastime. (See *Sport*.)

MARINE LIFE

The marine fish of the waters adjacent to Jamaica include kingfish, barracuda, snapper, marlin, dolphin and numerous types of jacks. Fresh water fish are the hog nose, the calipoeva and the mountain mullet. There are innumerable varieties of ticky-ticky, many very beautiful and only found in Jamaica.

The bath sponge, known to most of us solely by its skeleton, cleaned and often bleached, gives us a poor idea of the living creature. The sponge ranges in size from a pin's head to a huge mass weighing over a hundred pounds, and comes in varying shades of brown, yellow, orange, pink, red, lilac, blue and green. Those most commonly seen belong to the group of Horny Sponges.

The sponge is useful to its undersea companions. It sometimes serves as a living thicket. Certain species of crab which live in Kingston Harbour are in the habit of using sponges to conceal themselves from enemies. They deliberately plant small sponges on their backs and legs and allow them to grow and flourish. When his foe approaches, the crab merely pulls in his limbs and presents the tough and unappetising surface of the sponge to the danger.

JELLYFISH

One may often find thick, rather shapeless blobs of jelly lying along the beach. That these masses are animals and probably

alive a few hours before, is hard to believe. We call them Jelly-fish. They are certainly jelly but they have no connection with fishes.

Jellyfishes are abundant in warm waters, occuring singly or in vast schools. They float quietly at or near the surface of the sea and although they can swim feebly, they are largely at the mercy of currents and waves. Jellyfishes or *medusae*, as they are scientifically called, are amongst the ocean's loveliest orna-ments.

The most common jellyfish in Jamaican waters, particularly in Kingston Harbour, is the blue-white Aurelia or Moon Jelly. It resembles an inverted soup bowl.

It is easily recognisable by the four reddish horseshoe-shaped structures in the central region of the 'umbrella'. These are the sex organs and are arranged with their open ends facing the centre. The Jellyfish deposits the eggs into the digestive cavity where they are fertilised.

One of the most remarkable jellyfish is undoubtedly that called the Portuguese Man-of-War. These fairy craft present a very beautiful sight on the surface of warm seas all over the world, but it is not a very welcome sight to swimmers as the trailing tentacles can inflict a serious and painful sting. It is hard to believe that these floating colonies are not single animals but are composed of many different sorts of polyps which co-ordin-ate their functions and activities.

INSECTS

As in all tropical countries, the ants in Jamaica are innumer-able; the duck ant, which builds tremendous nests in trees, is probably the most interesting to the visitor.

Termites are very destructive but, strangely enough, one of the worst kinds was introduced to the island in imported lumber. The drywood termite is often looked upon as public enemy number one. It is the only termite which does not need to channel its way to water, and can thus live very happily 'eating' away the inside of any wood into which it has penetrated.

Cockroaches, whose name is legion, are as numerous and

Planning a Cattle Drive on the Good Hope Range   *Tourist Board*

Reflections in a quiet stream

Tourist Board

widespread as anywhere in the Tropics. There are small 'roaches' and large roaches, red roaches and brown roaches. One very rarely seen is the grey brown roach, the size of a small mouse, which makes its home under very old wooden buildings.

BUTTERFLIES AND MOTHS

There are just over one hundred recorded species of butterflies in Jamaica, ranging from the large Swallow Tail down to the tiny Blue. The most spectacular one is the giant Swallow Tail or *Papilio homerus*, which lives in the mountainous regions near Bath and in certain parts of the Cockpit country. Measuring about six inches across the wings, it is the largest butterfly in the Western Hemisphere and is found in no other part of the world but Jamaica. The commonest butterfly is the black and yellow striped Zebra which can be seen in hills and plains alike. It has an interesting habit, almost unique in the butterfly world, of collecting together in swarms each evening to roost on some branch, preferably a leafless one overhanging a stream. It is a lovely sight to see them assembling in great numbers and dancing in the air before settling down for the night.

One of the most striking Jamaican moths is the Hawk, a strong flying and swift variety that resembles a miniature aeroplane. The larger moths and butterflies are called bats by the local people, the true bat being called the rat-bat to differentiate it.

There are about sixty different species of dragonflies and damselflies in the island, two of which exist only in Jamaica. They are locally called Needle Case, Devil's Darning Needle, Horse Stinger and Snake Doctor. The two last names apparently come from the utterly false idea that the dragonfly stings, and from the superstition that he ministers to snakes. Some of the peasantry preserve the dragonfly in rum to prepare a lotion against the imagined sting or any other aches or pains.

There are two types of firefly, click beetles known as Peenie Wallies and smaller ones called Blinkies. The ability of these insects to produce a heatless light is one of the many marvels of nature, an achievement which man himself has not yet attained.

The flashes of the fireflies are mating signals, and it is extra-ordinary that a male firefly can distinguish between the signals of an attractive female of his own kind and that of other males. He does this by the fact that the female will time her flashes to occur at precisely the same interval as his. The other males, apparently not being interested, do not bother to utilise this accurate timing.

There are countless spiders in Jamaica, the large brown house spider being commonly identified with Annancy, the chief character in Jamaica folklore and nursery stories. More can be read of Brer Annancy in another part of this book. The only dangerous spider in Jamaica is the Black Widow. The Jamaican form never exceeds half an inch, with long slender legs which fold against the body. It can easily be identified by the red hour-glass spot which frequently occurs on the under side. The name Black Widow comes from the fact that the female usually devours the male after mating. Fortunately, this spider is an infrequent biter, and some authorities maintain that they only bite when they believe food is available. For instance, if one were to strike a web, the spider might rush out ready to bite, under the impression that an insect had been caught. The visitor will often be shown the home of the trap-door spider.

One member of Jamaica's nature underworld is the shade of brown or black, several inches in length, with long claws like the lobster, four pairs of walking legs and a jointed flexible tail with a sting at the end—the scorpion. They are not frequently found, as they tend to hide themselves away in dark places. The local way of extermination is to cut it in half with a pair of scissors, repeating all the time 'Our Father, Our Father'!

CORALS

Jamaica is not a coral island such as Bermuda and the Bahamas (and Cayman) but examples of all the varied coral are found along its shores. The Staghorn, the Star and Brain corals are the most common. Living corals are all colours from delicate shades of pink and blue to yellow green violet and brown. Along the north coast, particularly at Montego Bay, one can float over the coral reefs and see the beautiful sea gardens—coral castles adorned and surrounded by waving growths of varied hue and infinite grace. These growths are commonly known as sea fans, sea feathers, sea pens or sea bushes. Many of the dried specimens can be purchased from the boatman or the itinerant trader in the streets.

SEA AND LAND SHELLS

One probably never loses the interest one acquires in early childhood for sea shells with their intricate designs and delicate colours. These shells—the homes of over one hundred thousand known species of molluscs—are always fascinating, and Jamaica has her full share of beautiful varieties.

Prevalent in Jamaica are tusk shells, delicate tubes curved and tapering to resemble a miniature elephant tusk. These are found buried upright in the sand with just the tip of the shell projecting.

The visitor will be told that oysters grow on trees in Jamaica and strangely enough this is more or less true. The tiny tree oysters are found in mangrove swamps clinging to the mangrove roots.

The squid and the octopus are molluscs which, having merely been freed from the hampering armour of the external shell, are able to live an active and vigorous life.

Some snails have developed lungs enabling them to leave the water and live on land. Jamaica is particularly rich in land snails, there being over eight hundred different species. Slugs might be mentioned here, as they are land snails which have lost their shells.

The West Indian spiny lobster is actually a marine crawfish, lacking the pincer-like claws of the true lobster. In the rivers are shrimps and fresh water crayfish. Hunting for the tiny shrimps called 'Jonglers' by the Jamaican fisherman at night with lanterns and torches is interesting sport.

There are sea and land crabs. The largest of the West Indian shallow water crabs is the brick coloured Queen, often used for food. Very difficult to see are the ghost crabs which wander quietly along the sea bottom at night, and interesting is the swimming crab with its oar-like feet. On the sea shore one finds many sea shells acting as homes for the hermit or soldier crab. Of the Black and White land crabs, the black is considered a delicacy. These crabs live away from the coast, burrowing in the earth inland. Each year they make a migration to the sea to lay their eggs. It is an astounding sight to see them on their journey as, in mass formation, they move slowly across a wide area. When houses are in their way they have been known to climb up one side and down the other. When the young crabs are ready to walk, the parents lead them out of the sea back inland, often as far as the mountains.

TORTOISES AND TURTLES

There are no true land tortoises in Jamaica, but there is a common native pond turtle which is really a Terrapin, found in the lowlands in swampy areas and along rivers.

In the waters around Jamaica true turtles are well represented. Hawksbills are common and fishermen are always on the lookout for them, as the shell is very attractive in colour and is used to make the tortoise shell of commerce.

CHAPTER TWENTY-ONE

Industries

AGRICULTURE

Jamaica is an agricultural country, and agriculture is likely to remain the main industry. It is aided by generally favourable climatic conditions, but is subject to the disadvantages as well as the benefits of the tropical belt in which the island lies. In some districts, there are long periods of drought; and when the rain falls, it is sometimes so heavy that it carries away the surface soil. To the obstacles provided by Nature, man has made his own contribution; deforestation, soil erosion, fragmentation of estates, overworking of the land, unscientific farming, especially of the small settlements . . . these have reduced the fertility and the value of the land. Once, Jamaica owed its comparative prosperity to the existence of big, well-run estates (which incidentally provided part-time employment and money wages for many small owners) and to the fact that a large and satisfied peasant population was able to maintain itself in comparative comfort on its own holdings (see *Introduction*). Later in this chapter, some of the chief agricultural industries are described. In another chapter (*The Property Market*) the novice is given some hints relative to running an estate in Jamaica.

Because of two factors, the agricultural industry can no longer adequately support the population of the country. The population has increased (and is increasing) at a rate really alarming (see *Appendix*). The land asset, because of the reasons suggested above, has declined in value and even in size, despite a certain amount of swamp reclamation. The population problem is indeed depressing; it is the barrier to all the welfare and social improvement schemes. But the improvement of the land asset is a practical question which can be faced.

Improvement in agricultural techniques is essential, not only on the big estates, where private ownership can be depended

Coral specimens at Sunset Lodge

Carmen Pringle

A good catch

Abrahams

upon for maximum efficiency (and perhaps these are the only genuinely economic units). Administration is by means of a strange system, with the Government (Department of Agriculture) and the Jamaica Agricultural Society holding the reins in uneasy partnership. The Society, which employed the Agricultural Instructors, is gradually waning in influence, and repeated attempts have been made, and at last look like succeeding, to end the anomalous position in the interests of efficiency.

The Department of Agriculture is alive to the needs of the case, and investigation and research are constantly being pursued. All British West Indian agricultural bodies work in conjunction with the Imperial College of Tropical Agriculture (in Trinidad); and in the field practical experimentation by the large planters is continuous. It is the small man who needs educating and watching, and there are two opinions as to the wisdom of the continuous parturition of estates into freehold small settlements (nearly all property is freehold in Jamaica and there is strong opposition whenever leasehold tenure is suggested), with few stipulations as to proper husbandry.

However efficient the running of the agricultural industry might be, the fact remains that without special concessions, preferences and quotas Jamaica would be in a bad way, and it is impossible to see how she could maintain her economy without such aids. Her relationship to Britain, of which she is a colony, has saved her from economic disaster. Modern conditions have lost her some of her best markets, notably the United States and to a large degree Canada; but export of agricultural commodities to the Dominions is now increasing, Australia and New Zealand being Jamaica's newest customers, and also suppliers. Efforts are being made to resurrect Canadian reciprocal trade.

No small agricultural community can exist today except by the help of a beneficent protector, and this applies in particular to insular communities, far from the sources of raw material and cut off by vast sea distances from their customers. The necessity for other industries to supplement—for they cannot replace— the agricultural industry is well recognised, and in recent years many efforts have been made to realise this goal.

TOURIST INDUSTRY

The chief industry outside agriculture, and one which by persistent and imaginative development could outstrip it (though nothing can replace it) is the Tourist Trade, which has made enormous strides in recent years but which has not reached a figure commensurate with its potentialities. There are still many openings, and will continue to be as long as people live in the northern lands and have time and money to seek a delectable winter resort (which is also desirable in the summer). Jamaica has proved her possibilities in this respect, but she has only skimmed the first cream off the trade. It is certain that it will increase enormously in the years to come. The subject is exhaustively explored in the course of this book, but we should like to mention here the substantial concessions and privileges offered by the Government to this and other industries.

CONCESSIONS

Persons engaged in the hotel industry, whether as newcomers or as established owners, are given valuable tax concessions. A rebate of income tax is given for five years out of the first eight, to the extent of twenty per cent of the invested capital, so that an enterprise which earns twenty per cent on its investment can repay the capital in five years (out of the first eight). In addition, all supplies, including furniture, are admitted free of duty. This is a fine gesture made by the Government in order to support the growing industry; and the immediate effect of the legislation which permitted it was the upspringing of a number of new hotels (including Sunset Lodge and Tower Isle) and improvements to many existing hotels (including the substantial additions to Casa Blanca).

PIONEER INDUSTRIES

Later, similar facilities were provided for enterprises coming within a category known as 'pioneer industries'. Formerly, such industries were protected against undue and destructive competition by being listed in a schedule which permitted a partial or total monopoly for a period of years (an example is the Match Industry, which compensated Government for the loss of customs revenue by the payment of an excise duty).

Individuals or companies wishing to engage in new industries in Jamaica are advised to make full enquiries through a good solicitor. Some lawyers specialise in this type of work, and the advice of one of them should be obtained.

LABOUR

The labour question is a vexatious one, but this can easily be exaggerated, and it is doubtful if the trouble is greater than in any industrial community. Indeed, regimentation by the unions is less complete than in large centres, partly because trade union activities in Jamaica, though highly competitive and even ferocious, have not progressed far beyond the amateur stage. The unions divide themselves into two groups, one politically related to the Jamaica Labour Party (the Bustamante group); the other akin to the People's National Party (the left wing group) (see *Introduction*). The sugar industry and many of the large industries are dominated by the former; the clerical workers by the latter. There are few general labour practices; big employers of labour are the happy hunting ground, and the little man is usually left undisturbed. This naturally makes for ruinous competition between the man who is forced to pay high wages and to provide good working conditions and the man who runs his enterprise in a back street without interference. Let it be said, however, that improvements in labour conditions and rates of pay were overdue, that on the whole the unions are performing a useful service, and that the faults are largely faults of quick growth and inexperience. Outbreaks of hostility and violence occasionally occur, the unions are undisciplined, and the leadership is not all that it should be; but the Government is alert to abuses, and the situation will improve.

Wage rates are very much lower than in the big industrial countries, but this is misleading, as the production average of the worker is low. In order not to be misled by figures, the intending investor should make full enquiries, on the spot if possible.

Basketmakers carrying their wares on bamboo poles   *Tourist Board*

Peace   *J. Dougall*

NEW ENTERPRISES

A number of important industries have sprung up since induce-
ments were given, and there is still room for a number of minor
industries, especially for the manufacture of articles for local
consumption.

GENERAL

As has been said, matches are manufactured in the island, as are
shoes and shirts, and these industries have been established for
some years. A textile factory has been erected near Spanish
Town. The Jamaica Cement Factory has been recently established along the Rockfort Road near to Kingston and a little
further out are the premises of Bellrock Caribbean Ltd., which
not only manufactures building panels of gypsum but is exporting the gypsum rock and plaster-of-paris to the West Indies and
the United States. A number of other patented building
materials are being made in the island.

Perhaps the most important development is the finding of
substantial deposits of Bauxite, in which the Reynolds Metal
Company, the Aluminium Co. of Canada and the Kaiser Aluminium and Chemicals Corporation have invested large sums
of money. These companies expect to export Bauxite in large
quantities and a fine pier has been constructed by the Reynolds
Metal Company at Ocho Rios. The Aluminium Company of
Canada proposes not only to mine Bauxite but to partly process
it in Jamaica.

Canning has made considerable progress and several items
are preserved, including tomatoes and a number of fruits. Citrus
pulp for the making of marmalade is usually processed and
shipped in kegs. The Government operates a cornmeal factory.
One of the oldest factories in Jamaica is the condensery, owned
by the Nestle combine, and situated at Bog Walk. Confectionery
is made and exported and biscuits are manufactured for the
local trade. Mention must be made of the famous Picka Peppa
Sauce, which is manufactured from a secret recipe.

The new Ariguanabo textile mill is now in operation and there
is also a knitting mill, which manufactures knitted underwear,

shirts, socks and so on. The garment industry, which is quite a considerable one, might be described as a cottage industry. Most of the work is done by men and women in their own homes and it is estimated that ten thousand tailors, dressmakers, shirt makers, hatters, embroiderers and other workers are engaged in this trade. Many of them market their products through the retail stores.

There is a small cosmetic industry and two well-known firms manufacture perfume, the best known of which is Khus Khus, made from a fragrant native grass.

An interesting industry is the extraction of dye from the log-wood tree. Logwood was introduced into the island from Honduras in 1715 and has remained an important item of export. In the early days the wood itself was shipped, but in recent years the dye is extracted locally and shipped in crystallised form.

There is a thriving box-making industry and a factory for the making of tin containers has recently been established.

CRAFTS

For many years furniture of good quality and design has been made in the island (see *Housekeeping* and *Shopping*).

NATIVE CRAFTS

Jamaicans are good craftsmen, and there are many native crafts, some of which suffer, however, from lack of artistry in design. Skilled tuition and direction are needed. The Jamaica Women's League was begun as a charitable enterprise (it owed its origin to the work of several philanthropic women, including Mrs. Gloria Guinness, who had learned the technique of the craft in Puerto Rico). It is now self supporting, and delightful work, in the form of embroidered linen towels, table napkins, table-cloths, handbags and so on, is turned out. Numerous articles of woodwork, pottery from native clays (this is a skill which ought to be developed), beautiful silver work (mainly by the Indians), baskets and hats are among the numerous items to be classified under local crafts. They are sold in the big stores, in the markets, and on the streets, and the prices (and sometimes the standard of workmanship) vary accordingly.

C.D.C. AND C.D. AND W.

The Colonial Development Corporation has not been very active in Jamaica. The Turks Island salt industry is being assisted by means of this British governmental organisation, and a cold storage plant for the preservation of local commodities awaiting shipment has been provided in Kingston. The island does not lend itself to large-scale industries of the nature contemplated under this plan, like the ill-fated ground nuts scheme in Africa and the contemplated cattle-raising scheme in British Honduras. There are no large available areas for the cultivation of new crops, and there is little space for the development of pioneer farming enterprises.

Colonial Development and Welfare, which has contributed a large sum in British Government funds to a local Ten Year Plan (now well advanced in age if not in execution!) made provision for various schemes, including irrigation.

POWER AND LIGHT

Electric power and light, with one or two small local exceptions, are supplied by the Jamaica Public Service Company Ltd., which has affiliations with the Jamaica Public Service Company of Canada (Montreal) and with Stone and Webster of New York City. It operates under a long term franchise.

TELEPHONE

The telephone system is operated by the Jamaica Telephone Company, Ltd. It has operated the Kingston system for several years, and in 1945 took over the All Island system, the nucleus of which was installed some years earlier by the Government, which was losing money heavily on the enterprise. It is now in sole control of telephone undertakings throughout the island under a long-term Government licence. The system is a dial type system of the most modern kind.

CABLE COMMUNICATIONS

Cable and Wireless Ltd., now a part of the world-wide British Government-owned organisation, handles the overseas telegraphic system.

RADIO

The Jamaica Broadcasting Company, established in 1950, when it took over the Government operated system, has a monopoly of broadcasting under a licence. It uses commercial sponsorship for its programmes, according to conditions laid down in the licence. A proportion of the broadcasting time is reserved under the law for the Government, and a nominee seconded from the British Broadcasting Corporation advises the Government upon the use of its time.

SUGAR AND RUM

Sugar and Rum come under the control of the Sugar Manufacturers' Association, which is composed of the owners of the twenty-four sugar estates in the Island. The sale of sugar for the local market is handled by the Association, and since 1939 England has arranged for the acquisition of the remainder under a

collective system of purchasing for the entire British Commonwealth. This purchasing includes the crops of all the other
British West Indies and British Guiana. The present agreement
will extend for a number of years. In Jamaica, a percentage of
the price secured is returned to the industry for rehabilitation
and welfare.

The Sugar Manufacturers' Association also controls the quantity of rum produced each year and its marketing; selling it to
rum merchants who age, blend, bottle and sell it under various
brands.

The story of rum is the story of sugar, its origin going back to
unrecorded time in Southern Asia. Rum was probably first
brought to Europe by the invading armies of Genghis Khan.
In Solomon's discourses with the Queen of Sheba, there are
references to what may well be rum, and it may easily be that
Mark Anthony sipped cooling rum drinks while floating down
the Nile. Rum did not become important to the Western Hemisphere until the time of Columbus, who, gathering sugar cane
in the Canary Islands, transported it to Santo Domingo, whence
it spread to the other West Indian Islands.

No definite decision has even been reached as to the origin of
the word rum. One school of thought states it comes from the
Latin word *saccharum* for sugar. English sailors of the day called
it *Rumbowling*, which gradually became *Rumbo* and then rum.
An old history relates 'the chiefe fudling is *Rumbullion* and this is
made of sugar cannes distilled a hotte hellish and terrible liquor'.

Rum gradually lost its fiery nature. The sailors of the many
ships spread its fame, to say nothing of the pirates who took
Yo-ho-ho and a barrel of it to their wicked hearts. Byron once
wrote:

> *There is naught no doubt the spirit cheers*
> *As rum and true religion . . .*

Rum found a ready and stable market. It became a recognised medium of exchange. So many slaves were worth a barrel
of rum, so much land for so many puncheons. The slave trade
was in full bloom when the essayist Cowper wrote:

I own I am shocked at the purchase of slaves
And fear those who buy them and sell them are knaves.
What I hear of their hardships
Their tortures and groans
Is almost enough to draw pity from stones.
I pity them greatly, but I must be mum
For how can we do without sugar and rum?

Jamaica rum is still made on the old pot-still method. To describe it without going into technical details, the process begins when the cane is cut in the fields and taken to the sugar factory by every possible means, bullock cart, mule-drawn dray, trucks, miniature railways. There, it is put through crushers and rollers to extract the juice. The remaining pulp, called bagasse, is used as fuel for the boilers. The juice is then pumped into large tanks, heated, clarified and allowed to settle. This allows the clear juice to be decanted to evaporators to remove the water and then to vacuum pans for crystallising the *sucrose* content. The crystals, however, are floating around in molasses. The mixture is therefore brought to the whirling screens of the centrifugals, where the molasses is thrown off and the light brown sugar trapped by the screens, after which it is weighed into bags for the refinery.

The molasses is then mixed with water and dunder to make what is called 'wash', and pumped into two and three thousand gallon vats, where it is left to ferment. Natural fermentation takes about seventy-two hours. The wash is then run into the pot still, where it is heated to form vapours, which pass through low-wine and high-wine retorts, where the characteristic flavour of Jamaica Rum is acquired. A condenser then turns the vapours into a crystal-clear liquid, which bubbles forth from the still as Jamaica Rum. Years of ageing in oak puncheons, hogsheads, casks and vats now follow.

The oldest firm in the Jamaica rum trade is J. Wray & Nephew, who started business in 1825. The 'Nephew' was the Colonel Ward who later gave the Ward Theatre to the people of Kingston. Their Dagger Rums are well known in the world market and a household name in Jamaica. They also produce, on their own estate, 'Appleton', the lightest-known type of Jamaica pot-still rum, bottled under the name 'Appleton Special'. Unfortunately, the old records of the Appleton Estate were destroyed in the 1907 earthquake, but it is known that the estate was owned by an English family of that name. Colonel Ward acquired it in the early nineteen hundreds.

Despite their early start, the company employs modern methods of efficiency and is the only rum firm which transports its rum in steel tanks from the estate to its enormous private bonded warehouses overlooking Kingston Harbour. The rum is stored and aged in white oak vats of five and ten thousand gallon capacity, and in puncheons and casks.

The world-famous House of Myers has its headquarters at The Sugar Wharf, in the western end of Kingston, facing the sea. The Myers' family is one of the oldest in Jamaica and the present business was founded by the late Frederick Louis Myers in 1879. It was the age of colonial expansion and the beginning of the great families of merchant princes. It was the age of Clive and Rhodes. Young Myers, with great courage and enterprise, ventured into business for himself, a business which has steadily developed through three generations. The original premises, with enormous quantities of stock, were destroyed by earthquake and fire in 1907, and that is when the Myers' family bought a stretch of land on the harbour front at the west end of the city. The debris from the fallen buildings was used to reclaim an extensive area from the sea. The premises now contain a wharf, offices, warehouses running four to five hundred feet in length, and a fully-automatic bottling plant. The Sugar Wharf has its own post office and at the entrance there is the interesting Planters' Punch Inn, one end of which is shaped like a large vat, with steel hoops. The back wall is panelled with staves like the inside of a huge hogshead and the tables and chairs are cut out barrels. Most people who have heard of Jamaica have heard of Myers' Rum.

Close to Kingston's busiest intersection of King and Harbour Streets stand the offices of the producers of Coruba

*The Kingston offices of the Rum Company (Jamaica) Limited,
producers of Coruba Rum*

Jamaica Rum. The Company was founded in 1889 by a Swiss, Jules Fiechter of Basle, in which city the Company still has its European office. Now one of the largest of Jamaica's Rum exporting firms, it has been developed and expanded to its present size in Jamaica by R. J. Waeckerlin, also a Swiss, but now living in the island. The Company has an international market and Coruba can be found practically all over the world.

There seems no better way to end this section than to quote the words of some wag, who apparently felt called upon to defend the cause of alcoholic beverages:

> *The horse and mule live thirty years,*
> *And nothing know of wine and beers.*
> *The goat and sheep at thirty die,*
> *And never taste of Scotch or Rye,*
> *The cow drinks water by the ton,*
> *And at eighteen is nearly done.*
> *The dog at fifteen cashes in*
> *Without the aid of Rum or Gin,*
> *The cat in milk and water soaks,*
> *And then in twelve short year it croaks,*
> *The modest, sober, bone dry hen*
> *Lays eggs for nogs, then dies at ten.*
> *All animals are strictly dry,*
> *They sinless live and swiftly die*
> *But simple, Ginful, Rum-soaked men*
> *Survive for three score years and ten.*
> *P.S.—And some of us the mighty few,*
>   *Stay pickled till we're ninety-two.*

BANANAS

The once flourishing banana trade dropped from a high peak of 28,000,000 stems in 1928 to 6,700,000 in 1949, owing to the inroads of Panama Disease and, to a lesser degree, of Leaf Spot Disease. Panama Disease is a disease of the soil for which no cure (except the discovery of an immune banana!) has yet been discovered. Leaf Spot can be controlled by spraying with chemicals. This, though expensive, is an economic proposition if organised on a large scale. Small planters are assisted by Government organisation and, on the whole, the disease is kept under control.

Up to recent times, after Panama Disease appeared, the soil could not again be used for growing bananas; and consequently the decline of the banana trade was compensated for, to an extent, by the conversion of large areas of land to sugar cane. A year or so ago, after many years of research work, the Lacatan Banana was introduced to replace the popular Gros Michel variety. The Lacatan is resistant to Panama Disease but has not been as intensively planted as was anticipated because of the scarcity of suckers.

The acreage under Lacatan cultivation is gradually increasing, and the variety is now shipped regularly to Britain.

The United Kingdom buys the entire banana crop from Jamaica on an f.o.b. basis. In turn, the Jamaica Government pay the producers a specified price and bear all incidental expenses. The three organisations engaged in the banana industry in Jamaica are the United Fruit Company, the Jamaica Banana Producers' Association, Ltd., and the Standard Fruit and Shipping Company. The two last-named organisations own their own ships and the bananas of the United Fruit Company are transported to the United Kingdom by Elders and Fyffes.

The Gros Michel banana, for which Jamaica became famous, was brought to the island in 1835 by a French refugee from Haiti, Jean François Pouyat, who himself secured it for Martinique. Other varieties were already in the island in 1796, possibly brought by Captain Bligh of the *Bounty*, who introduced the breadfruit into Jamaica.

No story of the banana trade in Jamaica, or in the Caribbean and Latin America generally, could conceivably ignore the work of the United Fruit Company. This company is responsible for putting the banana on a commercial basis; and in doing so it brought progress, civilisation and security into the areas in which it operated. Vast expanses of hitherto useless tropical jungle were converted into productivity. Sparsely settled regions were made habitable and thousands of people given employment and a new standard of living. It did much to eradicate yellow fever, smallpox, dysentery, hookworm and malaria.

The company put its ships upon the sea and, while carrying its bananas, built up a tourist trade in the tropical south. Its research stations made possible a thriving and remunerative trade in the banana. The United States never had a better good-will ambassador. This is indeed a fine record for the company which was brought into being in 1899 by the shrewd hard-headed New England business man Andrew Preston, the explorer pioneer Minor Keith, and Captain Lorenzo Baker, schooner skipper and Yankee seaman.

The United Fruit Company as early as 1904 introduced radio communication between its plantations and its Tropical Radio Telegraph Company is now one of the main sources of radio communication in the middle Americas.

The Jamaica Banana Producers' Association grew out of a co-operative association which was formed in 1927. In 1936 it was incorporated as a limited liability company following the recommendations of a Commission which was sent out by the British Government to investigate the growing, shipping and selling of bananas.

The third of these organisations is the Standard Fruit and Shipping Company, a branch of the Standard Fruit Company in New Orleans.

The first bananas shipped to the United Kingdom were carried in the 'Port Moran' beginning an association with the Jamaica banana trade which has been maintained by the shipping firm of Elders and Fyffes ever since.

COFFEE

The largest coffee growing area in Jamaica is on the plains and foothills of the mountains running from the west in Saint Elizabeth almost diagonally across the island, to Saint Mary in the east, or across what might be described as the island's backbone. The famous Blue Mountain coffee, however, is only grown on the slopes of the Blue Mountains and has for many years been one of the highest-priced coffees on the world market. It is main-

Photo: Elders & Fyffes

*Loading the first cargo of bananas for the United Kingdom at Kingston
in March 1901, on the s.s.* Port Morant

tained that the temperature and humidity of the high mountains combine to bring out the quality for which it is so highly prized.

In the Spring of the year, coffee trees are beautiful with star-like white blossoms, after which the green berry appears. When matured, these berries turn a bright red and are usually gathered in October, November and December. They are then processed in pulping factories and dried in big barbecues preparatory to milling.

The Government has established a Clearing House through which all coffee designated for export must pass. Here, picking, cleaning, and grading ensure a standardised product and this control has done much to increase the market value, possibilities and reputation of Jamaican coffee. Comparatively speaking, the coffee crop in Jamaica is not a large one, but the Government's Agricultural Department is doing much to expand the coffee-producing areas.

Used in Ethiopia from the earliest times, coffee was introduced into Arabia by the fourth century, soon spreading to the rest of the East. Rauwolf made it known to Europeans by an account of his travels printed in 1573. The plant was taken from Mocha to Batavia by Wieser, Burgomaster of Amsterdam in the seventeenth century, and thence spread to Martinique from France in 1720. It has flourished in the West Indies ever since.

The most important types of coffee are the Mocha from Arabia, with yellowy brown beans; the Java with the large yellow beans; the Jamaican and East Indian which have large blue-green beans; the Surinam which has the largest beans; and the Bourbon with pale, yellowish white beans.

TOBACCO

The tobacco industry in Jamaica dates back to the 1870's and can thank the Manxman, Simon Soutar, and the Cuban Revolutionary War for its vigorous beginnings. Flying from the chaotic political upheavals and disasters, the expert cigar-making family of the Machados came to Jamaica, and their name has been closely associated with the tobacco trade ever since It was they who told Simon Soutar that his estate, Temple Hall, was an ideal place for the growing of cigar tobacco . . . and it has remained so to this day.

Simon Soutar, who came to Jamaica from the Isle of Man in 1858, was a man of many parts. He became a highly successful business man in the flourishing trades of sugar, rum, logwood, coffee and cocoa, owned wharves and steamships, and introduced the first tobacco-growing on his Temple Hall Estate in the Wag Water Valley running through the Blue Mountains, spectacularly beautiful country through which the visitor passes on the Junction Road going from Kingston to Port Antonio or Port Maria. The estate can trace its history back to 1728.

Internally disturbed Cuba was not in a position to retain her export cigar market and, with many more political refugees coming to Jamaica, the cigar industry grew in strength and stature and gradually established itself as a valuable export commodity of the island. The granting of Cuba's independence, however, brought her back into the world market and this, together with the fact that many of the cigar-making Cubans returned to their homes, forced the Jamaican industry to a low level. When the Second World War came, a shortage of dollars in the United Kingdom pushed the trade to boom proportions, and in the peak year of 1947 twenty-seven million cigars were exported. Subsequent increases in import duty, however, have made the Jamaican cigar a luxury item for the English public; and this in a flooded market, created a slump in the industry. It is not possible to assess what part the cigar can play in Jamaica's economy until conditions revert to normal.

In travelling through the island the visitor may see the large green leaves of the tobacco plants, especially in the region of Colbeck Castle (see Chapter 15 *Where to Go*). When mature, the tobacco is gathered and hung to dry on rails in palm-thatched barns, where it is left until the leaves and stems are dry up to the point where the stems join the main stalk of the plant. It is then made into a 'stick press', which is a stack with the stalks outwards and the leaves inwards, and left for a day or two. The leaves are then stripped off, graded for length, and made into heads of forty to fifty leaves. The heads are then stacked in piles of about six by ten by five feet which are called 'pilons', into which is let a hollow bamboo to accommodate a thermometer. Under close observation the tobacco is then allowed to ferment.

When the whole process of ageing and maturing is complete, and the tobacco has become a commercial article, the finest of it goes for the making of cigars. An inferior grade can usually be found at any Saturday market twined like a rope around and around the body of a higgler and known locally as 'jackass rope'. It is sold by the yard.

Cigars are made individually and consist of a core of tobacco which must be evenly packed to ensure uniform burning, enveloped in an inner and outer wrapper. The operator takes a quantity of tobacco sufficient for one cigar, wraps it in the inner wrapper, which is an oblong piece of leaf. The cigar is then rolled by hand to consolidate the tobacco and create the proper shape, after which it is placed in the outer Havana or Sumatra wrapper and rolled from the thick end to the pointed one. It is then finished off by a dexterous twist of the fingers.

Each firm has its brand names and the names such as Corona, Imperiales, Lonsdale, Churchill, which denote the size and shape, are universally used.

The modern factory and offices of the most important of Jamaica's cigar manufacturers—Machado's—are situated on East Queen Street at the bottom of South Camp Road. The name of Machado has remained closely associated with cigars since that day in 1875 when Benito and Juan Machado founded their small business. Today La Tropical deLuxe, La Tropical and Golofina cigars are known throughout the world, and the factory employs eight hundred workers.

Machado's also manufacture cigarettes for the local market, their Four Aces and Royal Blend brands having a very large sale.

On the Half Way Tree Road, near the entrance to Liguanea Club and Knutsford Park Race Course, are the offices and factory of Temple Hall. The pungent smell of good cigars permeates the premises.

Old Spanish Town

A meal in the charming patio of Gloucester House, Montego Bay

Driving up Constant Spring Road and looking to the right on Sandy Gully Bridge one can see the roofs of the Jamaica Tobacco Company, Limited, the cigar empire of James Gore, one of the most enterprising men in Jamaica. James Gore is the man behind the proposed building of a tourist city on the Health-shire Hills in Southern St. Catherine.

Any of the cigar factories in Jamaica will welcome visitors.

COCONUT INDUSTRY

The tall beautiful coconut palms which you will see around the coast are natives of the South Pacific, the seeds probably drifting to these shores with the assistance of the Trade winds, although some maintain they were brought by Captain Bligh of the *Bounty*. The name comes from the Portuguese or Spanish 'coco' meaning bugbear, hobgoblin, uglyface or bogey, because of the three circular dark marks or eyes at the end of the nut which give the appearance of a grotesque face.

The rather hairy-looking nut with which most northerners are familiar is really the kernel of the coconut. It is encased in a green and fibrous outer shell, from which coir is made, and these large green nuts are what the visitor will see at the heart of the graceful palms swaying in the breeze. The coconut can be divided into three sections—the green outer casing, the hard brown shell of the kernel and the jelly and slightly opaque water contained in the kernel when the nut is young. Incidentally, it is when the nut is in this condition that it is called a water coconut and offered as a drink. In the streets of Kingston you can often see the 'cokee man' shouting his wares in his sing-song voice. For a few pennies, he will trim and pierce a coconut for you and cut a spoon with which to eat the 'jelly'. But it takes a little expert manipulating to drink the liquid from the 'wood'. The water and the jelly are both nutritious. Housewives grate the more mature flesh, and squeeze out a thick creamy fluid which is used like ordinary cream. When frozen, it makes a most delicious ice cream.

The method of natural seeding is interesting. The inside jelly becomes thicker and thicker and harder and harder, and, becoming heavy, falls to the ground with a small amount of water left inside, which by now is slightly fermented. It is then that one of the eyes starts to shoot. This shoot takes its nourishment from the hardening jelly and water which eventually congeal into what is called the 'flower'. The roots force themselves through the bottom of the hard kernel and husk and another palm begins its long and useful life of approximately thirty to forty years.

For commercial purposes the nut is usually picked before it is heavy enough to fall. The entire coconut is useful. There is a native legend that the coconut is God's greatest gift to the lazy man. He sleeps in the shade of the tree, is awakened when the nut falls, drinks the milk, eats some of the meat. He then feeds the balance of the meat to his chickens, which produce eggs; and so on *ad infinitum*.

The green husk is dried and then beaten and combed to become coir used for mats, mattresses and upholstery. There are three factories in Jamaica. The hard brown case of the nut is used as fuel to operate the copra driers, which dehydrate the meat of the matured nut, or it can be converted into carbon and used as a filtering agent. From the dried meat or copra is extracted oil, which is used as an edible fat, and as the base for laundry and toilet soaps, oleomargarine and lard. The trash obtained after the oil is extracted makes a wonderful feed for cattle and fowls, and is said to contain a higher percentage of proteins and carbohydrates than any other nutmeal.

During the Second World War, when the importation of edible oil products was restricted, the Coconut Industry Board was formed to control the industry, and protected by law to provide a guaranteed market for the primary producer, as under the law the Board must purchase all marketable copra offered it. The Board has built up a large products factory under the name Soap and Edible Products, Limited, which is the largest manufacturing entity in the British West Indies. In addition to its many products, it also manufactures, under franchise, Sunlight Soap, Lux and Lifebuoy Toilet Soaps, Palmolive and Odex.

There is also a privately owned factory—Caribbean Products

Co., Ltd., whose new premises are situated on Spanish Town Road.

CITRUS

Oranges, lime, lemon and citron were brought to Jamaica by the Spaniards, but the shaddock, from which it is believed grapefruit was developed, came from China.

In 1944, the Citrus Growers' Association was formed and it is largely owing to its work that the industry is in such a thriving condition today. No accurate figures are available, but it is estimated that when the Association began work on the 1945-46 crop, the production of sweet oranges from wild seedling trees was less than half of what it had been in the early 1930's. Lack of markets and low prices did not encourage the grower to increase his acreage, and what was worse, caused him to neglect his trees. The advent of the Association and bulk purchasing by England brought safer markets and better prices. Assisted and encouraged, the growers began to resuscitate their existing trees and make new plantings. By 1948-49 the output was up to 512,000 boxes of sweet oranges and 235,000 boxes of Marsh seedless grapefruit. The Association then obtained a ten-year contract from the British Government for sweet orange juice, which has given the industry great impetus and security. A co-operative factory has been erected by the Association at a cost of £150,000.

Plans were made for greatly increasing the plantings and there will be at least one million new trees by the end of 1951. It usually takes at least five years for a tree to bear, but the Association, by means of fertilising existing trees and teaching growers to institute better methods of orchard practice, is producing quicker results. It has also organised an extensive campaign of top-working uneconomic trees to sweet oranges, which should result in bringing these trees into economic production in three years. Top-working is the system of grafting buds on to fully grown trees. It is anticipated that the 1956-57 crop will supply over four million boxes of sweet oranges; and grapefruit production should reach 500,000 boxes in 1951-52, at which figure it should remain static.

TOURIST GUIDE
AND
GENERAL INFORMATION

JAMAICA

The 5 Vacation Resort Areas of Jamaica

Offer
the greatest diversification and value of any Caribbean Holiday Resort

Remarkable Climate and Sunshine

Magnificent Scenery

Hotels to suit every fancy and pocket

Mountain and Seaside Resorts

Bathing every day on exquisite beaches

Every sport, recreation and entertainment

Easy to reach from all countries by many

Air Lines and Steamship Services

★

Tourist Guide
and
General Information

POPULATION

The population question in Jamaica is one of its most grievous problems. The rapid increase is out of all proportion to the ability of the country to support it, and it is the stumbling block in the way of all plans, all schemes, all proposals for the economic and social advancement of the people. The general standard of living cannot be high, the overall picture cannot become happy and gay, the efforts of those who strive for improvement must be vitiated . . . all from the same cause. There are too many people.

Possibilities of emigration are limited, except in time of war, when the armies and the industries of the fighting nations need man-power. Birth control and other reform measures have made little headway, because of the opposition of the Church and the increasing poverty of the masses of the people . . . increasing as the mass becomes more dense. Improvements in health and nutrition are largely neutralised because the mass continues to grow, its mass ever increasing by the access of the new generations. Employment and relief measures, inadequate in a poor country, become hopeless in face of the continuous upward graph of the population figures.

There is no way but Nature's way to stem the increase. The alternative, to build up the country's economic assets in order to meet the need, is doomed at least to partial failure because of the unstemmed increase in the number of people. Nevertheless, in face of the insoluble problem, efforts continue to be made to reconcile the country's means with the task to be attempted.

Jamaica had a population of 1,237,063 inhabitants at the last census in 1943. The population has reached this figure from an estimated 60,000 persons in 1494—a period of approximately four and a half centuries. This period can be broadly divided into two sections, the first under the Spanish rule, the second under the British. From 1494 when Christopher Columbus discovered Jamaica, until 1655, the Spanish had possession of the island, the native population being Arawak (Red) Indians. In about fifty years the Arawaks had completely died out owing, it is alleged, to the rigorous form of rule and labour enforced by the Spaniards. (See Chapter One.)

In 1655 the British took the island by conquest, and it was later formally ceded to England by Spain. It has remained British ever since.

The population is of mixed racial origin, predominately Negro, as the following official table compiled after the 1943 census, will illustrate :

Black	965,000	Portuguese	130
Coloured	216,348	Spanish	1,139
White	4,803	Chinese	6,886
English and Welsh	3,847	Chinese coloured	5,508
Irish	472	East Indian	21,393
Scottish	1,077	East Indian coloured	5,114
German	581	Syrian	834
Italian	287	Syrian coloured	171
Jewish	1,067	Other races	1,456

Negroes first came to the island in 1517, being brought from Africa as slaves by the Spanish (see *History*). In 1580 Portugal became attached to Spain and soon afterward many Portuguese came to Jamaica, among them being many Jews. After England took possession of the island in 1655, English, Irish and Scottish settlers came to the country in large numbers, being mostly soldiers and sailors sent by Oliver Cromwell. Although the Spaniards brought the first Negroes, England is responsible for importation of the majority of Africans into the island. In 1845, East Indians were brought in under a Government labour recruiting scheme which lasted until 1869. This indentured labour, after ten years of working on an estate, was given the option of repatriation to India or five acres of land. The majority elected to remain in Jamaica and today are mostly engaged in market gardening, for which they have a great aptitude.

In 1884 many Chinese were indentured from Hong Kong as labourers on the sugar estates, but today no Chinese can be found working on the land, and the wholesale and retail food and grocery trade is almost entirely in their hands. They are good citizens, but the criticism is made that the money they earn is sent to China, instead of being invested in Jamaica.

POLITICAL CONSTITUTION

From 1866 to 1944 Jamaica was governed as a Crown Colony of Britain although the Constitution allowed for a number of elected members with restricted powers.

The new Constitution, which came into effect in 1944, provides for the following machinery of Government :

The Governor, appointed from England.

The Privy Council, consisting of six members having limited powers, mainly to deal with the exercise of the prerogative of mercy and with disciplinary matters relating to Civil Service.

The Executive Council consists of three ex-Officio members, two nominated members and five members elected by the House of Representatives. The elected members are given portfolios relating them to various Government departments whose business they conduct in the House of Representatives. They have the courtesy title of Minister, but have no actual authority over

LIGHT AND POWER

An efficient and economical electric service is provided by the Jamaica Public Service Company Ltd. in the main tourist resorts throughout the Island.

The Company owns and operates generating plants in Kingston, Montego Bay, Port Antonio, Roaring River, White River, Bog Walk, Falmouth, Lucea and Black River, and holds franchises for the supply of electric service over its own distribution network in the parishes of Kingston, St. Andrew, St. Catherine, St. James, St. Ann, St. Mary, Portland, Trelawny, Hanover and St. Elizabeth.

The construction of a further Hydro-Electric generating plant, on the Lower White River in the parish of St. Ann, is in progress and the generating capacity of the Kingston steam plant will shortly be considerably increased. This is in keeping with the Company's policy of providing ample and efficient electric service for the residential, commercial, industrial and agricultural development of the Island wherever economically possible.

The Company provides, from time to time, opportunities for sound and attractive investments. Particulars of such investments are readily available from the Head Office of the Company in Kingston.

the departments. The Governor has only a casting vote in this body but has reserve powers in regard to matters of outstanding importance. The Executive Council is the principal instrument of policy.

The Legislative Council, consisting of three ex-officio, not more than two official nominated members and not less than ten unofficial members. This Council is the Upper House, corresponding roughly to the House of Lords. It considers legislation passed in the Lower Chamber (House of Representatives) and gives its assent or refers the matter back to that House. But if a Bill is twice passed by the House of Representatives and twice rejected by the Legislative Council, it can, after a specified lapse of time, be submitted for the Governor's assent without the concurrence of the Legislative Council.

The House of Representatives, consisting of thirty-two members, elected from the thirty-two Constituencies of the island on a basis of universal adult suffrage. The House of Representatives has ultimate control over financial matters and therefore it is the more powerful Chamber. The Upper House merely provides safeguards. The Constitution is now under revision.

FINANCE AND CURRENCY

The local currency is based on the British system : pounds, shillings and pence. The Jamaican Government issues notes to the value of five pounds, one pound, ten shillings and five shillings. British silver coins are used : threepence, sixpence, one shilling, two shillings (florin) and two shillings-and-sixpence (half a crown); also the British bronze threepenny-piece. Pennies and halfpennies cause some confusion to the visitor as there are three varieties in circulation, the British copper penny and halfpenny (and farthing), the Jamaican bronze alloy penny, halfpenny, and farthing; and the old Jamaican nickel penny, halfpenny and farthing (becoming rather rare). Visitors are inclined to confuse the latter coinage with silver, mistaking the halfpenny for a shilling or a quarter-dollar (25 cents) and the penny for a two shilling piece.

There are no restrictions on the importation of money from abroad. Passengers from the United Kingdom will find they are limited as to the number of actual Bank of England notes or other cash currency they are permitted to bring, but there is no limit whatsoever to the amount of money they can bring into the island, either in traveller's cheques, letters of credit or by means of bank transfer. Indeed capital investment is encouraged. Visitors from the United States who have any Bank of England notes in their possession are required to deposit them with the Customs. They are given a receipt and the money is refunded upon their departure. Travellers from England must take any such notes back with them. They cannot be used in the island or exchanged. Returning residents must exchange any in their possession at the offices of the Finance Board, 78 Harbour Street, Kingston. No Jamaican Government notes may be brought in by visitors and none should be taken out. Dollars can be used freely in the island for any purpose.

Courtleigh Manor Hotel
Kingston

You will find every comfort and perfect food in a lovely garden setting in the most charming residential district of Kingston.

•

COURTLEIGH MANOR HOTEL
KINGSTON

Telegrams: 'Courtleigh, Jamaica'   Telephone 8579

BANKS

There are branches of four large Banks in the island : Barclays Bank (Dominion, Colonial and Overseas), the Bank of Nova Scotia, the Royal Bank of Canada and the Canadian Bank of Commerce. Each has its head office in Kingston, and one or more is represented in the chief towns of Jamaica. The international banking service is equal to that in any part of the world.

CUSTOMS DUTIES

Rates of duty on commercial goods coming into the island vary from ten up to fifty per cent (in a few cases), but purely personal effects of visitors (clothing, jewellery, toilet goods) enter free. Cameras and binoculars are allowed in free for temporary use. Spirits to the amount of eight ounces and cigarettes to the amount of half a pound weight are permitted. Settlers' effects (meaning personal household goods which have already been in use) are allowed in free during a period of six months after a settler's arrival in the island.

Dogs may be imported only from Great Britain and Ireland and then must be accompanied by a certificate of health from the Board of Agriculture and Fisheries. Quarantine is not usual, but may be required. It is necessary for a Jamaican Veterinary Officer to inspect animals arriving in the island.

PASSPORTS

No passports are required by British subjects, Canadian or U.S.A. citizens entering Jamaica as tourists for any period up to six months, providing they produce a return ticket as evidence that they have come direct and will return direct to their own country at the end of their stay in Jamaica. British subjects or Canadian citizens will require a passport and visa if they should decide to travel home by an indirect route—by way of the United States, for instance. Citizens of all other countries will be required to produce passports and visas.

HEALTH REGULATIONS

No health certificates are required from persons entering Jamaica, except from time to time from countries where the incidence of communicable disease has been reported as high. Transportation companies are always fully informed on this subject and so are the Jamaica Tourist Bureau in New York and the West India Committee in London.

PERMANENT RESIDENCE

British subjects in possession of valid passports are permitted to enter and remain in Jamaica, provided they are not suffering from any communicable disease, and if they are in a position to satisfy the authorities that they are in possession of sufficient funds for their maintenance. There are no restrictions against British subjects engaging in business or other vocations or in acquiring property or taking employment. Indeed there are special induce-

GRAHAM
ASSOCIATES LIMITED
REAL ESTATE

Insurance
Investments
Travel
Commercial Intelligence

26 DUKE STREET, KINGSTON, JAMAICA, B.W.I.

20 MARKET STREET, MONTEGO BAY, JAMAICA, B.W.I.

DIRECTORS
Lord Ronald Graham · G. B. Girardet
H. V. Southby (Montego Bay) · C. Dampier-Bennett

ments for those wishing to invest money in hotels or industries. (See *Industry*).) It should be pointed out to those seeking employment, however, that the local market in most occupations is fully supplied. There is a shortage of technicians and other experts in some departments, but full preliminary investigation is advised. Aliens who wish to work must obtain permission from the Colonial Secretary.

INCOME TAX

Residents of the island and British subjects are allowed (as at January 31, 1951) an exemption of £200 in respect of incomes of £700 and under; and £150 in respect of incomes over £700. Allowances for wife and children under sixteen are allowed on the following basis :

Wife	£80
First Child	£40
Each other child	£20

Allowances within certain limits are allowed in respect of insurance premiums.

Rates of Income Tax are (as at January 31, 1951) :

On every pound of the first £100 (after exemptions)			7d
do	next	£100	1. 2
do	do	£100	1. 9
do	do	£100	2. 4
do	do	£100	2. 11
do	do	£100	3. 6
do	do	£100	4. 1
do	do	£100	4. 8
do	remainder		7. 6

Incomes of individuals in excess of £2000 are subject to a super-tax at the following rates :

For every pound of the first	£1000 of such excess			1. 3
For every pound of the next	£1000 of such excess			2. 6
do	do	£1000	do	3. 9
do	do	£1000	do	5. 0
do	do	£1000	do	6. 3
do	remainder		do	7. 6

Companies are taxed at the rate of 7/6 in the pound.

No temporary visitor or tourist is, of course, liable for Income Tax. If, however, the visitor becomes a permanent resident, he is liable for Income Tax only on such portion of his income as is received in Jamaica, on the above basis. The visitor is not considered a resident unless he has been in Jamaica for a period of six months or periods equal in the whole to six months of the Income Tax year. If, however, he maintains a place of abode in the island, he is regarded as a resident for any year in which he pays a visit, no matter how brief. Also, he is regarded as a resident if he comes to Jamaica year after year and his annual visits are for a substantial period of

time. The matter, however, can only be decided in each individual case by the Assessment Committee, but it may be said that they regard three months as a substantial period after four years.

There is provision for the relief of double taxation between Jamaica and the United Kingdom and other Empire countries.

In the case of persons not ordinarily resident in the island, death duties are only payable on property in the island.

POSTAL, TELEGRAPH AND TELEPHONE FACILITIES

Post Offices are found in all townships. The hours in Kingston are 8 a.m. to 4 p.m. (Parcels office and Money Order offices 9 a.m. to 3 p.m., and 9 a.m. to 1 p.m. on Saturdays.) Country Post Offices are open from 8 a.m. to 5 p.m., telegraph offices from 7 a.m. to 5 p.m. 'Porterage' is charged if destination is over a mile from the Post Office.

Air mails leave daily for the United States and Canada, and three times a week for England.

Postal rates are as follows (as at January 31, 1951) :

Surface mail. Inland letters 2d. for the first two ounces, 1d. for each additional two ounces.

Postcards 1d. Printed matter 1d. for two ounces, ½d. for each additional two ounces.

British Empire. Letters 2½d. for first ounce, 1d. for each additional ounce.

   Postcards 2d. Circulars 1d. for 2 ounces.

Foreign (including U.S.) Letters 5d. for first ounce, 3d. for each additional ounce.

   Postcards 3d. Circulars 1d. for 2 ounces.

Air mail

United Kingdom 1/6d. per ½ ounce.

U.S.A. 8d. per ½ ounce.

Canada 8d. per ½ ounce.

All European countries 1/6d. per ½ ounce.

Africa and Eastern Hemisphere 3/3d. per ½ ounce.

Air Letters (6d.) can be sent to all parts of the British Empire, and to some European countries.

Cablegrams may be sent all over the world, either at day rates or in the form of Night Letter Telegrams and Greeting Telegrams.

Telephone facilities exist between most towns and to the United States, Canada, Britain and many neighbouring countries.

Inland telegrams cost one shilling for the first twelve words and one half-penny a word thereafter.

A telegraph *Money Order* system is in operation between the United Kingdom and Jamaica, as well as Money Orders by post to nearly all countries.

MOTOR CARS

The Jamaica Automobile Association is affiliated with Automobile Associations throughout the world, and a traveller who wishes to bring his

own car is strongly recommended to place himself in the Association's hands. Visitors' motor cars are permitted entry duty free for ninety days by the giving of a bond for 45% of the c.i.f. value (which can be arranged through the Bank); or the deposit of the full amount of the duty according to the assessed value of the car. This is refunded upon re-embarkation. The traveller should provide himself with a written estimate of the value of his car from the manufacturers, dealers, or a reputable garage. Extension of the ninety-day period is granted in special circumstances. Drivers' Licences are obtainable and drivers should bring their International Driver's Licence and/or the driver's licence of their country or state. There are numerous garages and service stations throughout the island for the maintenance and repair of all types of British and American cars. The Shell Company in particular has a fine island-wide organisation. The Jamaica Automobile Association will test cars and supply drivers.

Motor cars can be hired with chauffeurs in the principal towns, at both contract rates and on a mileage basis. Standard makes of most British and American cars can be hired by the week or by the day on the drive-yourself principle.

EDUCATION

There are good kindergarten, elementary, preparatory schools and high schools (some of which call themselves 'colleges') in Jamaica. The standard of education is good in the better class schools and the University College of the West Indies provides higher education for a limited number of students.

There are three school terms a year, the approximate fees a term for day scholars being :

Kindergarten	£10
Preparatory	£16
High School	£12 to £21

Several of the better class schools take boarders. The cost of board and tuition for children of the High School standard ranges from £75 to £100 per annum. The standard is high.

Students may now take up studies in three Faculties at the University College of the West Indies—Medicine, Natural Science and Arts. Fees are £120 a year for board and lodging (residence is compulsory) and teaching fees vary according to the Faculty—£50 for Medicine, £25 for Natural Science and £20 for Arts. Students come mainly from the British West Indies, but entry is based on qualifications of applicants.

MEDICAL AND DENTAL SERVICES

Good surgical and medical attention is available but specialisation is rather limited. The dental facilities are good and adequate. There are three large private hospitals (as well as a number of nursing homes), and one General Public Hospital in the Corporate Area. The Public Hospital (in North Street, Kingston) exists mainly for the use of poorer residents; there are, however, limited facilities for paying patients, fees for private room being at

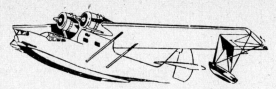

the rate of 7/6 per day, plus cost of any extra food or extra nursing attention. It is hoped that the University College Hospital at Mona, St. Andrew, will open in the near future.

The three main private hospitals are the Nuttall Memorial Hospital, Cross Roads, whose fees range from £6 6 0 to £12 12 0 a week; St. Joseph's Hospital (Roman Catholic), Deanery Road, Vineyard Town (£5 5 0 to £10 10 0); and Andrews Memorial Hospital (Seventh Day Adventist), 27 Hope Road, Half-Way Tree (£5 5 0 to £10 10 0).

CLUBS

There are some good clubs in the metropolis. The principal club in Kingston is the Jamaica Club, which may be described as a down-town business men's luncheon club. Liguanea Club, run on country club lines, situated in the residential suburbs on the main Half Way Tree Road, has a twelve-hole golf course and is an excellent sports and games centre with tennis, billiards, bridge and poker. Liguanea Club has a bar and a dining room and is open to both men and women. There are residential facilities for members. It adjoins the Knutsford Park Race Course, where polo is played. St. Andrew Club, for both men and women, provides tennis, billiards and card playing. There is a well-stocked bar but no restaurant. The Constant Spring Golf Club has a beautiful eighteen-hole course, and is open to both men and women.

The Royal Jamaica Yacht Club is at the eastern end of the Harbour. Membership fees are as follows :

	Entrance Fee	Annual Sub.	
Jamaica Club	£2 2 0	£8 8 0	(Town)
Special (temporary) subscription £1 1 0 monthly			
Liguanea Club men	£5 5 0	£10 10 0	,,
do. women	3 3 0	5 5 0	,,
Special (temporary) subscription £2 2 0 monthly			
St. Andrew Club men	£5 5 0	£4 4 0	,,
do. women	3 3 0	2 2 0	,,
Special (temporary) subscription £1 11 6 for a period of 3 months.			
Constant Spring Golf Club men	£6 6 0	£8 0 0	,,
Constant Spring Golf Club women	3 3 0	4 0 0	,,
Special (temporary) subscriptions 10/- a day : 30/- a week			
Royal Jamaica Yacht Club men	£1 1 0	£5 5 0	,,
Royal Jamaica Yacht Club women	1 1 0	2 2 0	,,
Special (temporary) subscription £1 1 0 for a period of 6 months.			

256

There are golf and country clubs in Mandeville (the Manchester Country Club and the Mandeville Club) and at Montego Bay (the Fairfield), a tennis club in Port Maria and other clubs throughout the island. All welcome visitors and have temporary subscription rates for their convenience. Various outdoor sports and games may be enjoyed at moderate cost and are described in the chapter on *Sports*.

There is a very active Angling Association, and in July of last year the Portland Fishing Club was formed. With headquarters at the Titchfield Hotel, Port Antonio, this club is able to offer excellent deep sea fishing to members. A survey was lately carried out to prove the fine sport which can be had in all seasons in this area. The ordinary subscription to the club is two guineas a year and one guinea entrance fee : special arrangements are made for temporary membership, which can include use of guides, boats and equipment. Application should be made to the Secretary at the Club's headquarters.

PRESS

There is a lively and independent Press in the island. The only morning newspaper is the *Daily Gleaner*, founded in 1834 by the deCordova family. The journal has high standing in the Caribbean area, and its news on current affairs is widely read and respected.

The *Chinese Public News* appears three times weekly.

There are a number of weekly publications :

The *West Indian Review*, established 1934 (as a monthly). This paper has exceptionally high prestige and is very popular with visitors. It is read in New York, London, Canada and throughout the West Indies for its editorial opinions, photographs and entertaining articles. The West Indian Publishing Company Ltd., who publish this Review, also produce *Jamaica Annual*, a yearly magazine.

The *Jamaica Times*, old-established, reviewing the week's news, with editorial opinion, has a country circulation, especially among teachers.

Public Opinion, mainly political, the organ of the Socialist party (People's National Party).

The *Agricultural Advocate* (sponsoring farmers' interests).

Other publications, appearing fortnightly or monthly are :

Spotlight, a challenging review of personalities and events on the lines of *Time* Magazine.

West Indian Sportsman.

Pagoda (Chinese interests).

There are some religious papers; also provincial papers.

Two publishing houses have recently set up in business :

The Arawak Press, West Indian Publishing Company Ltd., 44 East Street, Kingston, and the Pioneer Press, Gleaner Company Ltd., Harbour Street, Kingston.

HOTEL
CASA BLANCA
MONTEGO BAY

Overlooking the crystal clear waters of the Caribbean

•

CASA BLANCA is the only Hotel adjoining the
world famous Doctor's Cave Bathing
Beach. Its terraces overhang and
are literally built right into
the ocean.

•

The rendezvous of a distinguished clientele the CASA
BLANCA has always been an intimate and
friendly place to live.

•

For reservations: Write to the Manager

•

Cables: 'CASABLANCA MONTEGOBAYJA'

CONSULAR AND COMMERCIAL REPRESENTATION

Representatives of many nations have offices in Kingston. The United States Consulate is situated at 33 Duke Street. The United Kingdom Trade Commissioner's office is in the Royal Mail Building, 8 Port Royal Street, and the Canadian Trade Commissioner is housed in the Canadian Bank of Commerce Building, Harbour Street, all in Kingston.

Following is a list of the offices of Consular Representatives in Jamaica :

Belgium	5 Port Royal Street, Kingston
Chile	8 Port Royal Street, Kingston
Colombia	10 Duke Street, Kingston
Costa Rica	78 Orange Street, Kingston
Cuba	10 Duke Street, Kingston
Denmark	134 Harbour Street, Kingston
Dominican Republic	98 Orange Street, Kingston
Finland	8 Port Royal Street, Kingston
France	19 Duke Street, Kingston
Greece	62 Port Royal Street, Kingston
Haiti	11 Duke Street, Kingston
Honduras	78 Orange Street, Kingston
Luxembourg	5 Port Royal Street, Kingston
Netherlands	14 Port Royal Street, Kingston
Nicaragua	78 Orange Street, Kingston
Norway	134 Harbour Street, Kingston

(with Vice Consulates at Montego Bay and Savanna-la-Mar)

Panama	30 Upper South Camp Rd., Cross Roads
Peru	33 Lyndhurst Road, Cross Roads
El Salvador	54 Port Royal Street, Kingston
Spain	135 Harbour Street, Kingston

(with Vice Consulate at Port Antonio)

Sweden	8 Port Royal Street, Kingston
Switzerland	6a King Street, Kingston
United States	33 Duke Street, Kingston
Venezuela	Room 8, Coronation Bldg., Kingston

There is a flourishing local Chamber of Commerce which has an office above the Bank of Nova Scotia, King Street, Kingston, where visiting business men can receive assistance and information.

The Tourist Trade Development Board, 80 Harbour Street, Kingston, can supply visitors with all the information they require, and agents for airlines and shipping companies are all in the immediate vicinity.

COMMUNICATIONS

Following the advance of civil aviation, Jamaica has become the pivot point for air travel in the Caribbean. It is adequately served by airlines from England, the United States and Canada and offers excellent communications for Central and South America. Steamship passenger service from New York

COLUMBUS INN

Discovery Bay

magnificently situated, beautifully appointed, private beach, fresh water pool. Horseback riding. Suites or bungalows, also cottage homes and beach sites for sale. Water and electricity now on property.

This Volume has been printed by

ROBERT MACLEHOSE & COMPANY, LIMITED

of

GLASGOW, SCOTLAND

Agents in Jamaica

THOMSON HANKEY & COMPANY, LIMITED

12 PORT ROYAL STREET,   KINGSTON

has not yet been resumed but during the winter there are usually a number of luxury cruises. A regular passenger service is operated from New Orleans. From England there is a steady year-round service. Details are given below.

Airlines operating from Miami to Jamaica, which is three flying hours away, are Pan American World Airways, K.L.M. (Royal Dutch Airlines) and British West Indian Airways, all of which make connections with National and Eastern Airlines for New York. The Chicago and Southern 'planes fly via Havana to New Orleans and Houston with connections throughout the Middle West. Avianca offer a direct flight from Kingston to New York. B.O.A.C. fly their double-deck stratocruisers from New York to Nassau, with a connection by Constellation for Jamaica. Trans-Canada Airlines fly to Toronto and Montreal via Tampa.

British Overseas Airways (B.O.A.C.) offer accommodation to London, generally via Nassau and Bermuda. The flying time is twenty-eight hours. Pan American also accept bookings for London via New York, their Transatlantic 'planes having sleeping accommodation. K.L.M. fly to Amsterdam via Havana, New York and Newfoundland.

British West Indian Airways, a subsidiary of B.O.A.C., serve the Caribbean generally, offering service to the other islands and the north coast of South America. There is also an internal service between Montego Bay and Kingston.

Pan American Airways give excellent service to all Central and South American countries : K.L.M. operate to the Dutch West Indies. Caribbean International Airways run a weekly service to Jamaica's dependency, Grand Cayman and also fly to Tampa, Florida and Belize, British Honduras.

Fares ruling on the main air routes as at January 31, 1951, are set out below.

PAN AMERICAN WORLD AIRWAYS
Miami to Kingston

Single, Ordinary (daily)	£22 3 0	($ 62.00)	de luxe service and
Return „ „	£39 17 0	($111.60)	meals. Best connections
Single, Tourist (Tues. & Sat.)	£18 19 0	($ 53.00)	
Return „ „ „	£35 19 0	($100.70)	

Miami to Montego Bay

Pan American Airways run this service daily and duplicating the daily service when necessary. The fare is $7 less than to Kingston.

New York to Kingston
(via National and Eastern, air coach, to Miami, twice weekly)

Single	£38 0 0	($106.35)
Return	£74 1 0	($207.40)

(See also AVIANCA Service)

GOOD HOPE

An 18th Century Great House

with all the amenities of a modern hotel on a 6,000 acre estate, famous for all the best of Jamaica life, with mile long, private, tropical beach, swimming pool, fishing, tennis courts, more than 50 horses and 200 miles of riding trails.

For information and reservations apply to your own
Travel Agent or Good Hope

FALMOUTH   11 EAST 44th STREET
JAMAICA, B.W.I.   NEW YORK CITY 17, U.S.A.

References Required

B. & J. B. MACHADO
TOBACCO CO. LTD.

Cigar Manufacturers

•

La Tropical de Luxe

•

La Tropical Golofina Special

•

The finest in the World

London to Kingston
(via New York and Miami, daily)

Single   £152 10 0 ($427.00)
Return   £235 5 0 ($658.60) off season
to   £274 10 0 ($713.60) on   ,,

AVIANCA

Pan American World Airways are the agents for this service which runs a direct flight weekly (Saturday) from New York to Kingston, leaving at 1 a.m. arriving Kingston 9.40 a.m.

Single Fare   £46 16 0 ($131.00)
Return ,,   £89 1 0 ($249.40)

K. L. M.
(ROYAL DUTCH AIRLINES)

Miami to Kingston
Five times weekly

Single   £18 19 0 ($53)
Return   £35 19 0 ($100.70)

New York to Kingston
(via National and Eastern to Miami, five times weekly)

Single   £38 0 0 ($106.35)
Return   £74 1 0 ($207.40)

London to Kingston
(via New York or Havana, four times weekly)

Single   £152 10 0 ($427.00)
Return   £235 5 0 ($658.60) off season
to   £274 10 0 ($713.60) on   ,,

This line makes connection with B.W.I.A. for Montego Bay and also serves the Caribbean area, particularly the Dutch Islands.

CARIBBEAN INTERNATIONAL AIRWAYS
Tampa to Kingston
(via Cayman, every Friday; return flight Tuesday)

Single   £24 7 6 ($68.25)
Return   £43 17 6 ($122.85)

Kingston to Cayman (every Tuesday; return flight Friday)

Single   £9 4 0 ($25.75)
Return   £16 11 0 ($46.35)

This line also serves Belize (Honduras), doing the circular trip —Kingston, Cayman, Tampa, Cayman, Belize; returning Belize, Cayman, Tampa, Cayman, Kingston. It also caters for charter flights.

CHICAGO AND SOUTHERN AIRLINES
New Orleans to Kingston
daily

Single, Ordinary	£35	0 0	($ 98.00)
Return „	£66	10 0	($186.20)
Return Excursion	£54	3 0	($151.60)

Chicago to Kingston
daily

Single, Ordinary	£46	15 0	($131.00)
Return „	£89	9 0	($250.50)
Return Excursion	£69	18 0	($195.70)

New York to Kingston
daily

Single, Ordinary	£45	19 0	($128.70)
Return „	£87	7 0	($244.60)

TRANS-CANADA AIR LINES
Toronto to Kingston
Twice weekly

Single	£49	3 0	($ Can. 143.00)
Return	£88	8 0	($ „ 257.40)

Montreal to Kingston
Three times weekly

Single	£52	5 0	($ Can. 152.00)
Return	£93	19 0	($ „ 273.60)

BRITISH OVERSEAS AIRWAYS CORPORATION

London to Kingston direct
(by way of Lisbon, Azores, Bermuda, Nassau)
Twice Weekly

Single	£152	10 0	($427.00)
Return	£235	5 0	($658.60)
	off season*		
to	£274	10 0	($713.60)
	on season		

London to Kingston
(via New York and Miami or via New York and Nassau three times weekly)
same fare as above

New York to Kingston (via Nassau)
Three times weekly

Single	£46	16 0	($131.00)
Return	£87	0 0	($244.80)

Nassau to Kingston
Three times weekly

Single	£15	8 0	($43.10)
Return	£27	14 0	($77.60)

BRITISH WEST INDIAN AIRWAYS

Miami to Kingston
daily

Single	£18	19 0	($53.00)
Return	£35	19 0	($100.70)

BEACH VIEW HOTEL

MONTEGO BAY . JAMAICA . B.W.I.

•

Perfectly situated directly opposite Doctor's Cave Bathing Beach. American plan including Meals, Room Service, Swimming and Membership of the Fairfield Country Club.

•

For Reservations write
MANAGER, BEACH VIEW, MONTEGO BAY, JAMAICA
or consult your local Travel Agent.

RICHMOND HILL INN Montego Bay

Old Colonial Guest House and detached bungalows 300 feet above sea level overlooking the Town and Bay. Free Transportation to Beach.

'The Hotel with the view'

MOUNT MANSFIELD
GORDON TOWN
- Good Food
- Good Music
- Darts
- Fully Stocked Bar

In the
BLUE MOUNTAINS
overlooking Kingston Harbour
BAMBOO LODGE HOTEL
Irish Town P.O.

LIGUANEA TERRACE HOTEL, Modern Hotel and Service Flats
125 Hope Road, ST. ANDREW

THE WEST INDIAN REVIEW
Keep in touch with Jamaica by taking a subscription . . . 35s. (5·00) yearly,
post free anywhere in the world.
THE WEST INDIAN PUBLISHING CO. LTD., 44 EAST STREET, KINGSTON, JAMAICA.

New York to Kingston
(via Eastern Air Lines and Miami, daily)

Single £38 0 0 ($106.35)
Return £74 1 0 ($207.40)

Kingston to Montego Bay daily, either way

Single £3 0 0 ($8.50)
Return £5 8 0 ($15.30)
Special
Excursion £3 15 0 ($10.50)
(15 days)

* All airlines have a system of reduced fares to and from Europe in 'off peak' periods (December 1st to June 30th westbound, and September 1st to March 31st eastbound). Most offer special excursions from time to time, and all connect with European lines.

B.W.I.A. have a network of lines serving the whole Caribbean, Kingston being the central point.

As mentioned above, there has as yet been no revival of the regular steamship passenger service between New York and Kingston. There are, however, fairly frequent cruises during the winter months which are well advertised. Full details can be secured from any travel agent.

The Alcoa Line run a regular service to Jamaica and other West Indian Islands from New Orleans. The ships are modern and air-conditioned and most staterooms have private baths or showers. The accommodation is luxurious with swimming pool and other amenities. From England, Elders & Fyffes run a regular passenger and freight service at about fortnightly intervals. These are their refrigerated banana-carrying ships and carry about seventy passengers. The Standard Fruit & Shipping Company and the Jamaica Banana Producers' Steamship Company also have ships on this run at less regular intervals.

The French Line have recently inaugurated a service running from Le Havre and Southampton to Kingston, calling at Martinique, Guadeloupe, La Guaira, Curacao, Trinidad and Barbados and returning to Plymouth.

Royal Mail Lines, Limited, have operated a regular service from the United Kingdom to Jamaica and the West Indies for over a century. Comfortable accommodation is available on some of their cargo ships on this service, also on their vessels on the North Pacific run. The latter service is at monthly intervals by new vessels carrying twelve passengers only, under luxury conditions, sailing from London and calling at Bermuda, Kingston, Cartagena, through the Panama Canal to Los Angeles, San Francisco, Victoria and Vancouver. Homeward bound, these vessels do not call at West Indian ports, proceeding direct to the United Kingdom or the Continent.

Royal Mail Lines, Limited, are agents in Jamaica for the Pacific Steam Navigation Company, only one of whose large passenger ships has returned to the run since the war, the 17,500 ton luxury liner, *Reina del Pacifico*. The itinerary is Liverpool, La Rochele-Pallice, Santander, Coruna, Bermuda, Nassau, Havana, Kingston, Cartagena, Cristobal, Balboa, La Libertad, Callao, Arica, Mejillones, Antofagasta, Valparaiso, and usually the same ports of call homeward bound to Plymouth and Liverpool.

The Canadian National Steamships run from Halifax to Kingston once

a fortnight during the winter season using 7,000-ton Diesel motor vessels and carrying twelve passengers only.

The schedule of steamship fares is as follows as at January 31, 1951.

ENGLAND to JAMAICA

Steamship Line	Sailing Interval	Single Fares
Elders & Fyffes, Ltd.		
(agent, United Fruit Co.)	Fortnight	£70-£90 (First class only)
Standard Fruit & Shipping		
Company	Six weeks	£60 ,, ,, ,,
Jamaica Banana Producers'		
Steamship Company	Three weeks	£45-£80 ,, ,, ,,
Royal Mail Lines, Ltd. :		
Small freighters	Fortnight (approx.)	£50-£60 ,, ,, ,,
Twelve passenger Vessels	Month ,,	£75-£80 ,, ,, ,,
Reino del Pacifico		£105 (First Class)†
(Pacific Steam Navigation		£80 (Cabin) †
Company)	three months ,,	£39-£50 (Third Class)†
*French Line	40 days	£125 upward (First Class)
		£80 (Cabin)
		£60 (Tourist)

NEW ORLEANS to JAMAICA

Steamship Line	Sailing Interval	Fares
*Alcoa Steamship Co.	two weeks	$240 upward (First Class)

HALIFAX to JAMAICA

Canadian National		(December to April only)
Steamships	two weeks	$215- $270 (First Class)

The S.S. Caymania provides a connection with Jamaica's Dependency, Grand Cayman, running a three-weekly service.

* Connecting Jamaica with the Eastern Caribbean.
† These fares are higher on the homeward journey.

INTERNAL TRAVEL

Travel within the island is generally by the automobile. Cars can be hired from reputable firms whose names appear elsewhere in this book or will be supplied by the Tourist Trade Development Board, 78 Harbour Street, Kingston. The usual touring rate varies, depending on distances and whether there is a return trip or stop-overs. The total fee should be definitely and clearly arranged before proceeding on a journey. There are Drive-Yourself agencies from which cars can be rented by the day or week. There is also a daily limousine shuttle service to the North Coast in which seats can be booked. Visitors may bring their own cars, according to regulations which

will be found elsewhere in this book. There are no petrol restrictions. The cost of petrol (at January 31, 1951) is three shillings a gallon.

The Jamaica Government Railway provides train service to Montego Bay, also to Port Antonio and to Mandeville. Though travel may seem slow, hot and rather primitive, the first class is not uncomfortable and if sufficient people are available it is hoped that Diesel trolleys to accommodate from fourteen to sixteen people will be available. This form of travel is comfortable and fast. The journey by ordinary train to Montego Bay (113 miles) is scheduled to take six-and-a-half hours, that to Port Antonio three-and-a-half hours.

There are 'country 'buses' in all parts of the island but the conditions are rather rough.

The B.W.I.A. 'plane service between Montego Bay and Kingston, already referred to, flies daily.

There is no difficulty in securing transport in any part of the island and most hotels provide free transportation to their private beaches. All hotels and guest houses arrange transport for visitors through accredited drivers.

Mileage Table

* KINGSTON TO MONTEGO BAY, VIA MONEAGUE

KINGSTON to	miles		miles
Spanish Town - -	13	Moneague - - - -	42
Bog Malk - - -	23	Fern Gully - - - -	54½
Natural Bridge - -	29	Ocho Rios - - - -	59
Linstead - - - -	26	Dunn's River - - -	61
Ewarton - - - -	32	St. Ann's Bay - - -	64

* or MONEAGUE TO ST. ANN'S BAY VIA CLAREMONT 60

Runaway Bay - -	74	Rose Hall - - - -	112
Dry Harbour - - -	78	MONTEGO BAY - -	121
Rio Bueno - - -	83	Lucea - - - - -	146
Duncans - - - -	90	Green Island - - -	158
Falmouth - - -	99		

* KINGSTON TO MANDEVILLE

KINGSTON to			
Spanish Town - -	13	Porus - - - - -	50
Old Harbour - - -	25	Williamsfield - - -	56
May Pen - - - -	35	MANDEVILLE - - -	61

* MANDEVILLE TO MONTEGO BAY

MANDEVILLE to			
Santa Cruz - - -	21	Black River - - -	39
Bamboo Avenue - -	29	Savanna La Mar - -	68
Middle Quarters - -	31	MONTEGO BAY - -	86

* KINGSTON TO PORT ANTONIO VIA JUNCTION ROAD

	Miles		Miles
KINGSTON to		Annotto Bay - - -	31
Cross Roads - - -	2	Buff Bay - - - -	41
Half-Way-Tree - -	3	Orange Bay - - -	44
Constant Spring - -	6	Hope Bay - - - -	49
Stony Hill (top) - -	9	St. Margaret's Bay - -	53
Castleton Gardens -	19	PORT ANTONIO - -	60

* KINGSTON TO PORT ANTONIO VIA MORANT BAY

KINGSTON to		Rozelle - - - -	28
Bournemouth Bath -	2½	Morant Bay - - -	31
Rockfort - - -	4	Port Morant - - -	38
Dry River Bridge - -	6	Golden Grove - -	44
Cane River - - -	7½	Hector's River - -	50
Bull Bay - - - -	10	Manchioneal - - -	56
Albion - - - -	17	Priestman's River - -	65
Yallahs - - - -	19	Blue Hole - - -	71
White Horses- - -	26	PORT ANTONIO - -	77

* KINGSTON TO BUFF BAY VIA HARDWAR GAP

KINGSTON to			
Cross Roads - - -	2	Newcastle - - -	19
Matilda's Corner - -	2	Hardwar Gap - -	21
Papine - - - -	6	Silver Hill Bridge - -	34
Cooper Ridge - - -	7½	Buff Bay - - - -	42

* KINGSTON TO MONTEGO VIA JUNCTION ROAD

KINGSTON to		Ocho Rios - - -	64
Cross Roads - - -	2	Dunn's River - - -	66
Half-Way-Tree - -	3	St. Ann's Bay - - -	69
Constant Spring - -	6	Runaway Bay - -	79
Stony Hill - - -	9	Dry Harbour - - -	83
Castleton Gardens -	19	Rio Bueno - - -	88
Annotto Bay		Duncans - - - -	95
cross roads turn left -	28	Falmouth - - - -	104
Port Maria - - -	44	Rose Hall - - -	117
Oracabessa - - -	52	Montego Bay - - -	126

* KINGSTON TO MILK RIVER VIA THE ALLEY

KINGSTON to			
Spanish Town - -	13	The Alley - - -	42½
Freetown (turn left) -	27	Rest - - - -	53
Salt River - - -	36½	Milk River Baths - -	55

In the heart of Jamaica's
beautiful mountains at 2,200 feet

HOTEL

MANCHESTER

MANDEVILLE

The best golf and tennis in the island
in a superb setting

A first class hotel with first rate
accommodation and excellent cuisine

CABLES: 'HENRYEVE, JAMAICA'

Jamaica Food: Recipes

JAMAICA PEPPERPOT SOUP
(Myrtle Bank Hotel recipe)

Cut into small pieces a large onion, chop fine a quantity of callalu (the local spinach), blanch and cut fine some Indian Kale. Add dried or fresh shrimps (the shells of shrimps will add to the flavour), season with salt and hot red pepper to taste, add beef or chicken stock. Boil all ingredients together, and add cream when cooked. Mix thoroughly and serve very hot.

ACKEE SOUP

Take twelve ackees, pick them carefully, rejecting the pink parts and using the creamy section around the seed. Tie them in a piece of muslin, and boil. Put in one quart of water, one pound of beef, a small quantity of salt beef and salt pork, add seasoning, thyme and escallion. Mash the ackees smooth, mix them with the soup and boil all together.

BANANA STUFFING
(To be served with roast duck)

¾ cup butter	½ cup chopped celery
¼ cup chopped onion	2 tablespoons chopped parsley
1½ quarts bread cubes	1 cup diced ripe bananas

Seasoning of salt, pepper, sage, thyme, nutmeg and cinnamon.

Melt butter in frying pan, add onion and celery and cook on low flame for about ten minutes. Mix bread and bananas with parsley and seasoning in mixing bowl. Add cooked celery (the local variety is good for flavouring) and onion and mix thoroughly.

Fill cavity of the duck with the stuffing and roast without cover, breast up. When nearly cooked, slice two or three bananas and spread on top of duck. Pour a cupful of orange sauce over and roast for another ten minutes.

SHRIMP SALAD CREOLE

Cut two stalks green escallion, including tops, mince quarter cup celery. Add quarter cup salad oil, one tablespoon prepared mustard, two tablespoons lemon juice, half teaspoon salt, quarter teaspoon pepper; beat together. Add half lb. cooked shrimp; toss well. Cover, chill two hours, so the shrimp acquires the zest of the salad dressing. Mix lightly before you place the shrimp on crisp shredded lettuce. (Three servings.) Delicious with potato chips.

276

SCALLOPED MOUNTAIN CRAYFISH
(As served at the Ethelhart Hotel)

Boil the crayfish, then slice and place in scallop shells. Make a sauce from tomato puree heated together with a spoonful of butter and a spoonful of ground onion, flavoured with celery salt. Pour the sauce over the fish, top with breadcrumbs and a sprinkling of paprika. Bake.

TURTLE STEW
(Native Style as served at Myrtle Bank Hotel)

Slice onions and saute until they are brown. Fry the turtle meat. Add some finely chopped tomatoes. Sprinkle lightly with flour, add stock and cook until meat is tender.

PLANTAIN PUDDING

6 ripe plantains	1 cup milk
½ cup flour	2 tablespoons butter
2 teaspoons vanilla	1 egg
Salt to taste.	

Peel and crush plantains. Mix dry ingredients and add to plantains alternately with milk, stirring until smooth. Add vanilla and fold in stiffly beaten egg immediately before baking in moderate oven.

RED PEA SOUP

Put one pint of red peas in two quarts of cold water and boil for three hours until the peas are soft. About two and a half hours after boiling has begun, add a small piece of salt pork with seasoning. When quite cooked, press the peas through a colander and serve the soup with diced dry toast.

RICE AND PEAS

½ lb. red peas	1 lb. rice
1 coconut	Salt pork
Salt and pepper to taste	

Boil peas until soft. Grate coconut and extract milk, using half pint of water. Add to peas with salt and pepper. Cube salt pork and brown, then add to peas and, when mixture is boiling vigorously, add rice. Cook on a low flame until rice is cooked.

STAMP AN' GO FRITTERS

½ lb. salt codfish	Minced onion, tomato, Scotch
¼ cup water	bonnet pepper or 'country' pepper.
4 tablespoons flour	

Cook fish and flake finely. Mix in flour, seasoning and water and fry by tablespoonfuls in very hot fat until brown and crisp.

THE
CITRUS GROWERS ASSOCIATION
OF JAMAICA

Assures the buyer and the consumer of the finest quality fresh fruit and juices

Office: **72 LAWS STREET, KINGSTON, JAMAICA, B.W.I.**

Cables: ' CITGRO, JAMAICA '

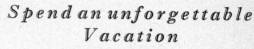

SALTFISH AND ACKEE

1 lb. codfish	1 dozen ackees
1 onion, 1 medium tomato	1 Scotch bonnet pepper or 'country'
Salt pork	pepper

Boil fish and flake. Remove pink part of ackees and boil separately in salted water. Cube salt pork and brown. Add coconut oil and fry onions, tomatoes and pepper, which have been sliced thin. Combine fish and ackees and pour the seasoning and oil over it. Serve hot. (The coconut oil gives the authentic flavour to this dish.)

BAKED LOBSTER (CRAWFISH)

Select two large crawfish. Boil and remove flesh from shell, clean and mince, mix in one cupful fine breadcrumbs, seasoned with salt and pepper to taste. Add finely chopped half of onion, diced small hot red pepper and a tomato. Divide each shell in four and fill with mixture. Sprinkle with some more breadcrumbs and bake in hot oven. Serve hot.

BAKED BLACK CRAB

Take landcrabs instead of crawfish and prepare as above. It takes about twelve crabs to fill four shells. Local taste likes this delicacy very highly-seasoned.

CURRIED GOAT

1 lb. goat mutton	$\frac{1}{2}$ teaspoon allspice (pimento)
1 pint stock	1 oz. dripping
2 large onions	1 dessertspoon desiccated coconut
1 tablespoon pure malt vinegar	1 large teaspoon curry powder

Brown meat in smoking hot dripping. Remove and add peeled and sliced onions, and when clear but not browned, stir in curry powder, allspice and coconut. Stir for a moment or two. Add stock, vinegar and salt to taste. Return mutton to pan. Simmer slowly for two hours. Serve in a border of boiled or fried rice.

MATRIMONY

Mix the pulp of the starapple with small pieces of the ordinary sweet orange. A dash of sherry will improve this delicious dish.

RUM ICE CREAM

Beat three eggs and add four tablespoons of sugar.

Add one pint of warm milk, and boil the mixture.

Allow it to cool, and then add one-half pint of cream and two tablespoons of Myers's Jamaica Rum.

Stir well and churn in ice cream freezer. Cherries or other fruit may be added.

(*Note*: If preferred, three half-pints of milk and four eggs may be used instead of cream.)

PLUM PUDDING, JAMAICAN STYLE
(for eighteen people)

One pound of beef suet; one pound of raisins;
One pound of currants, one pound of prunes;
One pound of citron; one pound of bread crumbs;
One pound of brown sugar.

One teaspoon of salt; one tablespoon of mixed spice; four tablespoons of flour; one grated lime; eight eggs.

Add one-quarter pint of Myers's Jamaica Rum, and one wineglass of Brandy.

Prepare the fruit, remove skin from suet and chop finely.

Mix all dry ingredients together. Add grated lime; sieve and sprinkle flour. Beat eggs well; then add rum and brandy to eggs. Pour into well buttered mould and boil for five hours.

RUM TOFFEE SAUCE

1 tablespoonful Dagger Rum
1 cup light brown sugar
1-3 cup cream
2 tablespoonsful butter

Boil sugar, cream and butter together for three minutes. Allow to cool and stir in Dagger rum.

RUM PUDDING SAUCE

2 teaspoonsful rum
1 egg
2 egg yolks
½ cup sugar
½ cup cream

Beat egg, sugar and cream together. Place in double boiler and continue to beat until mixture is hot. Stir in rum. Serve hot.

RUM FONDANT ICING

2 tablespoonsful Dagger Rum
2 cups confectioner's sugar
2 tablespoonsful cream

Add cream and rum slowly to the sugar, stirring until smooth.

HARD RUM SAUCE

1½ tablespoonsful Dagger Rum
1¼ cups confectioner's sugar
½ cup butter

Cream butter and add sugar slowly. Whip mixture until it is light and creamy. Add rum slowly and beat again.

282

JAMAICA DRINKS: RECIPES
MYERS'S PLANTERS' PUNCH
(The Old Jamaica Plantation Formula)

ONE OF SOUR (one part fresh lime juice)
TWO OF SWEET (two parts sugar)
THREE OF STRONG (three parts Myers's Jamaica Rum)
FOUR OF WEAK (four parts water and ice)

Add a dash of Angostura Bitters. Stir.

Serve very cold in a tall glass with cracked ice. Add a Maraschino Cherry.

MYERS'S COBBLER

Put two teaspoons of pineapple juice or one teaspoon of Curacao into a shaker.

Add half a cocktail glass of Myers's Jamaica Rum.

Put in plenty of ice and shake well. Strain into a tall glass filled with finely chopped ice. Decorate the top with slices of fruit. Pour a little port wine on top and serve with a straw.

MYERS'S HOT BUTTERED RUM

Pour one jigger of Myers's Jamaica Rum into a tall glass.

Two or three teaspoons of sugar.

Two teaspoons of butter.

Add one-half teaspoon of mixed spices (cinnamon and cloves) if desired.

Fill glass with boiling water. Stir well and sip slowly.

MYERS'S RUM SWIZZLE
(For twelve people)

Mix in a deep glass jug or bowl :

Four teaspoons of sugar,
A few sprigs of mint,
Add the juice of six limes or lemons,
Six ice cubes.
Add sixteen ounces of Myers's Jamaica Rum
(about eleven jiggers).

Use a swizzle stick and swizzle by rolling between the hands until the mixture froths over. (*Note* : If lacking a swizzle stick, stir rapidly with a long spoon.) Serve in cocktail glasses.

MYERS'S RUM AND BRANDY PUNCH
(For eight people)

Use a punch bowl or a deep glass bowl.

Pour in one-third pint of lime or lemon juice.

Add three-quarters of a pound of sugar dissolved in water.

Half a pint of Cognac.

One-quarter pint of Peach Brandy.
One-quarter pint of Myers's Jamaica Rum.
Two and a half pints of iced water or carbonated water.
   Add a large lump of ice. Stir thoroughly and serve in punch or cocktail glasses.

MYERS'S RUM BRULOT

Place a half lump of sugar in a teaspoon.
Pour Myers's Jamaica Rum over sugar to fill the spoon.
Ignite with a lighted match.
Let it burn until sugar dissolves.
Then pour into a demitasse of black coffee.

DAGGER KINGSTON COCKTAIL

Juice of half a lime (or lemon)
1 teaspoonful Grenadine (or powdered sugar)
1 oz. Dagger Jamaica Rum
½ oz. London Dry Gin
Ice and shake well.

RUM AND VERMOUTH COCKTAIL

1½ oz. Dagger Rum.
¾ oz. Dry Vermouth.
   Pour over ice cubes in shaker, stir well and strain into cocktail glass, the lip of which has been bruised with a slice of fresh lime (or lemon) peel. Twist peel over drink and garnish with it.

DAGGER RUM SOUR

Juice of half a lemon
½ tablespoonful of sugar
1½ oz. Dagger Jamaica Rum.
Ice and shake well. Strain into medium size glass. Add dash of soda water and garnish with half a slice of Orange and a cherry.

PINEAPPLE FIZZ

2 tablespoonful pineapple juice
½ teaspoonful powdered sugar
1½ oz. Dagger Jamaica Rum.
Ice and shake well into medium sized glass. Fill with cold soda water.

DAGGER MINT JULEP

4 sprigs of fresh mint
½ tablespoonful powdered sugar
1½ oz. Dagger Jamaica Rum.
   Use a long tumbler. Crush mint leaves and dissolve sugar. Add rum and fill glass with finely cracked ice. Allow glass to frost. Garnish with additional mint.

DAGGER RUM COLLINS

Juice of half a lime (or lemon)
Teaspoonful powdered sugar
1½ oz. Dagger Jamaica Rum

Place in large glass. Add cracked ice—soda water to fill. Garnish with slice of lemon, if desired.

CORUBA SOUR

One measure sugar or sugar syrup
Two measures freshly pressed sour orange juice.
Two or three measures Coruba Jamaica Rum,
    light or dark.

Add plenty of ice and shake well until a good portion of the ice dissolves. Serve ice cold in punch glasses.

CORUBA COCKTAIL

Put one measure of sugar into the cocktail shaker, peel one lime or lemon and squeeze the rind, forcing the oil out. Then drop the whole rind on to the sugar. Take the lime or lemon juice and add it, making sure it is a full measure. Add six measures of Coruba Jamaica Rum, light or dark. Fill the shaker up with ice, shake well and serve ice cold in cocktail glasses.

WEST INDIAN REVIEW SPECIAL

(as printed in the *West Indian Review*)
(Invented by Orford St. John)

The most satisfying cocktail in the world. Our own particular blend of

3 parts Gin—for the strong line, the stimulating thought and the clear crystal quality of our policy.

2 parts French Vermouth—for the dry style and cosmopolitan background of our contributors.

1 part Peach Brandy—for the rich smooth flavour of our presentation.

And just a dash of bitters for piquancy. Not Angostura, though it is West Indian. That is too bitter for our point of view. Something more fragrant, shall we say just a zest of lime or lemon peel.

Do not deep freeze or the aroma will be lost. Stir lightly on ice like a Martini, and serve in generous helpings.

An Annancy Story

HOW MONKEY MANAGE ANNANCY

One day Annancy an him wife sidung under tree a chat, no kno say Monkey eena tree top a lisen. Hear Annancy, 'Me wife, ah want a likkle fresh.' Hear him wife, 'What kinda fresh?'

'Any meat at all. Ah tell yuh wha yuh mek we do. Mek we get a barren an put it pon de bed so cover it up wid wite sheet so mek it favour man. Dell wi can sen call Bro Cow, Bro Monkey, Bro Goat an Bro Hog. Wen dem come, we wi put dem inside de house an den you can tan een de room wid dem.'

So Bro Annancy send fe all him fren dem. An Monkey come too an Cow was de Minister. Dem all come fine Annancy a cry. Hear dem :

'No cry so much man, is all a we road.'

Annancy say, 'Ah, Bro Cow, yuh kno de feelins. As yuh is de parson tek yuh fren dem eena de house go see de ole man pon de bed."

Wen Cow go eenside an go fi raise up de sheet, Annancy wife stap him braps.

'Hm-hm, me husban say nobady fi look pon de face tell marnin." So Cow no badar.

But Bro Monkey did hear eberyting wen him dida hide een de tree tap an him an him wife ouldn go eena de house no cya how Bro Annancy beg dem.

Bro Monkey ongle say, 'Hm-hm, Bro 'Nancy me too easy fi cry. Ef me go een deh me a go bawl too much.' So Bro Annancy soon hafi lef out Monkey for him did too smart fi him.

Bi dis time, Annancy did hide him cutlass backa door an it wuz de ongle door de house hab so now him dis go backa it go cwinge up. Den Bro Cow start fi pray. Meanwile hima pray Annancy dah halla an Bro Hog start call out, 'Kip up Bro 'Nancy keep up Bro 'Nancy.' But Bro 'Nancy still a bawl.

After Cow done pray him raise one Ole Hundad hymn wha go so :

> Me gullen ho St. John,
> Me gullen ho St. John,
> Me see de last today ya,
> Me see de las puppa gone.

As Bro Annancy did wan fi kill Cow, him bawl out say him no like dat hymn an start bruk fight. Same time him lock de door an start weel him cutliss an as dem oddar one no hab nuttin fi fight wid him kill aff de whole a dem.

Nex day Monkey laugh say, 'Bro Annancy, a good ting me never come eenside yuh house. But bi dis time Annancy did eat him likkle fresh an him belly full so him gi Bro Monkey piece meat. Jack Mandoora me no choose none.

Bibliography

A SELECT LIST

All the books enumerated below can be seen at the Institute of Jamaica, East Street, either in the General or West India Reference Library. A visit to the Institute's Libraries is essential to anyone interested in the history of Jamaica.

GENERAL (MODERN) REFERENCE

Handbook of Jamaica. Edited by W. A. Cover, 1949-50.

Jamaica To-day. Revised edition by P. M. Sherlock of Frank Cundall's *Jamaica in 1928.* Published 1940.

Guide to Jamaica. By Phillip P. Olley (Tourist Trade Development Board), 1947.

The Truth about Jamaica. By Esther Chapman, 1938. A pamphlet consisting of three articles reprinted from the *West Indian Review.*

Reference Book of Jamaica. Edited by Wyatt Bryce, 1946.

Colonial Office Annual Report on Jamaica, 1948. Published 1950.

Jamaica the Blessed Island. By Lord Olivier. Faber, London, 1936. A sociological history of the island by a past Governor.

Historic Jamaica. By Frank Cundall, West India Committee, 1915.

A perusal of the above books will give the visitor a good general idea of Jamaica. Historians and specialists will find much else of value in the volumes enumerated below.

HISTORY: GENERAL

History of Jamaica, or a General Survey of the ancient and modern state of that Island. By Edward Long, 1774.

The History, Civil and Commercial, of the British Colonies in the West Indies. By Bryan Edwards, 1819.

The Annals of Jamaica. By the Rev. Wilson Bridges, M.A., 1820.

Jamaica: Its Past and Present State. By the Rev. James M. Phillipo, 1843.

The West Indies and the Spanish Main. By Anthony Trollope, 1859.

A History of Jamaica, from its Discovery by Christopher Columbus to the Present Time. By the Rev. W. J. Gardner, 1873.

The English in the West Indies. By J. A. Froude, 1888.

The Story of the Life of Columbus and the Discovery of Jamaica. By Frank Cundall, 1894.

Jamaica under the Spaniards. By Frank Cundall and Joseph L. Pietersz. Institute of Jamaica, 1919.

Chronological Outlines of Jamaican History, 1492-1926. By Frank Cundall, 1927.

HISTORY: SPECIAL ASPECTS

SLAVERY AND APPRENTICESHIP

Death Struggles of Slavery (being a Narrative of Incidents which occurred . . . during the two years . . . preceding Negro Emancipation). By Henry Bleby, 1853.

Emancipation and Apprenticeship in the British West Indies. By W. L. Burn, 1937.

MAROONS

The History of the Maroons. By R. C. Dallas, 1803.

The Maroons of Jamaica. By Joseph J. Willams, S. J. Anthropological Series of the Boston College Graduate School, 1938.

Journey to Accompong. By Katherine Dunham. Henry Holt and Co., New York, 1946.

POLITICAL

The Constitutional Development of Jamaica, 1660-1729. By Agnes M. Whitson, M.A. Manchester University Press, 1929.

CHURCHES AND MISSIONS

There is in the Institute a fairly comprehensive historical record of the various religious denomnations and missions in Jamaica during the nineteenth century—the Roman Catholic Church, the Church of England, the Baptist, Moravian, Wesleyan, Methodist Churches; and the Jews. Also several memoirs of William Knibb and Thomas Burchell, Baptist missionaries.

MILITARY

There are some volumes on the history of the West India Regiment, and of Jamaica's Part in World War I.

Also see *The Jamaica Historical Review*, published by the Jamaica Historical Society, 13 East Street, Kingston.

BIOGRAPHY

Wonderful Adventures of Mrs. Seacole in Many Lands. Edited by W. J. S., 1857. Mary Seacole was a Jamaican nurse who served in the Crimean War.

The Myth of Governor Eyre. By Lord Olivier. Hogarth Press, London, 1933. Governor Eyre was the Governor of Jamaica during the Morrant Bay Rebellion of 1865.

Sir Henry Morgan, Buccaneer and Governor. By W. Adolphe Roberts. Hamilton, London, 1933.

The Life of Sir Henry Morgan, with an Account of the English Settlement of the Island of Jamaica, 1655-1688. By Brig. Gen. E. A. Cruikshank. Macmillan, Toronto, 1935.

The Governors of Jamaica in the Seventeenth Century. By Frank Cundall. West India Committee, London, 1936.

The Governors of Jamaica in the First Half of the Eighteenth Century. By Frank Cundall. West India Committee, London, 1937.

The Family of the Barrett. By Jeanette Marks. Macmillan, New York, 1938. Elizabeth Barrett Browning's family owned large properties in Jamaica from the date of the English invasion in 1655.

Sir Henry Morgan. By Rosita Forbes. Cassell, London, 1948.

SOCIOLOGY AND FOLKLORE

Jamaica Song and Story, including Annancy Stories, Digging Songs, Ring Tunes, etc. Edited by Walter Jekyll. David Nutt, London (for Folklore Society), 1907.

Jamaica Negro Proverbs and Sayings. By Izett Anderson and Frank Cundall. West India Committee, 1927.

Jamaica Folklore. By Martha Warren Beckwith. G. E. Stechert and Co., New York (for the American Folklore Society).

Black Roadways. By Martha Warren Beckwith. University of North Carolina Press, 1929.

Annancy Stories. By A. J. Newman and P. M. Sherlock, 1936. There are a number of other volumes of Annancy Stories.

The Aborigines of Jamaica. By Philip M. Sherlock. Institute of Jamaica, 1939.

Place-Names of Jamaica. By Frank Cundall, revised by Philip M. Sherlock, 1939.

Journey to Accompong. By Katherine Dunham. Henry Holt & Co., New York, 1946. Accompong is a Maroon village in the Cockpit district of Jamaica.

RACE RELATIONS AND SOCIAL THEORIES

White Capital and Coloured Labour. By Sydney (Lord) Olivier. Published by the Independent Labour Party, London, 1906.

Black Jamaica, a Study in Evolution. By W. P. Livingstone, 1889.

Race Crossing in Jamaica. By Davenport and Stegerda. Carnegie Institute of Washington, 1929.

The Marginal Man. A Study in Personality and Culture Conflict. By Everett V. Stonequist. Charles Scribner, New York, 1937.

The Truth about Jamaica. By Esther Chapman, 1938.

SCIENCE AND NATURAL HISTORY

A Voyage to the Islands Madeira, Barbados, Nevis, St. Christopher's and Jamaica, with the Natural History of the Last of those Islands. Illustrated. By Hans Sloane, M.D., 1707. Sir Hans Sloane was Medical Attendant to the Duke of Albemarle, Governor of the island at the time of the Port Royal earthquake of 1692, and wrote an eye-witness account of that catastrophe. His collections, made while abroad, are said to have formed the nucleus of the foundation of the British Museum in 1759.

The History of Jamaica. By Edward Long, 1774 (Volume III).

The Civil and Natural History of Jamaica, containing an Accurate Description of that Island, its Situation and Soil. By Patrick Browne, M.D., 1789.

A Naturalist's Sojourn in Jamaica. By Philip Henry Gosse, F.R.S., assisted by Richard Hill, 1851.

Aboriginal Indian Remains in Jamaica. By J. E. Duerden, A.R.Sc., with a note on the Craniology of the Aborigines of Jamaica. By Professor A. C. Hadden, M.A., D.Sc. Journal of the Institute of Jamaica, 1897.

The Birds of Jamaica. By Philip Henry Gosse, assisted by Richard Hill, 1847.

Birds of the West Indies. By James Bond. Macmillan, New York, 1936.

Flora of Jamaica. By William Fawcett, B.Sc., and Alfred Barton Rendle, D.Sc., in Natural History Series of the British Museum, 1910-1936.

The Principal Timbers of Jamaica. By C. Swabey. Department of Agriculture Bulletin (New Series), No. 29, 1941.

A Montane Rain Forest. A contribution to the physiological plant Geography of Jamaica. By Forrest Sheve, Carnegie Institute of Washington Pub. No. 199, 1914.

The Herpetology of Jamaica. By W. Gardner Lynn and Chapman Grant. Bulletin of the Institute of Jamaica. Science Series, No. 1, 1940.

The Herpetology of the Cayman Islands. By Chapmen Grant, with an appendix on the Cayman Islands and Marine Turtle. By Bernard Lewis, 1940.

Collection of Fishes from Jamaica. By Uluis Howell Rivero. Handbook of Jamaica, 1936.

The Rainfall of Jamaica (1870-1929). By J. F. Brennan, 1933.

Meteorology of Jamaica. By Philip Henry Gosse, assisted by Richard Hill, 1847.

Agriculture. See Journal of the Agricultural Society, 1897 onwards, and Bulletins of the Department of Agriculture, Jamaica.

Geology, Entomology. There are a number of publications on the Institute shelves dealing with the Geology and Entomology of the Island. See also Natural History Society notes, Institute of Jamaica.

MEDICINE AND HYGIENE

The Medical Assistant, or Jamaica Practice of Physic, designed chiefly for the use of Families and Plantations. By Thomas Dancer, M.D., late Physician to the Bath, and Island Botanist. London, 1819.

Yellow Fever in the West Indies. By Izett Anderson, M.D., Edin. London, 1898.

Medical Services in Jamaica. By Mary Manning Carley. Social Survey Series, No. 2. Institute of Jamaica, 1943.

EDUCATION

Education in Jamaica. Report of the Education Society, connected with the Jamaica Baptist Union. London, 1866.

Some Notes on the History of Secondary Education in Jamaica. By Frank Cundall. Institute of Jamaica, 1911.

Education in Jamaica. By Mary Manning Carley. Social Survey Series, No. 1. Institute of Jamaica, 1942.

Educational Supplement, Daily Gleaner, July 23, 1950.

DIARIES AND TRAVEL BOOKS

The Present State of Jamaica, with the Life of the Great Columbus, the first Discoverer; to which is added an Exact Account of Sir Henry Morgan's Voyage to, and famous Siege and Taking of, Panama from the Spaniards, 1683.

A Trip to Jamaica. By Edward Ward, 1698.

An Account of Jamaica and its Inhabitants. By a gentleman long resident in the West Indies (J. Stewart), 1808.

A Tour through the Island of Jamaica from the Western to the Eastern End, in the Year 1823. By Cynric R. Williams, 1826.

A Picturesque Tour of the Island of Jamaica, from Drawings made in the years 1820 and 1821. By James Hakewill, 1825.

Tom Cringle's Log. By Michael Scott, 1833. An account by a young merchant seaman of his adventures in West Indian waters in the early nineteenth century.

Journal of a West Indian Proprietor, kept during a residence in the island (1815-17) by Matthew Gregory Lewis (popularly known as 'Monk Lewis'), 1834.

Lady Nugent's Journal (in Jamaica, 1801-1805). Privately printed, 1839. Republished by the West India Committee, 1907. A very popular and amusing account of the island by a Governor's wife of the time.

Mrs. Russell Gurney's Account of her Visit to Jamaica, in 1866. Her husband, the Recorder of London, was a member of the Royal Commission appointed to enquire into the Morant Bay Rebellion.

Letters from Jamaica, the Land of Streams and Woods. By Charles Rampini (a High Court Judge in Jamaica), 1873.

Letters to Jane from Jamaica, 1788-1796. Edited by Geraldine Mozley. Published 1938.

Where the Twain Meet. By Mary Gaunt. Murray, London, 1922.

Revels in Jamaica. By Richardson Wright. Dodd, New York, 1937. An account of the gay life and theatrical circles in old Jamaica, 1682-1838.

Caribbean Nights. By W. J. Makin. Robert Hale, London, 1939. Written after the distrubances of 1938.

Black Caribbean. By R. W. Thompson. MacDonald, London, 1946.

West Indian Summer. By James Pope-Hennessy. B. T. Batsford Ltd., London, 1943.

Lands in the Inner Sea. By W. Adolphe Roberts. Coward-McCann, Inc., New York, 1948.

Jamaica Journey. By W. J. Brown, M.P   Allen, London, 1948.

The Land of Look Behind. By W. J. Brown, M.P. Latimer House, London, 1949. Private accounts of journeys, containing little about Jamaica.

Island in the Sun. By Rosita Forbes. Evans, London, 1949.

Haunts of High Adventure. By Col. P. T. Etherton. John Long, 1950.

The Traveller's Tree. By Patrick Leigh Fermor. John Murray, London, 1950

Note: There are many more books of this description in the West India

Reference Library, some slight, some more comprehensive, some of great antiquarian value. Also old 'Almanacks' and registers.

FICTION

Jane's Career. By Herbert G. de Lisser, 1913. Editor of the *Jamaican Gleaner* for many years and a keen observer of Jamaican life.

Susan Proudleigh. By Herbert G. de Lisser, 1915.

Triumphant Squalitone. By Herbert G. de Lisser, 1916.

Revenge. By Herbert G. de Lisser, 1919.

Punch and Judy. By Esther Hyman (Chapman). Constable, London, 1928.

Study in Bronze. By Esther Chapman. Constable, London, 1929. A study of mixed race relations by the Editor of the *West Indian Review.*

The White Witch of Rose Hall. By Herbert G. de Lisser. Benn, London, 1929.

Far Enough. By Helen Ashton. Benn, London, 1928. The experiences of a schoolmistress.

A High Wind in Jamaica. By Richard Hughes. Chatto and Windus, London, 1929. The rather horrifying travel adventures of some colonial children in the early nineteenth century; little about Jamaica.

Banana Bottom. By Claude McKay. Harper, New York, 1933.

Luminous Isle. By Eliot Bliss. Cobden-Sanderson, London, 1934. A good descriptive account of social life in the island.

Go Down Moses. By Jane Rees Wogan (Janet Cousins). Hutchinson, London, 1936.

Under the Sun. A Jamaican comedy. By Herbert G. de Lisser. Ernest Benn, London, 1937.

New Day. By Victor Reid. Alfred Knopf, New York, 1949. A story spanning the period from the Morant Bay Rebellion to the present day.

The Shadow and the Peak. By Richard Mason. Hodder and Stoughton, London, 1949.

Creole. By Lucille Iremonger. Hutchinson, London, 1950.

Dark Drums. Based on the Rose Hall legend. By Wenzell Brown. Appleton Century Crofts, 1950.

POETRY

Jamaica. By T(om) R(edcam), 1899.

Songs of Jamaica. By Claude McKay, 1912.

Voice from Summerland; an anthology of Jamaican poetry. Edited by J. E. Clare McFarlane. London, 1929.

Daphne. By J. E. Clare McFarlane. Fowler Wright, London, 1931.

The Moth and the Star. By Una Marson, 1937.

Wings of the Morning. By Vivian L. Virtue, 1938.

Flaming June. By Constance Hollar, 1941.

Jamaica (Dialect) Verses. By Louise Bennett, 1942.

First Poems. By George Campbell, 1945.

Treasury of Jamaican Poetry. Edited by J. E. Clare McFarlane. London, 1950.

GOVERNMENT PUBLICATIONS

The Report of the West India Royal Commission, 1938-39 (appointed as a result of the distrubances of 1938).

Reports on Agriculture, Economics, the Ten Year Plan, and many other official publications.

Note: All Government Publications, including the following, can be found at the Institute, or at the Stationery Office:

Proceedings and Debates of the old Assemblies, Legislative Councils and present Governing Bodies.

Accounts of the Board of Trade and Plantations (precursor of the Colonial Office).

Government Gazettes.

Colonial Office Annual Reports.

Census of Jamaica, 1943.

Reports of the Comptroller for Development and Welfare from 1943.

Reports of the Caribbean Commission from 1943.

Editor's Note: This Bibliography is necessarily incomplete. The above titles are selected from the large library of literature relating to Jamaica and the West Indies as most likely to be of general interest.

Index

Index to Advertisers

MANOR HOUSE HOTEL
Constant Spring, Jamaica

The Hotel lies in an entrancing tropical setting, at the foothills of the Blue Mountains, six hundred feet above sea-level. Here is the ideal place for a holiday in Jamaica at all seasons of the year, for although only six miles from Kingston, the temperature is fifteen degrees cooler, and the situation of the Hotel in its extensive grounds ensures a delightful atmosphere of quiet and peaceful seclusion. And yet everything that goes to make a perfect holiday is close at hand: an eighteen-hole Golf Course, considered to be the best in the West Indies, adjoins the Hotel property. The Hotel has its own Tennis Court, and a delightful fresh-water Swimming Pool.